*The Patterson E.*

# THE BREAD CRUMBS SERIES

## SUBSTANCE *for* SECURITY *and* SIGNIFICANCE

*Shawn & Kate,*
  *Please enjoy this 145 day manuel of nourishment... The Bread Crumbs. Writing the foreword was a complete honor of mine and truly believe this book will find you well.*

A DAILY DOSE OF MAKING YOU MAGNIFICENT

## C.J. Jackson

*I'm so thankful to know you both.*
  *My very best & with love, JP Thompson*

**Bread Crumbs Series Substance for Security and Significance**
Copyright © 2020 by **C.J. Jackson**

All rights reserved. No part of this publication may be reproduced, distributed or transmitted in any form or by any means, including photocopying, recording, or other electronic or mechanical methods, without the prior written permission of the publisher, except in the case of brief quotations embodied in critical reviews and certain other noncommercial uses permitted by copyright law.

Although the author and publisher have made every effort to ensure that the information in this book was correct at press time, the author and publisher do not assume and hereby disclaim any liability to any party for any loss, damage, or disruption caused by errors or omissions, whether such errors or omissions result from negligence, accident, or any other cause.

Adherence to all applicable laws and regulations, including international, federal, state, and local governing professional licensing, business practices, advertising, and all other aspects of doing business in the US, Canada, or any other jurisdiction is the sole responsibility of the reader and consumer.

Neither the author nor the publisher assumes any responsibility or liability whatsoever on behalf of the consumer or reader of this material. Any perceived slight of any individual or organization is purely unintentional.

The resources in this book are provided for informational purposes only and should not be used to replace the specialized training and professional judgment of a healthcare or mental healthcare professional.

Neither the author nor the publisher can be held responsible for the use of the information provided within this book. Please always consult a trained professional before making any decision regarding treatment of yourself or others.

*Cover design by* 100Covers.com
*Formatted by* FormattedBooks.com

ISBN: 978-1-7355849-0-4

# DEDICATION

This book is dedicated first off to His Majesty, King of Kings, and Lord of Lords, Jesus Christ. He has not only laid a path for me to follow, but he provided "Bread Crumbs" along each step of my journey. I give Him praise and thanks for opening my eyes to new sights and sounds! In addition, where would I be if not for my bride, Brenda Jackson? She has withstood the onslaught of handling everything I have faced physically, mentally, emotionally, and spiritually. In fact, her genuine support and shining spirit has been an encouragement whenever I was empty, tired, or drained from battling this world. To me, no man is genuinely happy until he finds a treasure like her! That is what God says, "The man who finds a wife finds a treasure, and he receives favor from the LORD" (Proverbs 18:22 TLB). Brenda has been that and beyond! Thank you, princess, for accepting my flaws and my failures, and accepting my fire from the Lord that hopefully stays ignited FOREVER!

# Contents

Foreword .................................................................................. XV
Introduction ............................................................................ XIX

1. Cream and Sugar ............................................................... 1
2. The Great Expectation ....................................................... 3
3. The Little Birds .................................................................. 5
4. Time to Leave the REST STOP ........................................... 7
5. Liar, Liar .......................................................................... 11
6. The COMFORT ZONE ..................................................... 15
7. Submergence ................................................................... 17
8. "Why Lord?" .................................................................... 21
9. Out of Nothing ................................................................ 23
10. A Divine Storm ................................................................ 25
11. Shining Star ..................................................................... 27
12. The Other Side ................................................................ 29
13. I Can See Clearly NOW ................................................... 33
14. LIMITLESS ....................................................................... 37
15. Unwrapped ..................................................................... 39
16. "How Do You Know?" ..................................................... 41
17. Humble... YOURSELF ...................................................... 45

| | | |
|---|---|---|
| 18. | Prescription for Instability | 47 |
| 19. | DISTRACTIONS | 49 |
| 20. | CONSUMED | 53 |
| 21. | Be Not Deceived | 55 |
| 22. | "On the Dunes" | 59 |
| 23. | He's Always Here | 61 |
| 24. | EVERLOVE | 63 |
| 25. | No More Running Away | 65 |
| 26. | Created for Authenticity | 67 |
| 27. | The Many Faces of Death | 69 |
| 28. | Journey to the CENTER of the HEART | 71 |
| 29. | The Truth about REJECTION | 75 |
| 30. | Who Are You? | 77 |
| 31. | TRUSTED | 79 |
| 32. | More Than a Word | 81 |
| 33. | "What Lies Below?" | 83 |
| 34. | Leaving the Land of Confusion | 87 |
| 35. | "Seeing the Invisible Things" | 91 |
| 36. | UNLIMITED Possibilities | 93 |
| 37. | Restless People | 97 |
| 38. | SIFTED | 99 |
| 39. | Spiritual Incarceration | 103 |
| 40. | Born to Bloom | 107 |
| 41. | The Expose of Perception | 109 |
| 42. | The Reconciliation Factor | 113 |
| 43. | I Am the Kingdom | 115 |
| 44. | Our Place of Peace | 117 |
| 45. | "TEMPTATION ISLAND" | 121 |
| 46. | "My Personal Trainer" | 125 |
| 47. | ROOTED and GROUNDED | 127 |

| | |
|---|---|
| 48. SOUR MILK | 129 |
| 49. "For The SEEKERS" | 131 |
| 50. "The FIG LEAF APPROACH" | 135 |
| 51. Discovering the REAL LIFE | 139 |
| 52. SOUL FOOD | 141 |
| 53. Having a Stronghold? | 143 |
| 54. "The Case on Gossip" | 145 |
| 55. "What Do You Produce?" | 147 |
| 56. "Your Authentic Identity" | 151 |
| 57. "The SEE-THROUGH MAN" | 153 |
| 58. "FIGHT" | 157 |
| 59. "Stormproof" | 159 |
| 60. "No More Repeats of the Old Nature" | 163 |
| 61. "CHRIST in YOU" | 165 |
| 62. The Perfecter of Faith | 167 |
| 63. Keys to the KINGDOM | 169 |
| 64. Beware of Dogs | 173 |
| 65. For His Pleasure | 175 |
| 66. BREAK the CYCLE | 177 |
| 67. BABY FOOD | 179 |
| 68. "THE SPIRITUAL CUISINE" | 183 |
| 69. "FAKE FRUIT" (Part I) | 185 |
| 70. "FAKE FRUIT" (Part II) | 189 |
| 71. "FLAWED" | 193 |
| 72. POISON | 195 |
| 73. An Expose of the Three Temperatures of People (COLD LOVE Part I) | 199 |
| 74. An Expose of the Three Temperatures of People (COLD LOVE Part II) | 201 |

75. An Expose of the Three Temperatures of People
    (LUKEWARM LOVE) ...................................................... 203
76. An Expose of the Three Temperatures of People
    (HOT LOVE) .................................................................... 207
77. Laying Aside Unresolved CONFLICT ................................ 211
78. DRIVING Through DISAPPOINTMENT ........................... 215
79. "Phases of the HEART" (Part I) ........................................ 219
80. "Phases of the HEART" (Part II) ....................................... 221
81. "Phases of the HEART" (Part III) ...................................... 223
82. "Phases of the HEART" (Part IV) ..................................... 225
83. The Believing Heart ......................................................... 227
84. "TRAPPED" ..................................................................... 229
85. Is it Possible? .................................................................. 233
86. "Superheroes and Sober-mindedness" .......................... 237
87. The COST ........................................................................ 241
88. The Good Shepherd ........................................................ 245
89. God Sees the Best .......................................................... 249
90. "DISTRACTED!" .............................................................. 253
91. Learning to Live in His Presence .................................... 257
92. The Futile Ground ........................................................... 261
93. The GREATER PLACE ..................................................... 265
94. CHECK YOUR ATTITUDE ................................................ 269
95. "Dressed Like a Wolf" .................................................... 273
96. "PREPARED for PROSPERITY" (Part I) ............................ 277
97. PREPARED for PROSPERITY (Part II) .............................. 281
98. "DON'T LET THE DEVIL DECIEVE YOU" ....................... 285
99. The AXIOM of HUMILITY ............................................... 287
100. Silence Your Enemies With PRAISE ............................... 291
101. "I SEE CHRIST!" ............................................................. 293

| | | |
|---|---|---|
| 102. | "On the Shores of STRIFE" | 295 |
| 103. | Be CONSIDERATE | 299 |
| 104. | UNCONDITIONAL GIVING | 303 |
| 105. | "HOLY" | 307 |
| 106. | DANCE! | 311 |
| 107. | "Moving Past Survive to THRIVE" | 315 |
| 108. | "PURSUE PEACE… With All Men" | 319 |
| 109. | SELF-RIGHTEOUSNESS | 321 |
| 110. | "Turning FAILURES Into FULFILLMENT" | 323 |
| 111. | "WALK THIS WAY" | 327 |
| 112. | 20 Feet Tall | 331 |
| 113. | "SQUEEZED" | 335 |
| 114. | Living in NEWNESS | 337 |
| 115. | "What Is Your FORM in God?" | 341 |
| 116. | DELIGHT | 345 |
| 117. | "Learn of ME" | 349 |
| 118. | "REJOICE: AGAIN and AGAIN!" | 353 |
| 119. | "HUNGRY?" | 357 |
| 120. | "Thinking Like GOD" | 361 |
| 121. | "MOVING OUT THE SPIRIT OF MAMMON" | 363 |
| 122. | GIVING UP (A Tale of Giving Up CONTROL) | 367 |
| 123. | The UPLIFTING QUIZ | 371 |
| 124. | "MY LIFE" | 373 |
| 125. | PURE | 377 |
| 126. | Thoughts in the Temple | 381 |
| 127. | "He's a Jealous GOD" | 385 |
| 128. | STILL STANDING | 387 |
| 129. | "Learning to WORSHIP in Any DISRUPTION" | 389 |
| 130. | "When Pride is HIGH" | 393 |

131. "YOUR WILL NOT MINE" ................................................. 395
132. "Managing Emotions Through the INNER-MAN" .............. 397
133. "The PALM TREE" ......................................................... 401
134. PEARLS ......................................................................... 403
135. "Greatness in Thankfulness" ........................................... 407
136. "WHAT'S GROWING... FROM YOU?" ............................ 411
137. "Thinking of YOU" ......................................................... 413
138. ELEVATE ....................................................................... 415
139. REAL LOVE vs. FALSE LOVE .......................................... 419
140. "DENIAL" ...................................................................... 421
141. NO WORRIES ................................................................ 425
142. "Are You Truly Ready to LOVE?" .................................... 429
143. "MIND MOVE" ............................................................... 431
144. "Self-Esteem in RECOVERY" ........................................... 435
145. "The Culture of the ANGRY" .......................................... 439

# Acknowledgements

When I was eight years old, my family was living in Los Angeles, California. My parents were not under the care of Christ at the time but under the cares of this world. In fact, I recall they knew more how to party than praise the Lord. Since they were still quite young parents, they spent a great deal of time going out on the town and having me stay usually with a babysitter. At first, it was several individuals that watched over me. From a young teen girl who lived down the street, to staying with a kid I went to school with whose Dad abused his wife nightly. Finally, my parents found someone that would alter my life to this day.

Her name was Mrs. Stivers, and she lived directly across the street. She was probably in her fifties at the time. She was a widow, and her husband had died some years before we moved into the neighborhood. She was a wonderful woman that was the initiator of introducing me to Christ! At first, I did not get all the devotion to this so-called Lord that she was so devoted too. She would pray every morning out on her patio before she began to work in her garden. She would share so many spiritual principles to me about a garden that I knew at eight years old that not only was God a gardener, but He made man to follow in His footsteps.

Mrs. Stivers went to church every Sunday, so when my parents were going out on Saturday nights, I knew that church was going to be taking place on Sunday mornings. What was so interesting was as I began to comprehend the bible and make practical sense of what was being shared with me. Oh, did I tell you that Mrs. Stivers was the Professor of Theology at Pepperdine University? In fact, we went to the church that most of the students went too as well. So, I began to hang around a bunch of theology majors at eight years old!

After a while, my Mom knew that Mrs. Stivers was more than a babysitter, she was my mentor, my teacher, and my friend. I spent hours and hours not only at her home, but in her classroom, and at study hall with her and the students. I loved Sunday school and worship. It became so much of a weekly operation that my Mom allowed me to hang out with Mrs. Stivers every Sunday. On one of those Sundays, I accepted Christ as my savior! Most thought I was too young to transition into giving my life to Christ, but what they didn't know was the living scriptures was brought to life to me from a little lady that allowed the Word to open my understanding.

For the next few years, something began to happen to me. I realized that I was no longer just a little boy, but that I was a little disciple. My Mom knew that something was stirring in me. Yet she still allowed this great friendship with Mrs. Stivers to take place. I really did not have any real friends around at that time, so the only person outside of my parents that gave intentional attention to me was Mrs. Stivers. She was the key catalyst of directing me on the journey to discover Jesus.

You may be saying, "Why exhaust so much attention towards this woman of honor?" Well, she was responsible for shaping my innocent little mind towards not only who Jesus is but what He came to do on earth, which was to make me like HIM! After all these years, I am still learning how to be like Him. Mrs. Stivers, whether she knew it or not, revealed from her life security and significance in Christ! Not in her possessions, her power on campus, or in her position as a professor, but as a child of God. I hope this book *Substance for Security and Significance* resembles the impact she made on my life!

Thank you, Mrs. Stivers! I will always remember you and love you!

C.J. Jackson "Coy"

# Foreword

## By J.P. Thompson

Significant Reader, I am so excited for you. The message you will receive in the contents of this book is so timely and special. Some would say these are the most confusing and terrifying times we have seen in decades. I have GOOD NEWS though; God has called someone to deliver a message to us. Are you ready to receive it?

Identifying the difference between success and significance in your life is vital to discovering your true purpose. Growing up and going through the different stages of life, I looked to the world to find what true success might look like as I transitioned into my career of serving people in personal finance. With this passion, I related well to the concept of people who "deposit" INTO your life and people who "withdrawal" FROM your life. I was beyond blessed to meet the ultimate depositor just within three months of starting my business and career, your author, Mr. CJ Jackson. This would prove to be the time when I transformed my mindset from success to significance.

There are many ways a person can pour (deposit) into someone. For example, two significant ways, which have rocked me to my inner core, are dedicating your time to that person and speaking truth into their life (Sometimes no matter how hard it may be for them to hear and receive the message). CJ will pour into you through the contents of these pages… but one thing that became completely evident to me is the question I had to ask myself, am I willing to receive it and put it into practice in my own life to achieve significance and stability?

Have you ever heard that the definition of commitment is simply just showing up? CJ taught me firsthand, that commitment is discipline, and discipline leads to discovering significance in your life. CJ's spiritual mentorship and our partnership took an agreed upon regiment of meeting consistently that we both committed to. I cannot speak for our author, but I would imagine, like other disciplines that we establish in our lives, it takes work and pure commitment from both parties to achieve significance. Life throws curveballs at you at every turn but establishing a game plan to stay committed and discipline will spotlight your path to significance and purpose. Here is what I will say, it truly did for me, in both moments of triumph and turmoil.

Celebrating triumphs in your life is obsessively wonderful. CJ bringing my wife and me to the Lord's altar (after great preparation!) as we made a covenant to each other in holy matrimony in front of the people we care about most is a moment that I replay in my mind constantly to bring immense joy and peace. Gripping and squeezing dearly my wife's left hand, while her mother opposite of me held tightly her right hand, as we brought my daughter into our family, fills me with every joyous emotion one could feel. Quite frankly, it's perfect rhythm and harmony that you wish to not end. Growing up in a small family steel business, I enjoy the "Everything is firing on all cylinders" mentality!

Finding purpose and significance through turmoil is another story completely. One moment you're down on one knee proposing to the love of your life, and the next you're telling your fiancé that you have just been diagnosed with Stage 4 Hodgkins Lymphoma and need multiple surgeries and chemotherapy to heal—Happy engagement Carter! Finding spiritual and personal growth through both triumphs and turmoil is necessary. This turmoil brought its fair share of pain, agony, and uncertainty, but throughout it all, my wife and I held sacred the foundation that CJ had laid for us in delivering God's word and depositing the Lord's significance into our lives.

CJ Jackson's message will serve as a restoration station for you to stop for a refreshing moment to explore the abundant significance in your life. In closing, Significant Reader, the contents of this book will simply get you excited about life again!

Godspeed,

JP Thompson
Mentee and Raving Fan of Coyvell "CJ" Jackson
Owner of Thompson Schoch Financial Advisors

# Introduction

After publishing my first book in 2016 entitled *The Bread Crumbs*, an interesting journey begin to develop in my life. First, I was diagnosed with cancer in April 2016. It was fourth stage cancer in my prostate. The surgeon would have to remove the large tumor that had grown so large it was causing challenges to my bladder and my kidneys. As I faced this first major hurdle in my health, I knew God was not only with me on this new course, but I knew through it my faith would forever be altered and modified because of this new road that laid before me.

My surgery took more than six hours, and after, my body immediately began to feel the pain of being worked on. In addition, apparently the doctors had forgotten to give me pain medication to reduce the pain after surgery. When I awoke, the pain was unlike anything I had ever faced! I began to groan and make all kinds of vocal noises because of the pain. My wife was anguished and fought back tears because of watching me struggle with this great pain. But as I began to deal with the pain, I heard a small voice share with me, "Open His word." So, I shared with my distraught wife to open the bible to Psalms Chapter 1.

As she began to read, I begin to recite the very words that were being amplified from my wife's voice, then I began to elaborate and prophesize with authority on what was being shared in my very hospital bed. As I began to share, nurses and doctors came in to see what the commotion was and were stunned to realize that amid my significant PAIN, I pursued to PRAISE His name. Then as I proclaimed His matchless name, something happened! The pain was removed without the use of any medications. It was a sign of where God was leading me towards a new path of deliverance that was beyond the natural order but functioning in the supernatural order!

It was a demonstration of power that moved everyone that was in that room. Including the entire medical staff! No one could doubt, diminish, or downsize what was uncovered in that hospital room. It was in this exact moment that I knew every aspect of my life in Christ was about to go to a different level, to a different dimension!

Little did I realize, in less than eight months later, that the cancer would return with a vengeance. But I had now stepped into the deep end of God's power, His protection, and His purpose! I had experienced a place beyond a church service and some great sermon. I had received a special reservoir of might that like the bible speaks, "It made mountains move." My mountain currently was my health.

So, when the doctors informed me and my bride that cancer had returned, I think they expected us to break down, lose ground emotionally, and begin to display outward beliefs of "I am going to die?" or "This is too much!" Nevertheless, the

Lord had revealed to me, "God is our refuge and strength, a very present help in trouble. Therefore, we will not fear" (Psalms 46:1-2). This was indeed a troubling situation, and I knew I needed God's very present help in my current circumstance. When the doctor told me I would need more than 40 treatments to remove the cancer over a period of two months, I knew that even though the doctors were doing their part, that Jesus had revealed, "I am the Great Physician."

Through this course, the Lord was telling me that my life would be a witness to His ability to HEAL, to HELP, and to deliver a HARVEST during what was deemed by some as a seedless season.

This prompted me to consider that *The Bread Crumbs* was more than a daily dose of nourishment of how God feeds you with His wellness to the totality of life. Little did I know that He was revamping, remaking, and recalibrating my entire position in how I saw myself through His eyes.

I realized that to truly see God, I must seek to look through His lenses and not my own. So, I was led to comprise a series of books that are geared towards reaching every area that God had intended for his children to become WHOLE. I guess like most people, earlier in my walk with God, I assumed I had reached the place where we deem we have arrived or we claim, "This is it." But I was in store for a rude awakening. I had not even touched the surface of what God had genuinely wanted to see manifested in my life. I assumed I was a whole person but realized as things that I faced exposed themselves, I was not whole but broken or in pieces.

I soon discovered that I was not alone, that many so-called believers had hid, covered up, and pushed down what they were facing or trying to deal with. This led me to this first book of the series, which is specifically designed to give application and teachable moments in security and significance. These special daily dishes in which I call "Crumbs" are designed to help shape, sustain, and stabilize places where we have tried to function without working or giving attention to the places where we hurt and go through pain without actually healing from it. Too often in life we attempt to cram tons of information pertaining to certain areas of the spiritual life down our throats and wind up feeling like we have never made much progress. This new daily devotional on "Substance for Security and Significance" is to magnify the places that many of us walk out within life. It is systematically arranged to give a daily spiritual meal that reaches to the depths of your heart and soul.

You will discover that from God's perspective, He has had a place ready for us to embrace since He sent His Son as the Redeemer. He has been waiting on us to stop the vicious cycles and motions of going through a thing and not becoming the thing. He intended for us to become the living examples of Abundance, Transformation, Balance, Openness, Power, and Love!

Many of us have spent enough time being surface dwellers in this so-called spiritual life and not venturing toward greater heights, greater depths, and places where we become completely awakened to the voice of God. This latest written piece is geared to cause real growth in the places where many walk with the struggle to see actual fruit and progression in this life, and they can begin to monitor and map out what the Lord truly desired to see magnified.

So, as you take your first step in taking a bite out of this book, I suggest you see it as daily operation where the outcome is to begin to witness results in areas where you have been dormant in growth or doubting things will ever change. This is your spiritual nourishment for establishing what may be lacking or missing from the Substance of Security and Significance!

## Day 1

# CREAM AND SUGAR

*"Taste the Lord and know that He is good."* (Psalms 34:8)

Lots of people enjoy drinking coffee or tea with cream and sugar. In fact, I have discovered that the craze with coffee shops across the globe is due to adding something in coffee or tea that makes it taste super special. Most people have found that when you add a little something to coffee, it makes it more delicious. From one flavor to another, people love adding something to their coffee. Every morning I witness long lines of people in coffee shops standing in line to add something to their day—preferably something great!

It is amazing how that something like cream and sugar can extremely alter the taste of something like coffee. The truth of the matter is that our Christian lives also desire for us to have something constantly added to it. For you see, the Bible shares, "We have this treasure in earthen vessels that the surpassing greatness of the power may be of God and not of ourselves" (II

Corinthians 4:7). No child of God was designed to live or exist any other way than what God envisioned, which was to be a "TREASURE."

A treasure is something desirable. It is something wonderful, incredible, and excellent! Every child of God should anticipate something glorious every day the Lord touches their life! Most people who desire an excellent cup of java taste it to confirm that its good. Our focus scriptures states, "Taste the Lord and know that He is good." God dispenses something awesome and attractive as a norm in every moment. It is in His nature to deliver something that contributes to our lives. So why don't we add to what has already been decided to those called "the earthen vessels"?

The difference with us and coffee shops is that people believe way before they even receive their cup of coffee that it is going to be GOOD. Why? Because they have had it before. They know what to expect. They have tasted it time after time. They have established the deliverance of something reliable.

Could one of the reasons why so many are missing something special day after day in the Lord be because they have never truly embellished the grace and favor of God? I mean, if we enjoy what is being poured into our lives daily, why not continue to wait with anticipation? When God is good, you always savor the moment!

## Day 2

# THE GREAT EXPECTATION

*"Now unto him that is able to do exceedingly abundantly above all that we ask or think, according to the power that worketh in us."* (Ephesians 3:20)

Today in prayer time the Lord revealed this, "Expand your EXPECTATIONS." The revelation He exposed though was that the great expectation comes when my life is about the pursuit of pleasing Him. The fulfillment of pursing Him is accomplished through OBEDIENCE. God operates in the environment of obedience, and if you want to catch Him, you must pursue Him in obedience. In my life, I have discovered that my pursuit at times has been for the Lord to fix and flourish my life without concluding that He works through my OBEDIENCE. When I pursue Him in obedience, then my EXPECTATIONS also expand.

"Now it shall come to pass, if you diligently obey the voice of the Lord your God, to observe carefully all His commandments which I command you today, and that the Lord your God will set you high above all nations of the earth. And all these blessings shall come upon you and overtake you, because you obey the voice of the Lord your God" (Deuteronomy 28:1-2).

Think about it; we desire for the Lord to do great things in every area of life, but did we ever consider that the favor of God is directly connected by what is coming out of us before His presence? Stop for a minute and consider our passage in a personal way, "Above all that we ask or think," God can go BEYOND that! In other words, whatever I imagine, dream, plan, process, or even consider as unreal, He is still able to go exceedingly beyond that!

No matter if you think your dream is just too big or too enormous to be revealed, it is still far below what God can deliver. For the Bible says He cannot do a little bit better or even a whole lot better, but ABUNDANTLY better. In fact, the word "exceeding" implies that abundant is not even a word big enough to describe what He can do.

Did you ever think that our expectations limit God? Why is that? Because He has no LIMIT! God's abundance is beyond our comprehension and understanding. So, I challenge you to go beyond what you expect from God and learn to EXPAND your EXPECTATIONS! The word "expand" means to ENLARGE or spread out. The word "expectation" means EAGER anticipation. When I expand my expectations, I am enlarging my anticipation. Now that is something to expect!

To expand our expectations requires us to think outside the box to begin to base our expectations on what HE can DO and not what we are able to think or do. BECAUSE HE can DO ABUNDATELY MORE!

## Day 3

# THE LITTLE BIRDS

*Inspired by my Bride Brenda Jackson*

*"Look at the birds of the air, for they neither sow nor reap nor gather into barns; yet your heavenly Father feeds them. Are you not of more value than they?"* (Matthew 6:26)

Recently my lovely wife shared something about "The Little Birds" that you and I witness in the sky every day. On one hand, it was simple, and yet on the other hand, it was significant! What she revealed to me was to learn a life principle the birds. She stated, "Have you ever noticed that birds live satisfied, secure, and simple? Birds don't get confused in life with stuff."

"Look at the birds," those were the exact words that Jesus instructed us to consider. In addition, He even wanted us to observe the actions that "they neither sow nor reap nor gather into barns; yet your heavenly Father feeds them." Birds do not normally check into the Betty Ford clinic, and we do not find them losing sleep over bills, or the lack of income in the bank. In fact, birds live a simple life! It is one where there is little if any frustration or aggravation. Birds live life with the absence of complication. We operate quite the opposite. With divorce, depression, and debt being how many function and flow daily, it is a wonder we do not pause and "look at the birds."

One of the first things to look at from the birds is they do not sow or reap. Birds do not plant or harvest their food. It is always accessible for them through means outside of their control. Birds do not hoard, hide, or connive to live. Birds exist with the realization that their needs will be addressed by the creator. Notice that the scripture states, "Nor do they gather food into barns." Birds are not hypnotized by the cares of this world. Birds care nothing about fashion, foreclosures, and finances. Birds are free to live for what they were created for! What about you and me? Are we living a life that was intended from God? Or has something caused an operation where we fuss and fret over everything down to what is on the menu? I suggest that we look at the birds.

Birds live with meaning. Birds live with purpose. Birds live with priorities! Think about it; birds spend their time living for their intended function. Your priorities reflect what is important to you in life. Jesus stated, "Where your heart is there also is your treasure." Priorities show up where we spend our time, our money, and our energy. Priorities determine what we will get out of life. Just as worrying reveals the evidence of things that stifle your life, priorities are the cement that proves what you hold of value.

No wonder Jesus commanded that we "seek first the Kingdom of God and all His righteousness." Because when we seek the kingdom of God, then the Kingdoms of this world (meaning the things of this world) will have no jurisdiction into God's intended function for His creation, namely His people. The birds understand their overall function, and they live like it. Perhaps here lies the reason why Jesus shared, "Look at the birds."

## Day 4

# TIME TO LEAVE THE REST STOP

*"The soul of a **lazy** man desires and has nothing; But the soul of the diligent shall be made rich."* (Proverbs 13:4)

The other day while sitting on my balcony, I noticed something that on any other day I would have most likely missed. But on this occasion, I got a glimpse of something that opened my eyes even further about God's creation. It was in the remarkable way Canadian Geese communicate. It was evident that a flock of geese had decided to use my backyard as a rest stop before heading south for the winter. We all have heard and even read of the fantastic voyage that these great birds make every year, but what I saw today left me with an even greater respect for the architect… "God." As I sat there admiring these great creatures, one in the flock (who appeared to be the leader) began to walk around the entire group as if to communicate that rest time was over. It was now time to fly!

Communication is a tool designed by God. The objective is to connect, unite, and understand another. In addition, it is only by some form of communication that we can comprehend our very existence. The fact that this leader of the flock knew when it was time to persuade the others to fly caused me to realize how often we deal with others in life but never help push, propel, or prepare them for their purpose. It is the design of God that in communication we receive from those that are close to us to have a powerful impact that bears fruit of prosperity. Those birds needed rest, but they also needed someone to share when it was **time to leave the rest stop.**

In my short time on earth, I have met thousands who have never left the rest stop.

In other words, they cannot seem to break free from procrastination or with just letting time slip away. They say, "One day I will make a change," but that one day becomes many days. They have great plans for new business ventures and talk of making moves that would change their current course in life, but they cannot get off pause. When do you know if your life has become a pattern of hanging out for too long at the REST STOP?

First, ask this question: Are you making a difference in the world? Those who linger too long at the rest stop are not able to make movements for someone else because they are so frozen on self, and they cannot provide service for someone else. There is a reason why the Word of God is so full on the topic of being lazy. The reason why is because the lazy spirit has a result, and it is that you never prosper. Our text states, "The soul of a **lazy** man desires and has nothing."

When we get comfortable at the rest stop of life, so much that we have all these great ideas but we have no follow through on them, then what we produce in the finality of life will result in revealing to us nothing! As I watched these great geese fly away with their leader holding the front position, I realized that maybe why so many people stay at the rest stop of life is because they refuse to follow those that God has placed in their lives as leaders. How can we break free from a lax world that wants us just to get by and settle for nothing if we are unwilling to follow the solid instructions of those that share when it is time to fly?

## Day 5

# LIAR, LIAR

I remember as a child when I first conjured up my initial attempt to lie. I had convinced myself that to escape the wrath of my parents over something I had done was to lie. It is interesting to note that the lie has become a fine art. Lying in our society is more recognized as a useful practice. The world as we know it has been convinced that the lie is a proven established way to function. From the White House to what appears to be nearly EVERY house we have witnessed, children, adults, parents, couples, spouses, businessman, government officials, and leaders all over the world use lying as a workable tool for personal convenience. The Bible pulled the mask off who is the culprit of lies in John 8:44 where it records that Satan was "a LIAR and the FATHER of LIES." Not only is he seen as a liar, but he is known as the Instructor of Lies. In other words, someone is schooling the world in lies. Someone is directing the hearts of mankind to be led down the road to consider lying is a viable option.

Lies are illusions. Lying is a trick, and a form of DECEPTION. In other words, lies approach those who dwell on some level of truth and then use lies to create an alternate route. Remember when Satan in Genesis Chapter 3 turned Himself into a snake (serpent)? That was really the first lie. He was using a mask to hide the truth of who he really was. Adam knew the truth about all the animals because God made him the official first zoologist in naming the animals. Adam had the insight (the truth) to know that when he named all the animals none of them could TALK. Yet he listened, he considered the information from a talking snake, because lies are attractive and alluring. But consider for a moment if he knew the snake, (and I believe that he did), then he knew words coming from a snake is not the TRUTH.

Today we allow things, situations, and circumstances to talk to us in ways that is not the truth like the snake. We allow ourselves to continue to absorb the perpetual release of information where the goal is to guide us towards the consideration of a lie. Everything lying is geared towards obtaining a GAIN. The devil wanted to gain the worship of mankind by having mankind worship himself. Remember they were convinced by the lie that "if they eat the fruit they would be like God" (Genesis 3:5).

The weapon God has given us to wage war against lies is the Word of God, which the scriptures declare as the "Sword of the Spirit" (Ephesians 6:17). Jesus said that His words "are Spirit and they are Life." In other words, Christ is declaring that His word is connected to His glory. His word is ALIVE (Hebrews 4:12). The Word is not only divine, but it possesses power to activate LIFE! Our text reveals that as the father of lies he (the Devil) has "desires" that we desire. The Instructor of Lies wants you to desire lies for what he believes you really crave to do. In addition, the Bible states that as the father of lies "he has been a murderer since the beginning," meaning he leaves Death and Destruction wherever he goes. Also, the Bible states, "He does not stand in the truth, because there is no truth in him."

In other words, when a person stands on something, they are firmly positioned in it. They are grounded and rooted in it. The father of lies cannot stand in the truth because there is no truth in him. Think about it, there is no truth in the spirit of the enemy. If there is no truth, then his quest is to take us where he already dwells, and that is with no TRUTH. If there is no truth, then there is no reality. Christ states on the other hand that "I am the way, the TRUTH, and the life" (John 14:6). He also stated that His Word was the TRUTH (John 17:17). So, the truth is the devil since the beginning of time has been tracking us to separate us from the truth. To separate us from the Lord. Today, seek for the truth, stand on the truth, search for the truth, and speak on the Truth!

## Day 6

# THE COMFORT ZONE

*"Now the Lord said unto Abram to get from out of his country, and from his family, and from his father's house, and go into a land that I will show you: And I will make you a great nation, and I will bless you, and make your name great; and you shall be a blessing."* (Genesis 12:1-2)

Today it appears we have a people that are more familiar with comforts than character. Think about it, when an infant begins to crawl and eventually attempts to take steps, they are not afraid to fall more than once. They keep getting up over and over!

Yet many people fail in life because they are unwilling to make changes. We refuse to change jobs, towns, or even friendships. We stay in the COMFORT ZONE.

Many evade and squirm around any kind of discomfort, not realizing like the infant that one must be willing to face some discomfort to experience a new level of life.

God had asked Abram to leave what he was accustomed to. He left his livelihood, family, and roots, and trusted the direction of that would lead him to have a great name and be a blessing.

One of the things I love about Jesus is that He always gives people something to do that they never did before. He knew that their obedience was the proof of their faith in Him. It is amazing that when we face calamities and challenges, we freak out, fall out, and let our feelings trip us out, when all this is remarkably like that child falling but getting back up because the baby has in fact faith to get back up.

When you want something you have never had, you must do something you have never done!

Thousands in this life will fail because they refuse to make changes. I want you to pray today that you learn to embrace whatever has impacted your life so that God breaks you from your COMFORT ZONES!

## Day 7

# SUBMERGENCE

> *"Whoever believes in me, as Scripture has said, rivers of living water will flow from within them."* (John 7:38)

On the last and greatest day of the Feast, Jesus stood and said in a loud voice, "If anyone is thirsty, let him come to me and drink. Whoever believes in me, as the Scripture has said, streams of living water will flow from within him" (John 7:38-39). By this he meant the Holy Spirit. It is interesting that God would use water to symbolize His Spirit. In the beginning (when God created the Heaven's and the earth), water was about all there was. It was not until the third day of creation God caused "dry ground" to appear. To this day, about 70 percent of the Earth is covered by water.

Water was one of the main elements God used in creation. For example, if you were to go outside and look at a tree in the field, that tree is made of at least 75 percent water. If you go down to the local KFC, their chickens (when they were alive) were 75% water. And the common pineapple has 80 percent water in it. Then of course… water comprises more than 60 percent of your body, 70 percent of your brain, 80 percent of your blood, and nearly 90 percent of your lungs. Most things are in fact submerged with water. The Bible tells me that God is omnipresent. Like water, He is everywhere! In fact, there is no place that we can go to get away from His Spirit.

David wrote in Psalms 139: 7-10, "Where can I go from your Spirit? Where can I flee from your presence? If I go up to the heavens, you are there; if I make my bed in the depths, you are there. If I rise on the wings of the dawn, if I settle on the far side of the sea, even there your hand will guide me, your right hand will hold me fast." Like water, God's Spirit is everywhere. And yet, that Spirit is not accessible to everyone. Jesus teaches us that ONLY those who believe in Him will have this fountain of living water within them. Like water, God's Spirit has been given to us so that our thirst can be satisfied, so that our lives or souls can be submerged in true satisfaction.

When Jesus talked with the woman at the well, He said to her, "Everyone who drinks this water will be thirsty again, but whoever drinks the water I give him will never thirst. Indeed, the water I give him will become in him a spring of water welling up to eternal life" (John 4:13-14). So, what kind of thirst does the Spirit satisfy? The truth of the matter is He helps our thirst to be connected to God and the thirst for righteousness. He fulfills the thirst to be purified, the thirst to be sanctified, and our thirst to be strengthened. Our thirst for comfort! The Bible tells me in Romans 8:26 that "the Spirit helps us in our weakness. We do not know what we ought to pray for, but the Spirit himself intercedes for us with groans that words cannot express." Even when I cannot find the words to express my emotions, God's Spirit steps in and "intercedes" for me; He understands my sorrows and difficulties and communicates those things directly to God.

Imagine that, we have a connection with the Holy Spirit where His intent is to keep me satisfied, saturated, and submerged with the ingredients of God. Why you ask? Because you were created and designed to reflect the nature of God. If this is our reality, I encourage you to open your life and await the POURING!

## *Day 8*

# "Why Lord?"

*"My God, my God, why have you forsaken me? Why are you so far from saving me, so far from the words of my groaning?"*
(Psalms 22:1)

Today we are going to dive into why so many days of our lives end in "why Lord?" Also, what should we do when the "why Lord" fills our minds?

Think long enough, and you will discover that we exist in this world asking the question—WHY? For instance, why I am all alone, or why did my spouse leave me? Some go farther with asking, why did my Mom leave this time side of life, and why was I born this way? We are born with a burning desire to know the "whys" of life!

The thing that many may miss along the way of seeking answers to the whys of life is that God knows all! If this is a reality to life, it is a reality for you personally. The confirmation that God has and is the ANSWER to everything is verified in His Word, His Will, and His WAY!

In other words, He knows tomorrow better that we know yesterday. And He can be trusted! God's Word is the voice and message of EVERLASTING that reveals His Will and His Way of acting and reacting with mankind. The will of God can never go against the Word of God! Every time God speaks from His Word, He is not only revealing His Will, but He is giving you the course to travel down towards His Way. We may never get every answer to every "why," but we can trust in God's Way!

*Day 9*

# Out of Nothing

*"Let there be Light."* (Genesis 1:3)

Did you ever consider a reality about the almighty God who has created and formed everything, that He manifested everything from nothing? It blows me away how often we are ready to give up everything because our current road of life sometimes goes directly to what appears as a dead end, not realizing that with God He makes roads! Today I humble myself to His greatness as I witness how many times the Lord has made SOMETHING… "Out of Nothing!"

Remember the Bible states, "In the beginning the earth was without form and void, and darkness covered the earth." Yet the Lord looked down on the earth's condition and concluded, "All it needs is a little light!" Like the earth, the Lord has looked down on you and me and determined, "All they need is my light." Let us face it; we were disconnected, confused, lost, wayward, and the Lord said, "They see nothing, but I'm about turn to that into SOMETHING!"

You may be asking today what the Lord will use to blossom life where there is no life. Here is your answer—"NOTHING!" The Almighty always begins His great, creative work with "NOTHING." How is this possible? Mainly due to the truth that He is the catalyst of what causes change where there was nothing, because He is our forever SOMETHING. No wonder the scripture shares, "If anyone thinks he is something when he is nothing, he deceives himself" (Galatians 6:3). We are something because of SOMEONE called Jesus!

It is amazing that all creation yields to the handiwork of the Lord, from a tree to a Tiger, but man seems to struggle with allowing the Lord to have his with what He has made. It is the Lord's responsibility to create and our responsibility to SUBMIT to His creating.

As Christians, if we think we are "something" so that we look down on others or we are wise in our own eyes, we deceive ourselves! The only something there truly is, is God.

The great Myles Munroe quoted on one occasion, "If you want to know how to run a thing, you don't ask another thing, you must ask the one who created the thing!" So often in this life when we face dead ends and distractions, we navigate through them by attempting to make our own detours, not realizing that even when it looks like we have just jumped into a bowl of nothing, God can still deliver something "OUT OF NOTHING!"

## Day 10

# A Divine Storm

*"Then the Lord spoke to Job out of the storm."* (Job 40:6)

What is the first thing you consider when you hear a storm is coming? Some of us start preparing for the worst. Others realize it is a sign for the weather to change in their lives. Have you ever thought that in the spiritual there are storms where it is used as a conduit for God to speak? Such is the case with the man called Job. God used the power of a storm to speak a powerful word that was relevant for his servant. It was a personal word that was specific towards what was to come in his life. Today God still speaks through storms. It may not be with natural thunder and lighting and wind and rain but with a force that is demonstrating the need for renewal and restoration.

Today there is a spiritual storm that is on the weather report of those anticipating God's ultimate grace. This storm is called… **The DIVINE STORM.** This is a storm that is directed by God. It is a storm that is under His power. It is a storm that God has decided for His chosen children to go through. Divine storms reveal to us that God is in control! Divine storms manifest in our lives for witnessing the all-consuming power of our God. Divine storms move in our direction to showcase God's protection, His provision, and His power!

The key for being a partaker of a divine storm is you must understand that it is not a storm to set you back but one designed to set you up. You may think the storm you're facing is taking you under, but it came to take you over. This is the outcome of a Divine Storm.

Often, we think that the weather conditions are changing in our lives because of the devil, but let me inform you that God intentionally sends storms our way. He sends divine storms because He has a new forecast in store for you. God spoke to Job in the middle of a storm. Jesus spoke to Peter in what appeared to him as one of the greatest storms he had ever encountered and said "COME!" Jesus wanted him to walk through storms. He wanted Peter to recognize that despite the storm, He was the NAVIAGATOR!

## Day 11

# SHINING STAR

*"And they that be wise shall shine as the brightness of the firmament; and they that turn many to righteousness as the stars for ever and ever."* (Daniel 12:3)

So many people desire to be stars for the world that encircles around their lives. God speaks from His word instructing us that His desire is for us to be eternal stars, meaning stars that impact this life and continue into the next!

Our text states, "Those who are wise shall shine." First off, the wisdom the writer is inferring to is the wisdom of God. Much too often though, most believe that any wisdom will do, or that wisdom is wisdom. The truth of the matter is that God says in I Corinthians 3:19, "For the wisdom of this world is foolishness with God." To God, foolishness compares with worldly wisdom. This wisdom is where the intent satisfies our own impulses and is not one that is centered on giving God the complete glory.

True wisdom, the Bible shares, "Comes from above." In other words, it not only resembles the giver of it (The Lord), but it also models its true origin from God. In addition, not only are they wise who truly shine, but they shine and portray righteousness to others! As stars, we are to radiate from our lives the quintessential characteristics of God that embody the light of God (His wisdom). True righteousness is not according to me, but according to the Lord! In fact, the Bible states, "Seek first the kingdom of God, and ALL HIS RIGHTEOUSNESS" (Matthew 6:33). There is an objective to seek not just any standard of righteousness but His Righteousness!

To turn towards righteousness, you must "let your light so shine before men, that they may see your good works, and glorify your Father which is in heaven." (Matthew 5:16). This is the reality of a SHINING STAR!

God stated we are "those who turn many to righteousness like stars forever and ever" (Daniel 12:3). According to scientists, we have observed more and more stars that have materialized than ever before. The galaxy is growing in the multiplicity of stars. In fact, one place is nicknamed "STAR CITY." Here they have discovered two previously undetected cities of stars known as global clusters, which are hundreds of thousands of stars.

God has created us to impact others with ability like the stars, in that the intent is to multiply His RIGHTEOUSNESS!

## Day 12

# The Other Side

*"This is the message that we have heard from Him and declare to you, that God is light and in Him is no darkness at all."* (I John 1:5)

Have you ever searched for something but the lighting was dim or dark in that place and you were unable to find it? I have discovered that when one is in the dark, they lack the insight or knowledge that exposes them to purpose. Darkness is more than the absence of light. It is more than not being able to see physically. It is the place where God is not. Darkness is a condition that keeps us from the revelation of God or the knowledge of God. From this understanding, we can conclude that darkness is ignorance. The objective of darkness is to keep the people of God from knowing the truth because the revelation of the truth can and will make you free!

You may recall when Jesus warned, "Take heed therefore that the light which is in you be not darkness" (Luke 11:35 KJV). It is quite apparent that the Lord wanted us to be in the zone with the fact that "there is a light in us." He wanted us to know the distinction of light from darkness. Many may think once they receive the light that there is no way they can succumb to the dark. The problem with that position is Christ made it vividly clear by saying, "Take heed," which means this was a warning.

The Lord wanted us to know what we claim as light may in fact be the dark! Satan has access to dwell in the domain of darkness, and we must grasp that point—the devil can traffic in any area of darkness, even the darkness that still exists in a Christian's heart. No wonder Jesus made it plain about being aware of the light that resides in us. The Bible shares, "The spirit of man is the lamp of the Lord" (Proverbs 20:27). Your spirit, illuminated by the Spirit of Christ, becomes the "lamp of the Lord" through which He searches your heart. There is indeed a holy radiance surrounding a true Spirit-filled Christian. But when you harbor sin, the "light which is in you" has become "darkened."

The challenge many of us face is how did we leave the presence of light and transition towards darkness? Jesus made it clear in Matthew 6:22-23, "The eye is the lamp of the body. If your eyes are healthy, your whole body will be full of light. But if your eyes are unhealthy, your whole body will be full of darkness. If then the light within you is darkness, how great is that darkness!" Jesus knew the key towards full illumination in the light had everything to do with what we have our eyes fixated on. In fact, He said, "The eye is the lamp of the body." Symbolically, the lamp illustrates guidance towards the knowledge and understanding of God, while the eye itself is pointed directly towards our desires. The Bible says, "You, Lord, are my lamp; the Lord turns my darkness into light" (II Samuel 22:29).**Cross references:** 2 Samuel 22:29 : Ps 27:1; Isa 2:5; Mic 7:8; Rev 21:23; 22:5When we allow our spiritual eyes to be affected by the flesh, it dulls our senses in the Lord. Our eyes convince us to use justification and rationalization in the promotion of that which we seek from the dark!

No wonder Eve shared "that the fruit of the tree was good for food and pleasing to the eye" (Genesis 3:6). The movement of darkness/ignorance is only possible because we adjust our lives to make it fit. The bible states, "You deceive yourselves" (James 1:22). In other words, we convince ourselves of our position. Satan is called the deceiver, and he is also called the prince of darkness, which is really the prince of IGNORANCE. His intent is to promote a person to refuse to comply. God desired that we be holy, sanctified, humble, true, and godly. If these attributes have left the residency of your heart, be aware you may be subjected to the other side!

## Day 13

# I CAN SEE CLEARLY NOW

*"Judge not, that you be not judged. For with what judgment you judge, you will be judged; and with the measure you use, it will be measured back to you. And why do you look at the speck in your brother's eye, but do not consider the plank in your own eye? Or how can you say to your brother, 'Let me remove the speck from your eye' and look, a plank is in your own eye? Hypocrite! First remove the plank from your own eye, and then you will see clearly to remove the speck from your brother's eye."* (Matthew 7:1-5)

Spiritually I have discovered that for a large portion of my life I have looked through a set of lenses I assumed were giving me ultimate clear vision, only to realize that until I was able to look through the eyes of God, I was still missing the glorious. Seeing with clear eyes spiritually is a part of what we call spiritual discernment. This is having the perception to see through the understanding of God. Some mainly think that spiritual discernment is the ability to see the difference between right and wrong. But it is so beyond that.

Spiritual discernment is the grace to see into the unseen. It is a gift of the Spirit to perceive the realm of the spirit. Its purpose is to understand the nature of that which is veiled. There is a process required to see clearly in the Spirit. Someone coined the phrase, "Beauty is in the eye of the beholder." The challenge we have with seeing through the lenses of the Spirit is that we have lived or worn spiritual glasses for so long in our current life that it has created an operation of what we deem as acceptable. Until there is a change within an individual, he or she will not even know that their current living may be CLOUDY.

There are many who suppose they are receiving the Lord's discernment concerning one thing or another. Perhaps in some things they are, only God knows. But many are simply judging others and calling it discernment. Jesus commanded us to judge not. He sends us into the world not as judges of man, but under Him as co-redeemers. We are not sent to condemn people but to rescue them. For us to see clearly in the Spirit, we must remove what causes our spiritual insight to be off-sighted. Remember, Jesus said, "First take the log out of your own eye, and then you will see clearly to take the speck out of your brother's eye." Notice, that until we can deal with what is preventing ultimate sight for us, we will not SEE CLEARLY! In other words, no matter what we do, our spiritual perception will be tainted until we remove what is the catalyst for causing us to be off-sighted. The way we help others is not by judging but by seeing clearly. This is the "righteous judgment" of which Jesus speaks in John 7:24. We do not "see clearly" until we have been through deep and thorough repentance, until that instinct to judge is UPROOTED! If all we are is the judge, the jury, and the verdict, we will never see clearly. In other words, we will never see what God has wanted to unveil. We will continue to look through a set of lenses that creates confusion and chaos and not conception and connection. Today, let us get our spiritual eyes examined and conclude if there is something preventing us from seeing the glorious!

## Day 14

# LIMITLESS

*"With men this is impossible, but with God ALL things are POSSIBLE."* (Matthew 19:26)

It is amazing that God allows us to peer into His unfathomable ability. The challenge for us is not what can He do but will He do it for you. What we miss is the reality from the Word of God that it is a seed that is searching for fertile soil (our lives) where it can BLOSSOM. We must change the condition of our lives so the seed can produce a Harvest. Everybody desires much, but how often are we checking out the growth of what we claim has been planted in our lives? Like a farmer, we must evaluate the soil before the seed can truly expand. Over and over we witness God trying to plant in our hearts what kind of harvest He has planned for us. He said in John 15:16 "that our fruit should remain." That means a continual perpetual operation. God envisioned His divine nature to be for us what it is for Him… LIMITLESS!

God stated to His children that "ALL things work together for those who love God, to those that are called per His purpose" (Romans 8:28). Jesus said, "ALL that the Father gives Me will come to Me, and the one who comes to Me I will by no means cast out" (John 6:37), and the Bible shares in John 3:35 that "ALL things are in His hand." If the Lord is trying to plant in us ALL that He has, let us prepare our lives and take Him at His word and witness that He is… LIMITLESS!

## Day 15

# Unwrapped

*"The Word [i.e. Jesus] became flesh and made His dwelling among us. We have seen His glory, the glory of the One and Only who came from the Father full of grace and truth."*
(John 1:14)

I am sure many of us remember *A Charlie Brown Christmas*. It's a great story about how the famous Peanuts gang discover that of all people, Charlie Brown is concerned about the meaning of Christmas. You may recall that he was first disappointed in Snoopy because of all the fancy lights and tinsel decked on his doghouse. Then the Peanuts gang share their concept of Christmas by Lucy sharing that she wants real estate. His sister Sally writes a letter to Santa that reads, "Dear Santa, I want tens, twenties, etc." After all this and more, Charlie Brown says, "Does anyone know what Christmas is about?" To Charlie Brown, Christmas had become an event instead of a personal experience!

God's message about Christmas is that the God of the Universe became flesh. More specifically, God became a man and went by the name of JESUS. The One we are looking for to save us from the mess our world is in has arrived already. The reason he has come is so that we can unwrap the greatest gift ever given. Here is a question, "Why would God give us such a gift?" The answer is… Because He loves us so much (John 3:16)! We are God's crowning achievement of His creation. God wants to bring us back from being lost from Him!

In addition, there is more that the Lord is also wanting us to unwrap. The Bible says, in Romans 12:6, "God has given each of us the ability to do certain things well." Not only has God given us the Gift of salvation, but He has also given us a gift that delivers a special purpose in the world today through us.

Now here is another question, "Have you unwrapped the gifts given to you by God?" I remember a tale where a child refused to open a gift because of the wrapping paper the gift was in. It was wrapped in a brown bag that one might use for their lunch bag. The child concluded that because of the observation of the wrapping paper the gift must be insignificant. But you see, God has always revealed it is what is inside the package that counts. Even on the birth of the Messiah, many mocked that a King would be born in a barn. They ridiculed the claim of a Savior being born in a manger because like the child with the gift wrapped in a lunch bag, it was not acceptable. Today the Lord is still leading many of us to paths where we come face to face with unwrapping a gift; He has specifically set it up for each of us. It may not be glamorous from our face value, it may not look appealing from the onset, but we must remember what God is concerned about. My friends, are we opening the gifts to see what is inside and using those gifts for His cause?

## Day 16

# "How Do You Know?"

*"Ask, and it will be given to you; seek, and you will find; knock, and it will be opened to you. For everyone who asks receives, and he who seeks finds, and to him who knocks it will be opened."* (Matthew 7:7-8)

Recently I met an old friend that I had not seen in quite some time. Much to my amazement, I was stunned to discover that it appeared that our entire dialogue seemed to focus completely on doubt, depression, delusion, distraction, and destruction. Every word spoken reverberated confusion and conflict from within. As I begin to get a word in edge wise, I realized that as I spoke on faith and having favor, my friend was perplexed and puzzled that I refused to be baptized into his current plight of anguish and anxiety. Many today struggle and fight against a word of DELIVERANCE mainly because they have been saturated by words of despair and deception. When

Jesus stated, "Seek and you shall find," we miss what lies behind what is entitled: The "SEEKING SPIRIT."

The Seeking Spirit is one where there is refusal to stop SEEKING. So many times I have heard from those going through mayhem and mishaps that they were determined to stay in that same old predicament. They make comments such as "There is no good in the world," and "I'm sick of fighting, what's the use?" not realizing what Jesus emphasized in our text, and that is it is the one that does not stop seeking that RECIEVES.

As my friend continued to spew words of agitation and aggravation, I noticed that I did not hear one time a word that pierced through his current barrier and obstacle. Notice that Jesus also shares, "Knock, and it will have opened to you." For many of us, we look over the fact that KNOCKING signifies the desire to enter.

Knocking means… In spite of what door may be preventing my entrance, it is my knocking that will cause the doors that are closed all around my life to OPEN!

Far too many in our world have not even the spiritual fortitude to knock. So, they stay behind the entrance of deliverance and dominion, not taking what God has already given, because they have been beaten down by past and current heartaches and hopelessness. So as my friend poured out what was on the inside of his heart, I knew that because he struggled to allow new words or new seeds to be planted into his heart, I had to take a real introspection into what I sought for his behalf. Despite his inability to push aside the debris that had become a standard in his life, I had to SEEK for his own benefit. I began to share, "How do you know that your circumstances will not be changed?" I told him, "Despite the chapters that you believe will be written for your life, I believe a new chapter is already being written for your future!"

He asked me, "C.J. do you really believe that change is on the way?" He asked, "HOW DO YOU KNOW?" My reply was, "I have witnessed the Glory of the Lord!" As my friend and I concluded our conversation, I told him I expect a DOOR to OPEN that has been closed. Nearly a week later, he called with great excitement about a current opportunity that had just showed up out of nowhere! He could not explain it, and he could only embrace it. Today, if you have been dealing with the attitude to give up or just exist in disappointment, I want to encourage you to KEEP SEEKING! KEEP KNOCKING! Believe that if you "Ask, it will be given unto you!"

## Day 17

# HUMBLE... YOURSELF

*"Therefore, humble yourselves under the mighty hand of God, that He may exalt you at the proper time, casting all your anxiety on Him, because He cares for you."* (1 Peter 5:6-7)

Did you ever consider that true humility is an act that requires a personal intentional pursuit? Which means it is not easily achieved due to the reality that for the child of God, we must break free from the clutches of carnality. True humility is not about us, it is about God using us completely for His purpose.

It is not natural for us as humans to be humble; on the contrary, we are usually trying to "achieve" or "stand out." However, humbling yourself can help you experience real joy, because real joy is not man-made or a tangible touchable natural quality of the earth. Real joy is DIVINE. No wonder Jesus said, "These things have I spoken unto you, that my joy might abide in you, and that your joy might be full" (John 15:11). The avenue Jesus used to grant great joy was His WORD. Not just His word though, but the obedience of His word translates us to place of great joy. But here is the thing—we cannot fully and realistically follow His word until we HUMBLE OURSELVES!

Notice that our text states, "Humble yourself UNDER the mighty hand of God." In other words, when I am UNDER something, it signifies that I am under its authority. To be under anything willingly is to submit to it. This is what John the Baptist meant when he shared, "He must increase, and I must decrease" (John 3:30). Humility is gained when we practice secret acts of service and then stand back so God can take over. When we do our part (whether publicly or secretly) and then stand back so that God can do His part, we are decreasing ourselves so He can increase. And when He does, wondrous things can happen for the Kingdom!

Humbling yourself is the equivalent of doing things in such a way that God gets the credit. In a world filled with wanting the glory or attention for ourselves, many seem to struggle even approaching God because of the overriding intention for personal modification instead of Lordship amplification. When the selfish spirit is pursuing to be filled, it craves for the credit, or it will even steal the credit. How we handle credit for things that we do is very telling of our character and has great impact on the results. To have true humility is a struggle when we thrive in environments where taking the credit is how we operate. It is better to give away credit than to try to take it. Credit taken is dangerous, but credit given away always comes back to you. As with hidden service, one of the best ways to build humility is to give credit away. There is no greater joy than to give credit away and watch as God gets the glory.

## Day 18

# Prescription for Instability

*"But let him ask in faith, with no doubting, for he who doubts is like a wave of the sea driven and tossed by the wind. For let not that man suppose that he will receive anything from the Lord; he is a double-minded man, unstable in all his ways."* (James 1:6-8)

Did you know that the Latin meaning for doubt is to have two minds? No wonder our text highlights, "But let him ask in faith, with no doubting, for he who doubts is like a wave of the sea driven and tossed by the wind. For let not that man suppose that he will receive anything from the Lord; he is a double-minded man, unstable in all his ways." Doubt is also known as hesitation, or disbelief. Doubt is the king of the unstable where we are often confronted with it along the journey of faith. Doubt is the opposite of faith.

Instability often opens us to being indecisive. In fact, the symptoms of indecisiveness are to be unsure, wavering, anxious, insecure, unpredictable, and lacking confidence. Faith is being sure that something is TRUE. No wonder the Bible shares, "Walk by faith and not by sight." When we walk by faith, we are living by faith. But "faith comes by hearing the word of God" (Romans 10:17). When we open our hearts and souls to the Word of God, we have also opened our lives to the same power that framed the worlds. The Bible states in Hebrews 11:3, "By faith we understand that the worlds were framed by the word of God." The Bible makes it clear that faith has SUBSTANCE and EVIDENCE (Hebrews 11:1).

Yet people struggle with DOUBT. Why is it that we waver with instability? Here it is: Doubt is not the absence of faith, it is a shortage of FAITH, and not having enough faith to establish God's ABILITY. The word "instability" has within it the word "ability," but to embrace that, we must know that God is ABLE! Unbelief is being sure something is not possible. Doubt is not being sure. When we have walked in doubt rather than faith then we have a boundary line for our faith that can only go as far as the threshold of where we are with DOUBT.

The Bible states, "It is impossible to please God without FAITH" (Hebrews 11:6). In other words, faith is a necessary ingredient to please the Lord. The enemy shouts, "God is not ABLE" and "God doesn't care." He attempts to position you to receive the messages that "Life is unfair" and "Praying is a waste of time." Many do not realize that DOUBT is the first seed the enemy is attempting in our minds. It begins with DOUBT, but moves to DISCOURAGEMENT, to DELAY, to finally DEFEAT. His goal is to remove FAITH! So, let us take our medicine for instability.

*Day 19*

# DISTRACTIONS

*"Trust in the Lord with all your heart and lean not on your own understanding; in all your ways acknowledge him, and He will make your paths straight."* (Proverbs 3:5-6)

One day a boy arrives home from school earlier than usual and decides to go into his Dad's office. Since Dad was still at work, he did not think it would amount to anything. But to his surprise, as he searched through the drawers of his Dad's desk, he discovered a strange magazine. This magazine was unlike any other he had ever found while scanning his Dad's office. This magazine was filled with explicit sexual material that when found the boy was confronted with a major distraction. Deep down he knew that this book was causing his desires to be awakened and triggered a pulling curiosity that was telling him his Dad would never find out if he looked just a little longer. He was dealing with a distraction.

A young lady who had multiple arguments with her husband found herself walking away feeling unwanted, unloved, and uncared for. But at work, her boss displays a daily presence where she witnesses sincere concern, care, and comfort on a regular basis. On this one day, her boss observes that she is distraught over her home life ordeal and decides to give her a rose to brighten her day. Upon receiving the flower, the young lady faces a feeling she never had before. This was the feeling that her boss had been everything she had ever wanted in a relationship. She was face to face with a distraction.

There is not a person on the globe who has not at some point had to get through a distraction. We do not ask for distractions, they just come into our lives. Think about this, have you ever done something where you got what you wanted but wished you never would have gotten it? For many of us, we want to do right. Our problem is that distractions will cause us to almost do the right thing. But almost doing the right thing is not the same as doing the right thing. Distractions make us think that it is not really that bad. Distractions can cause us to think it is okay not to completely do the right thing so long as we try a little bit. The Bible tells us what to do when times get hard. It says, "Trust in the Lord with all your heart and lean not on your own understanding; in all your ways acknowledge him, and He will make your paths straight" (Proverbs 3:5-6).

Here is our dilemma we "lean on our own understanding," and in doing so we often become pawns for distractions. Think about the owner of a lonely heart who is blinded to those who prey on their own insecurities of the heart. How about the person who constantly quits before they really begin not knowing that the culprit often is some unannounced distraction? Individuals like these succumb to being distracted because they are shallow in what is called spiritual resolve. This is the ability to be fixed or stuck on a position you have made based on your trust in the Lord. Our spiritual resolve is constantly being challenged by distractions.

Think of it this way, the people who looked at Jesus being crucified thought God was doing nothing when He did not come and take Jesus down from the cross. They thought God was doing nothing when they put Jesus in the tomb and sealed it with cement and put guards in front of it. While God was being accused of doing nothing, God was making it possible for us to be saved. God was giving us victory over death by sending Jesus to conquer death and hell. God was doing all this while people were thinking God was doing nothing.

Before you go run after a distraction and do something you ought not to do, do not say it is because God is not doing anything for you. God may be about to make you a winner in life. Just what you need might be about to happen. But if you choose to follow that distraction, you may lose what God wants to give to you. The key for a triumphant life over distractions is in putting your trust in God.

*Day 20*

# CONSUMED

*"Therefore, since we are receiving a kingdom that cannot be shaken, let us be thankful, and so worship God acceptably with reverence and awe, for our 'God is a consuming fire.'"*
(Hebrews 12:28-29)

In life, I had my opportunities to keep a campfire lit at night, and it does not stay lit continuously on its own. There is a pursuit that is needed to keep the fire fed. In other words, the fire will go out if it is not being ignited. In the Old Testament, God said to Moses in Leviticus 6:9, "Give Aaron and his sons this command: 'These are the regulations for the burnt offering: The burnt offering is to remain on the altar hearth throughout the night, till morning, and the fire must be kept burning on the altar.'" Verse 13 shares, "The fire must be kept burning on the altar continuously; it must not go out." This fire was a continuous fire. The application for us today is to make sure we keep the fires of God maintained in our lives. We are today living sacrifices (Romans 12:1).

If you are a child of God, I want you to ask yourself, have you ever been consumed by God? In other words, have you ever allowed your total inner being to be fully open towards God?

There are those who have allowed outside influences to affect the "consuming fire" that is accessible for all those that are connected to the Lord. Some have lost this fire's intensity to serve and to sacrifice for the Savior through you.

To consume means to "engage fully." There are a number of those who only come so close to the fire of God. What is the reason for this? One reason why is because there are those that only open so much to the full overflowing ability of God. This is due primarily because it is scary to open beyond our own control, or beyond what we feel we are not accustomed too. If we can control the heat and the intensity coming from God, then we do not mind being near the fire!

I believe some would rather be a "consumer" in the Lord verses being "consumed." When we are consumers, we control what we take in. Some exist as consumers of God's word, His will, His ways, and His wonders. But when you are consumed by God, He is the author and finisher of where He's going with your life! It is your choice to allow God your entire being. It is not God's responsibility to keep the fire burning in your heart… it is yours!

## Day 21

# BE NOT DECEIVED

*"Then the LORD God said to the woman, 'What is this you have done?' The woman said, 'The serpent deceived me, and I ate.'"* (Genesis 3:13)

How many times have you ordered something from a catalog that looks like just what you wanted, but when the product arrives, it does not look nearly as good as it did in the catalog?

Deception is a powerful ploy. Interestingly, deception is only an option for the Christian believer. Nonbelievers are "led astray." To be deceived, you must have some truth to measure the error by. In other words, people who are deceived are those that have some form of truth that has been twisted from then unadulterated truth.

Why does Satan deceive? First off, Satan cannot create anything. All he can do is manipulate and maneuver on what has already been created. Since he cannot match God's power,

Satan must maximize what he does have, and deception is his strong suit. He has turned deception into his greatest masterpiece.

Satan's weapon is his mouth. The word "Serpent" in Hebrew means one who whispers and suggests. With Adam and Eve in the book of Genesis, Satan made God words appear suspect, unclear, and leaving pertinent insight out of the equation, that prompted the Adam's family to consider the DECEPTION. Satan led one third of the angels astray from the very presence of God in heaven with deception and caused Eve to disobey in a perfect environment because of deception. Why? To thwart the plan of God! Ultimately the goal of all deception is to remove the elect of God away from where the power dwells. The Bible states in Psalms 62:11, "Once God has spoken; twice I have heard this: That power belongs to God." Since power belongs to God, and we are the offspring of the power source, it makes sense that deception is the tool to that is used to keep us from possessing it!

How do we effectively deal with deception? With Revelation Knowledge. This is not just ordinary natural communicated knowledge but knowledge that is supernaturally communicated through the same voice that spoke the worlds into existence. It is a knowledge that reveals the truth (the reality of all things) because of your personal encounter with the Word of Truth (which is Jesus Christ). Jesus said, "My word is truth" (John 17:17). When we are constantly being saturated in the Word of God; we are being submerged in the Truth.

Deception happens because of where we are in our hearts. Jeremiah 17:9 says, "The heart is deceitful above all things and desperately wicked." Deception preys on the heart. The heart that is influenced by deception is a heart that has need of the fertilization of the Word.

When a heart becomes stubborn, hard, or resistant, it is just like soil that has become absent of what it needs to allow anything to grow. God's word allows us to see how we were truly meant to function. If there lies any form of bitterness, doubt, instability, or internal anxieties within you, understand that its goal is to move you away from the TRUTH and shift you into a realm where deception becomes a way of life instead of the truth! Today, allow the Word of God to soften what has become hard and difficult, and learn not to be DECEIVED!

## Day 22

# "On the Dunes"

*"Behold, I will do a new thing; now it shall spring forth; shall ye not know it? I will even make a way in the wilderness, and rivers in the desert."* (Isaiah 43:19)

Before I begin to share in length about what lies in deserts, I want to share a current condition of our world. We are surrounded on every side by trouble, tragedy, misfortune, heartache, discouragement, consumption, decline, loss, destruction, decay, ruin, devastation, spoliation, desolation, refuse, rubbish, trash, and garbage. Ladies and gentlemen, we are in… DESERTS!

Webster defines a desert as "a wasteland, a place unsuitable for major life." Think about it; most of us do not see flourishing fruit trees and gardens when we reflect on deserts. We think of dehydration and starvation.

Deserts today are things, places, and circumstances that reveal hopelessness, panic, and abandonment. A desert is a living reality for the person saturated in frustration and emotional fatigue. All over the world today people are sighing, crying, and dying in this desert! Their hopes are dismantled, their dreams are destroyed, their prospects all but perished.

For some, the desert experience is a disease or sickness that has devastated the body and left individuals unable to function as they used to. And so, they have written themselves off as useless and hopeless. To others, your desert is a desert of depleted finances and resources. Perhaps your wasteland involves relationships. In this land, you feel useless and helpless. Your heart seems to be vacant of the nutrients of the soul such as joy, happiness, and contentment.

Notice in our text though that God will deliver a "River in the Desert." The text states, "I will make a way in the wilderness and rivers in the desert." In other words, God rescues, revives, and restores us no matter the desert experience!

On the DUNES of life, the Lord reveals His Will, reveals His Wonders, and reveals His Way! The challenge for those that are dealing and going through a desert is to focus not on the condition of the desert but on the Deliverer of that experience.

It is the AMAZING POWER of God to know that He is ABLE no matter if the world is looking like one big giant desert. The scripture states the Lord "Will do a new thing!" We must begin to trust the voice of God as we walk out our desert encounter and know that even though our lives may be dry and void of Abundant life on this current journey, the Lord is about to do something "On the DUNES!"

*Day 23*

# HE'S ALWAYS HERE

Today many think we can change the atmosphere and thereby make it more suitable for the Lord by the way we worship. The truth of the matter is that God is everywhere. We do not change the atmosphere, we change our heart of worship.

David realized this, and he wrote (Psalms 139:7 NIV) "Where can I go from your Spirit? Where can I flee from your presence?" It is us who needs to see Him! Just because He is there, it does not mean that we always experience the reality of His presence.

When we begin to praise and worship the Lord, the Holy Spirit begins to work within our hearts, and we become more aware of the presence of the Lord, which was there all along.

The reality is… HE IS HERE! Right now, He is everywhere. Jesus promised that when two or three believers gather in His name that He would be there with them (Matthew 18:20) "For where two or three come together in my name, there am I with them."

For us to experience the presence of the Lord that is truly ready to be viewed, we must worship Him! The bible states, "He inhabits the praises of His people" (Psalms 22:3). In other words, we not only become aware of His presence, but He exists with those that were created, designed, and purposed for His Glory to dwell in!

When we worship the Lord as a lifestyle, we embrace more of His presence than embracing our problems as a lifestyle. We do not dwell on ourselves, but on His supremacy. When the Lord reigns, then worship is more than an event. It is rather a response to His glory that is ALWAYS HERE!

## Day 24

# EVERLOVE

*"God is love. Whoever lives in love lives in God, and God in him. In this way, love is made complete among us so that we will have confidence on the day of judgment, because in this world we are like him. There is no fear in love. But perfect love drives out fear because fear has to do with punishment. The one who fears is not made perfect in love."*
(I John 4:16-18)

I have a question for you that I would like you to meditate on and that is, what is perfect love? To further reflect on this question, it is identified from the Lord that not only does it exist, but that this *perfect love* is attainable. First off, when anything is perfect there are no flaws. When something is perfect, it is complete, absolute, and made to be whole.

The challenge with mankind is that we have lived so long living and receiving something that is abstract of this love that God ordained, that many of us consider that the everyday love that runs its course throughout humanity today is synonymous with the EVERLOVE of God. But is it?

This love did not begin when God created the universe. It was already existing! This love is within the nature of God. He Himself is the personification of love. Within the Godhead there is love. This love finds its origin in God. We must realize that this love is not natural, it is supernatural. This EVERLOVE makes no sense in this world because it came not from this world. This love is not situational or based on meeting some level of expectation to receive it.

Notice from our text that this love can drive out FEAR. In other words, anything that has been hibernating and germinating the virus of doubt, depression, and division, this love can force it out! To drive something out is to possess a power to move it out of the way. Today, many relationships that want love, need love, and seek love discover after further observation that they may dealing with the disease of FEAR. When fear is prevalent, there is a desperation and a hopeless pursuit to avoid and escape what hurts by filling it with justification and rationalization. This is an artificial love.

We have been conditioned to believe that God's love is ANY kind of love. The truth is EVERLOVE has an objective, and that is to make you into something perfect. This perfect love is a "Deposit With No Return Expected" operation. In other words, it is where "God so loved the world that He gave His only begotten Son." God gave without expecting a return. This love was sacrificial, submitted, and SOLDOUT. This love was selfless versus selfish. This is divine love. Today love is confused as being conditional, temporary, and a fairy tale, but to those that have received the GREATEST LOVE through Christ, it is an... EVERLOVE!

## Day 25

# No More Running Away

*"Brothers, I do not consider that I have made it my own. But one thing I do: forgetting what lies behind and straining forward to what lies ahead, I press on toward the goal for the prize of the upward call of God in Christ Jesus."* (Philippians 3:13-14)

It is an undeniable fact that many of life's problems we grapple with in the present are the result of what has happened to us in the past, whether because of our own deliberate choices or because of circumstances, which were quite beyond our control.

The person we are today is a product of all our yesterdays. We can blame our genetic makeup or our environment for our problems. It is often easier for us to shift the blame of our problems on to others, but to be honest, to put it solely on this is to ignore our own actions or inactions.

More important than the circumstances of the past are the ways in which we have decided to react to them. Such behavior often crystallizes into patterns, which harden into settled convictions, which in turn condition and dictate our present feelings. One of my professors impressed upon my heart that we will never leave the PAST until God unlocks us to our PURPOSE!

When trouble comes to most of our lives, we can do one of three things: (a) endure it, (b) try to escape it, or (c) enlist it. Many have come to learn only to endure trials. When this takes place, then trials become our master, in other words, we allow the navigation of our lives to be dictated by the bumps and bruises life brings our way.

For those who attempt to escape their trials, they wind up often missing how the problem can disclose the purpose God wanted to achieve through their lives. Think about it; Noah preached to an audience of none for 120 years, yet God used his problem as a vehicle of purpose! Joseph was sold into slavery by his brothers, then was sent to prison over a lie, yet God used a man called a prisoner for PURPOSE!

Lastly, when we learn to enlist our trials, then trials become our SERVANTS instead of our MASTERS, and we will learn from them. The word "enlist" means to recruit or to use something for a purpose. Remember, it was the Lord that stated, "All things work together for our good and His glory" (Romans 8:28). Stop and consider for a moment that God can use ALL THINGS for our good and His glory. That means no matter what we face or confront there is no need to RUN AWAY!

*Day 26*

# CREATED FOR AUTHENTICITY

*"I hate all your show and pretense—the hypocrisy of your religious festivals and solemn assemblies. I will not accept your burnt offerings and grain offerings. I won't even notice all your choice peace offerings. Away with your noisy hymns of praise! I will not listen to the music of your harps. Instead, I want to see a mighty flood of justice, an endless river of righteous living."* (Amos 5:21-24)

Some years ago, while attending the San Diego County Fair, I happened to come across a special juicer that was being demonstrated on site. It looked like it could do anything and everything that I desired in a juicer. Little did I know that right after purchasing this eye-popping machine, I tested it at my home and discovered that it was not working like the salesman had demonstrated at the fair.

It could barely slice a banana! Eventually I had found out that I was not the only one who had discovered this. Hundreds of customers who had purchased this machine were awakened to a reality about this juicer and that it was designed primarily to capture an audience. It was created for show. It was not created for its true purpose.

In our text, we observe that the Lord is displeased with the operation of His people. He states, "I hate all you show and pretense." In other words, the Lord was witnessing a performance instead of a position in His presence. They were more infatuated with their demonstration than the divine glory of God. The question we should all ask is why? What causes a people to shift towards a camouflaged appearance rather than to be authentic people before the Lord? Ever since Adam and Eve covered up with fig leaves in Genesis Chapter 3, as a people, we have attempted to give a simulation to God. We have used a variety of things to cloak over what God is longing for. He desires a genuine operation. He desires a sincere servant.

In verse 24 of our text He states, "Instead, I want to see a mighty flood of justice, an endless river of righteous living!" God anticipates an operation of justice and of righteous living to such a degree that it cannot be contained. We were not designed to be artificial. We were designed to be authentic. When we are synthetic, we are never satisfied! When we have become an imitation, we fall short of the true design in His image. That juicer I bought at the fair eventually became a garage item put away because it never fulfilled its true purpose. I pray today that all God's children press pause on their lives for a moment and evaluate if the Lord is observing an authentic operation from their lives.

## Day 27

# THE MANY FACES OF DEATH

*"If any of you wants to be my follower, you must turn from your selfish ways, take up your cross daily, and follow me. If you try to hang on to your life, you will lose it. But if you give up your life for my sake, you will save it."* (Luke 9:23-24)

Death is one of most challenging things to deal with. Death leaves us feeling powerless. Death arrived on the scene of humanity when sin arrived. Since the Garden of Eden experience with Adam and Eve, we have had to deal with death. All through the scriptures we see a theme that for us to get back to what God envisioned, there must be a death.

Jesus stated in our text, "If any of you wants to be a follower, must turn from your selfish ways, take up your cross and follow me." In other words, anyone who wishes to truly follow Jesus must be willing to let some things die. Notice that this death is a personal decision on everyone. If you wish to follow Jesus, you must be willing to let something die. Another scripture states that we must "die daily." In other words, we must be willing to give something a death sentence.

This could be a death over bitterness, revenge, or envy. For others, it could be a death to selfishness and blaming others for where you are in life. There may be a need to die to what you refuse to believe what Jesus can do. Doubt and despair are things that need to die daily. If they thrive inside of us, we cannot live!

It could be a death to being totally absorbed on wanting your way in your marriage when the Bible shares, "Husbands love your wives as Christ loved the church and gave himself for it." In other words, Jesus was willing to die for love. He was willing to give up his all for love. The question all spouses should pose is what are we willing to let die that does not reflect the will of the Lord? In Christ, there is a constant wiliness to die to self. Today, open your heart to God and determine what you are willing to give a death.

## Day 28

# Journey to the Center of the Heart

*"I the LORD search the heart and examine the mind, to reward a man according to his conduct, according to what his deeds deserve."* (Jeremiah 17:10)

Have you ever considered that where you are in life right this second is a reflection and an examination of where you are in your heart? Whether we knew it or not, everyday something is attempting to impact our hearts from having a bitter heart, a wounded heart, and even a broken heart.

For some, it appears from physical appearance that all is well, but with the heart, often the impact of despair and damage doesn't reveal itself completely from the outside. On the contrary, it's a slow process that little by little eats away at our spiritual stability. All the while our outside life may seem legit, but our inner life is struggling to maintain focus.

I heard a story that transpired after a violent storm one night, where a large tree, which over the years had become a stately giant, was found lying across the pathway in a park. Nothing but a splintered stump was left. Closer examination showed that it was rotten at the core because thousands of tiny insects had eaten away at its heart. The weakness of that tree was not brought on by the sudden storm; it began the very moment the first insect nested within its bark. Like the tree, what has access to our hearts will impact our future. The question most of us have has always been the same, "What do I have to do for my heart to be right with God?" It is in our nature to feel that we must do some type of work or deed to earn God's pleasure, but the truth of the matter is "without faith it is impossible to please God" (Hebrews 11:6).

Charles Reade shared that if "I sow a thought I will reap an act. And if I sow an act, I will reap a habit. And if I sow a habit, I will reap character. And when I SOW character, I will reap a destiny." Whatever is sown in my heart has the potential to interfere with my destiny. Obviously getting rid of harmful influences will not change a corrupt heart into a purified heart. Outward acts cannot produce inner benefits. Eventually, whatever is at the CENTER of the HEART will reveal itself. The Lord's objective for the heart is to have one that "hungers and thirsts for righteousness" (Matthew 5:6). For an outward act to be effective, it must come from a heart that seeks to do God's will instead of its own. So, Lord, "Create in me a new HEART!" This is how we change from the inside out!

Matthew 15:18-20 shares, "But the things that come out of the mouth come from the heart, and these make a man 'unclean.' For out of the heart come evil thoughts, murder, adultery, sexual immorality, theft, false testimony, slander. These are what make a man 'unclean;' but eating with unwashed hands does not make him 'unclean.'" Notice that Jesus seems to emphasis that eating with unwashed hands has nothing to do with the heart. On the flipside, eating with washed hands has nothing to do with being cleaned as well. Being purified is a condition of the heart.

For far too long, many have hidden behind doing things as a statement of their true selves without ever truly taking a journey to what lies at the CENTER of the HEART. Pause right this second and ask yourself, do you recognize that you are striving to penetrate to the core of your heart? Or do you find yourself hiding the pain and perplexities that exist in your heart? We cannot please God unless our hearts are right with Him. Today, I encourage you to travel towards the depths within yourself that verifies you are venturing to the CENTER of the HEART!

## Day 29

# THE TRUTH ABOUT REJECTION

*"Praise be to the God and Father of our Lord Jesus Christ, who has blessed us in the heavenly realms with every spiritual blessing in Christ."* (Ephesians 1:3)

Rejection can be defined as the sense of being unwanted. You desire people to love you, yet you believe that they do not. You want to be part of a function, a family, or just healthy fellowship, and yet you feel excluded. Somehow there is a prevention of possessing what is the opposite of rejection, which is… ADMISSION. The understanding of this word deals with permission, meaning I am accepted! I am allowed! Yet many people struggle with admission or authority mainly because rejection has created an identity and not the Lord.

Almost all of us have experienced rejection at one time or another, but many of us have not understood its nature or its effects. Rejection was never part of God's plan. Rejection from its roots is about denial. The spirit of rejection is like a cancer hoping that any person open to its influences will also be contracted with a spiritual virus that leaves us in what I call the Phase of Refusal. The reason why is because we push, prevent, and propel anything remotely connected to what reminds us of the original rejection.

All rejection causes separation. Think about it. A husband who has been rejected from his wife is always feeling the effects of separation. How about someone in love who has discovered that their love was rejected, and now they deal with symptoms of being severed from what they assumed was whole?

Most people deal with rejection with putting a little Band-Aid over it. In other words, they dress it up and cover it up by attempting to avoid it. Others tell themselves that the only way to handle this is to maintain a position where they feel they must REFUSE to change the condition of their heart regarding this area or this person. This is the Phase of Refusal. Our focal scripture speaks loudly about what the Lord has blessed us with, "Every spiritual blessing in Christ."

If that is true, then how we combat rejection is with the TRUTH. Too often though we allow another relative of rejection to hold us captive. This is deception or a lie, the lie that it will always hurt. That it will always be the same. The lie that I must keep it hidden in the crevices of my heart. But to the Lord that is not the truth.

## Day 30

# WHO ARE YOU?

*"We are the clay, and You the potter; we are the work of Your hand."* (Isaiah 64:8)

Remember the story of Rudolph the Red-Nosed Reindeer? It is a great tale that describes the struggles of learning to appreciate who you are. For you see, Rudolph struggled with his identity. In fact, because he was so different, he and his parents decided to cover it up. They wanted him to fit in with everyone else. So, his special glow was hidden. It was deemed as unacceptable.

But did you know, it is only a matter of time when what you have been trying to cover up will at some point be exposed. Rudolph was faced with the result that his personal glow would be known by everyone in his life. So, traumatized Rudolph decided to leave his home. He decided to run and escape from his problem. Rudolph was convinced that he was a reject. He did not like who he was.

No matter who you are today, you must understand that every person on the globe is a person of design. Our scripture states, "We are the clay, and You the potter; we are the work of Your hand." If we are the clay and the Lord is the potter, then we must let Him SHAPE us. He is the artist and we are the masterpiece! God has the capacity to turn us into something special. But if the clay is resistant, then God as the Potter must take longer into transforming us into His intent. The goal is for us to YIELD. This means we must surrender to His will.

Who you are is not determined because of your surroundings, your situation, or your stuff. The Bible shares in Ephesians 2:10 that "We are His workmanship!" In other words, we were meant to be exquisite, excellent, and extravagant!

Long before an artist will paint on the canvas, he has the thought of the ending from the very beginning. The same is true with God. The Bible states that "He is the author and finisher of your faith." The Lord knows who you are because He made you. Not only that, but no matter what you are facing in this life, you must hold to the reality that He has seen what He intended for you.

Everything created by God was in His mind before there was even a world. That includes the purpose for you! Rudolph the Red-Nosed Reindeer was trapped in a state that he had become who he was because of what others said about him. Today we must fathom and embrace that who we are was purposed in the mind of God! So, WHO ARE YOU?

## Day 31

# TRUSTED

*"So, David went out wherever Saul sent him, and behaved wisely. And Saul set him over the men of war, and he was accepted in the sight of all the people and in the sight of Saul's servants."* (I Samuel 18:5)

Gaining credibility is like depositing money in the bank. In other words, you are not going to gain credibility without making some deposits. David who one day would become King was accountable to the King. He was reliable to the King. He was dependable to the King. He was responsible to the King. The thing is when you gain credibility you have gained a reputation. There is nothing worse than to have a spotty and shaky reputation. The reason being is you cannot be TRUSTED.

You can only draw on credibility if you have established the habit of making deposits into the world you have in front of you. My philosophy is "if you don't put anything into the account of being TRUSTED, you can't take it out when you need to make withdrawals." This is CREDIBILITY!

If you want people to believe in you, have trust in you, admire you, and have confidence in you, you must evaluate what you have given to establish that TRUST.

The Bible shares, "Confidence in an unfaithful man in time of trouble is like a bad tooth and a foot out of joint" (Proverbs 25:19). Being in the company of someone who has not proven they can be trusted according to the Proverbs writer is seriously PAINFUL. Think about a tooth ache; it is a nagging and lingering pain that plagues you until it is PULLED.

Too often the world reveals the aftermath of broken trust, severed trust, and misused trust. Could the answer to why we witness displaced trust be because we have lost the desire to make investments to be TRUSTED?

## Day 32

# MORE THAN A WORD

*"And now abides faith, hope, love, these three; but the greatest of these is love."* (I Corinthians 13:13)

If you truly possess the love of God, then you must understand that like God, the manifestations of what love truly does and demands is identified by those that claim they are filled with the Love of God. For you see…

Love never gives up.
Love cares more for others than for self.
Love does not want what it doesn't have.
Love doesn't strut.
Love doesn't have a swelled head.
Love doesn't force itself on others.

Love is not about "me first."
Love does not fly off the handle.

Love does not keep score of the sins of others.
Love does not revel when others grovel.

Love trusts God always.
Love always looks for the best.
Love never gets stuck in the past.

Love does not keep score of the sins of others.
Love will endure, encourage, and exalt others.
Love will give up the best.
Love will accept the truth.

Love is constant, committed, and courageous.
Love prays for enemies.
Love strives, seeks, and searches to please the Lord all the way to the end!

Love… It is More Than a Word.

## Day 33

# "What Lies Below?"

*"Search me, God, and know my heart; test me and know my anxious thoughts."* (Psalms 139:23)

Recently while working with a young man who was struggling with handling his feelings, I discovered that he had become accustomed to locking up within himself how he felt. He had concluded that when facing difficult feelings, the best policy was to hide them away and not find a way to work through them. He decided it was best to gloss over his feelings by staying busy at work. He felt it was more of a battle to bring the way he was feeling to the surface than to deal with it. So, he stuffed it away.

In the book *Men Have Feelings Too* by Gary Oliver, it discussed how many men have been conditioned towards not revealing their real feelings. Many men have found it easier to just hide their feelings. Upon further review though, what we find is that most men express more feelings of abandonment, distrust, loss, frustration, and hopelessness than women. It just happens to come out as the secondary emotion called... anger.

Most men who are angry find themselves in the stage of dealing with this secondary emotion because they could not figure out how to deal with their stress, their depression, and even the emotions that come after a calamity. The signs of the secondary emotions show up with loss, death, and changes in our relationships. So, what happens? Many truly hide how they really feel about it. In Matthew 26, before he would become the famous Apostle Peter, he experienced a moment where he was face to face with dealing with some tough stuff from inside his feelings. This occasion was when his Lord and his friend Jesus was taken away and arrested like a common thief. Peter never thought it would come to this. He could never imagine seeing the Lord of Lords in this state.

Think about the difficult scenarios we have in this life that manifest in our own lives. They catch us unaware, and often we are oblivious as to what we are about to face and how it will impact our feelings. Peter watched on that day as they dragged His Lord away like he was a common criminal, as if He were insignificant. As he stood in the shadows trying to play incognito, someone noticed him. They remembered him as one of the men that had become known as a follower of Jesus.

But when this person made mention of the fact of who he was Peter denied that he even knew Jesus. Not only that but he became furious and began to swear and curse to boot! Let us put ourselves in the shoes of Peter. His life had been changed in the last three years when this same Jesus took him and told him he would be responsible for the building of His church. This same Peter, who was a common fisherman, would now be a major ambassador for the Lord. To think that his feelings would not be going through some ebb and flow is an understatement. He was close, connected, and committed to Jesus. But Peter's feelings where going through secondary emotions because of what he was going through with watching the trial of the Messiah.

Peter attempted to cover up what the Lord knew was really going on in the inside. Remember it was Jesus who prophesied to Peter about the reality that he would deny him, and to prove this a rooster would crow three times. How many times have we tried to hide how we really feel when the Lord knows the truth? How many times have we tried to act like, "I'm fine, I'm okay," when we know the entire time that there is a whirlwind taking place with what lies below? For Peter, he realized when the rooster cut loose with crowing that Jesus knew of his hiding game. Perhaps you are walking through a tough time that has been trying to get you to cover up what is really at work.

Our scripture emphasizes the need for the Lord to search us entirely. As God's people, we must realize that when the Lord takes a stroll in our hearts, He knows where we are with our feelings. He knows what is heavy, hard, and hectic at times to walk through. The Bible says He is our creator and that we are made in His image. In other words, the Lord understands how we feel. He knows our emotions because He created that phase of our lives. Today, remove the curtain and cease the hiding of how you feel and allow the comforter to intervene. Learn of the power that is associated when we expose our true feelings to the one who cares about "What Lies Below."

## Day 34

# LEAVING THE
# LAND OF CONFUSION

*"For God is not the author of confusion, but of peace, as in all churches of the saints."* (I Corinthians 14:33)

There is a powerful spirit that is moving and shifting through the lives of men and women around the world, and it is called "The spirit of confusion." Many people miss the mark of the subtle ways confusion operates. Confusion is disorder, chaos, and a purposeless action. While order is about creating purpose, disorder is about the promotion of chaos. When we witness confusion in our marriages, confusion in our homes, confusion with our friends, and even confusion in our churches, it is the fruit of a SEED. The challenge is we are so prone to allow anything into our souls because we have not allowed God to be the GARDENER.

Jesus said, "I am the vine and my Father is the vinedresser" (John 15:1). A vinedresser is a Gardener. In other words, God is in the business to set the environment right for your life for you to grow. Think about a garden where there is no intended purpose and there is also no work in the soil prepared for the seed. In addition, there is no movement on the existing conditions of the garden. Meaning there is no pulling of weeds, rocks, and debris that may be in the soil. In the end, it will look like something where there was no order or preparation for something wonderful. If our minds are like the disorganized soil that is constantly in disarray, then it leaves us in a state of confusion. The Bible shares in Proverbs 4:5 that we should pursue to "Get an understanding." When we truly have an understanding, my good friend Keith Goosby shared with me that it means "now you can stand under it!" If I cannot stand under what the voice of God utters to my soul, then the opposite of understanding is at work which is confusion.

Notice that our scripture states, "God is not the author of confusion," which would lead us to consider that confusion has been written by somebody to be read. The problem we face when we navigate through this life is that we are so inclined to read from an author that promotes confusion that over time we succumb to it. The Bible says in I John 1 "Test every spirit." Even if it is what is working from within your own spirit.

There are many people who are oblivious to the fact that the spirit of confusion is at work in their lives. They think as they go from job to job, and spouse to spouse, and even church to church that it is someone else, when there is something at work within them that says they are in a state of confusion. James says, "For where envying and strife is, there is confusion and every evil work" (James 3:16). Every time we witness the activation of resentment or conflict within ourselves or with others it is the spirit of confusion that is seeking for more territory. One of the first things the enemy attempts when we contact the glory of God is to attempt to confuse us. Even Jesus before he set out on His great ministry encountered confusion from the enemy (Matthew Chapter 4). But Jesus revealed that He knew the glory of the Lord. Jesus like us today was offered to absorb the insight from the author of confusion. But He chose not to open it because He was the author and finisher of faith!

Today there is an epidemic of spiritual deafness among many children of God. They cannot hear from God because confusion has convoluted and complicated the realm of their souls. Jesus said that there would be those that would "Draw near to me with their mouths, and honor Me with their lips, but their hearts are far from me. In vain they worship me" (Matthew 15:8-9). That my friend is confusing! To have all the appearances of closeness being displayed with the Lord but face the sobering truth that your heart is far away from Him is a ploy from the spirit of confusion! So how do you claim victory over it? Our scripture says again that "God is not the author of confusion, but of PEACE." This is restoration. In other words, God is the author of making things better! God is the author of setting things right, He is the author of wholeness and of completion. If the Lord is the author of peace, it is imperative that we seek not only to believe that but to become what the author envisioned.

## Day 35

# "Seeing the Invisible Things"

Have you ever read *Where's Waldo?* It is a series of children's books created by British illustrator Martin Handford. The books consist of a series of detailed double-page spread illustrations depicting dozens or more people doing a variety of amusing things at a given location. The readers are challenged to find the character named Waldo who is hidden in the group.

The thing is if you do not know what Waldo looks like then everything on the page is just a blur. Everything appears to be blended on the page. The Bible states that Jesus "is the image of the INVISIBLE God, the firstborn of every creature" (Colossians 1:15). Perhaps some struggle with seeing invisible things in their lives because they have not really identified Jesus as Lord.

Faith in the Lord is nothing more than seeing the invisible. II Corinthians 4:18 shares, "While we do not look at the things which are seen, but at the things which are not seen. For the things which are seen are temporary, but the things which are not seen are eternal." Every child of God has been given the sight to see in the invisible. We must learn to trust in God and to see with the eyes of faith so we can have the faith that allows us to see the invisible.

## Day 36

# UNLIMITED Possibilities

*"And they limited the Holy One of Israel. They did not remember His power; the day when He redeemed them from the enemy."* (Psalms 78:41-42)

"If God is all powerful, why don't we see more miracles and healings today?" This question is asked not just by non-believers but by those who believe as well. All too often we are confronted with the bleak reality that our "beliefs" do not line up with the God we see in the Bible.

Our passage states that the people "LIMITED the Holy One of Israel. They did not remember His power; the day when He redeemed them from the enemy." The catalyst that was responsible for the limitation or the constraint of God's power was the people. They had allowed something to circumvent the true essence of God's glory in the lives of His people. This was… UNBELIEF.

Jesus said, "If you have faith of a mustard seed you could speak to this mountain and it would move, and nothing shall be

IMPOSSIBLE for you." (Matthew 17:20). How is it POSSIBLE in the mind of God to move mountains that are in our way, and we cannot believe we can even move small BUMPS on the road of life?

The Apostles were faced with a similar dilemma of belief, and they asked the Lord to "INCREASE our FAITH," because Jesus had asked them to be able to forgive someone to the point of 70 times 7, and that was beyond their limited depth of not only comprehension, but belief (Luke 17-4-5). My prayer today is that you would have a magnetized intensity from the Lord to grant you no stipulations or roadblocks towards accessing the power of faith so that you can REAP from the realm of UNLIMITED possibilities!

I can still remember the song we sang as children that went something like this; **"This little light of mine I'm gonna let it shine."** As a child I don't think I really understood the emphasis of the song. Today I now realize that without the light of the Lord the world would be in total darkness! Wherever God is not present there is darkness. Even in the creation of the earth in Genesis chapter 1 verse 2 the bible states: *"darkness was over the surface of the deep, and the Spirit of God was hovering over the waters."*

In other words, God was about to birth something or manifest His will over the earth. You see, the light of God is also the will of God. When the light of God shines from our lives just like it hovered over the earth in the beginning it is able to move and impact the lives of those we touch because of the brightness that shines from our lives! They are impacted by our character, our conviction, and our consistent allegiance with the

Lord. Did you ever consider that your little light can actually light the entire world?

When you are an illuminator of God you are in essence the conduit that God will use to deliver His light to those who are in the haze and the murkiness that dwells in this world. When we are the evidence of God's light. We are the shine and the glare of God's glory! We are the expressed illustration of God's power on earth! We are the continuation of God's generation, and the explanation to why He was willing to allow His Son to die! Our scripture highlights that: *"we in the midst of a crooked and perverse generation where we shine as lights."* The objective of the light of God we carry within ourselves is not something to be taken lightly or as insignificant. It is the expressed purpose of God to straighten out that which is crooked, and to move what has existed in a perverse state to a state of righteousness.

When you are an illuminator you brighten the atmosphere! When you are an illuminator you expose the greatness of God! You enlighten, encourage, and empower the people that God has brought in direct contact to your life. I want you to pause for a moment today and fathom the thought that you have been placed exactly where you are to show the presence of God by becoming an illuminator!

C.J.

## Day 37

# Restless People

*"If we confess our sins, He is faithful and just to forgive us our sins and to cleanse us from all unrighteousness."* (I John 1:9)

Webster's describes restlessness as "an uneasy continuous condition that evolves in the mind." Restlessness encompasses the lack of security and stability within us. Restlessness involves a constant conflict with what is raging inside of us. Because of this constant conflict, it transitions into a place of turmoil that is evident in the world around us. Many strive to fix it with seeking for outside relationships, not realizing that their current relationship with themselves is bound to reveal itself with others!

Tension, anger, anxiety, frustration, and fears follow the restless. The restless person is always moving to find something that will provide a reprieve from restlessness. There is a sense of incompleteness that seems to run wild with the restless. Because many believe there is no solution to their restlessness, they opt for personal isolation, not knowing that personally withdrawing from the world when restless often stifles any movement forward because we are saturated with it (restlessness).

The removal of restlessness is in seeking for wholeness. This begins with acknowledgement. We must acknowledge our restlessness. This requires a true assessment of you. This is being real about your life. For many that are walking through restlessness, this is not easy. In fact, it rocks the boat on what we have been using to camouflage our real inner struggles. True acknowledgment is confession. No longer do we pretend about who we really are or what we want others to think. Confession reveals who we really are. In addition, confession is a release from the damage of restlessness. Confession paves the way for God to work. Without confession, we will struggle with forgiveness even for ourselves.

Confession frees us to enjoy authentic fellowship with the Lord. It relaxes our souls and lightens our cares. Confession starts the rebuilding of security. Confession is the door towards inner peace and maximum joy! No wonder the scripture reads, "If we confess our sins, He is faithful and just to forgive us our sins and to cleanse us from all unrighteousness." The benefits that await us when we confess will open our lives where we will first be *forgiven*. Meaning that whatever has manifested because of the restlessness in our lives will now be pardoned with a new lease on life. Second, we will be *cleansed*. This means to be purified. In other words, the stains of the restlessness in our lives will be washed away! In closing, understand that the flesh nature does not strive to admit that anything is wrong. It does not want to yield towards confession. You must realize that pushing away confession keeps us restless and keeps us from having wholeness.

## Day 38

# SIFTED

*"Simon, Simon, behold, Satan has demanded permission to sift you like wheat; but I have prayed for you, that your faith may not fail; and you, when once you have turned again, strengthen your brothers."* (Luke 22:31-32)

Most of us remember Jesus warning His disciples about His crucifixion. "One of you will betray Me," He said. Yet, instead of turning to God in humility, an argument arose among the disciples as to which one was the greatest. Jesus, who sees both the natural and spiritual realms, addressed Peter (who evidently "won" the argument), "Simon, Simon, behold, Satan has demanded permission to sift you like wheat; but I have prayed for you, that your faith may not fail; and you, when once you have turned again, strengthen your brothers" (Luke 22: 31-32). This text reveals a profound insight into why the Lord allows battles in our lives. Jesus knows that His disciples are going to fail Him. Yet, think of this—He does not pray that

His followers do not experience failure. Instead, He prays that their faith does not fail. Jesus did not ask that God would keep Peter from battle but that Peter would come through the battle into a greater spiritual place.

We squirm and squeal and cry for God to save us from certain battles, but if we were able to pierce through, reach heaven, and hear Jesus, we would probably hear Him praying for us as He prayed for His disciples. The good news—indeed, our very confidence—is that in everything Christ is praying for us. We will get through to the other side of battle. Yes, there are times when we sin, when we make serious mistakes, and when there is pride or jealousy or ambition motivating us toward certain failure. We may fail, but the intercession of Christ will see us through.

It is amazing what God can do with human failures. Remember, Christ said, "Satan has demanded permission to 'sift you like wheat.'" Keep this in mind; Satan is not given permission to destroy but to sift Jesus' disciples. Each of us has two natures: one, a hard outer husk, which is an old nature, the other an inner softness, which constitutes our true self. The outer husk is that part of us that, while we are flesh-center beings, is used to protect ourselves from the harshness of our world. Before we come to Christ, that "husk" protects the inner softness, which otherwise cannot endure the struggles of life in this hostile, devil-filled world.

But when we come to Christ, the husk must be broken and die. We cannot rely on the lifestyles of the flesh to protect us; we must become Christ-centered. So, the Almighty allows the enemy to attack. Satan thinks he is destroying us. But God says, "All you can touch is his flesh!" God is thinking, "I wanted that removed anyway!" So, the battle is designed to sift (remove) your old nature. When something is "sifted," it is filtered. In other words, something that is needed will go through the filtering process to remove something that is no longer needed. Christ comes in our lives for a time of sifting. This sifting is for a greater glory. You are the greater glory!

## Day 39

# SPIRITUAL INCARCERATION

> *"The Spirit of the Lord God is upon me, because the Lord has anointed me to bring good news to the afflicted; He has sent me to bind up the brokenhearted, to proclaim liberty to captives, and freedom to prisoners."* (Isaiah 61:1)

The core of the ministry of Christ lies in our focal passage of the moment. Herein we discover that Christ came to heal all those that are brokenhearted. He came to release those who have been locked in some form of bondage that has kept them in a position where they are unable break free. Jesus came not to condemn us of stains or of our sins. He came to shatter the chains of our faults and failures.

The Bible shares in 2 Corinthians 3:17, "Now the Lord is the Spirit; and where the Spirit of the Lord is, there is liberty." In other words, the purpose of the Messiah was not to just help us get through some tough times regarding the condition of our hearts, or to just help us get through a season where we feel like we are shackled, but on the contrary, the objective was to bring ultimate liberty! Jesus came to release us from the curse of sin. What is the culprit behind broken hearts and spiritual captivity? It is sin.

From the very beginning with Adam in Genesis Chapter 3 when sin was released, we recognize the effects of it. Adam and Eve after sinning ran from the presence of God instead of running towards His presence, because sin separated them from God. In addition, they found fig leaves for clothing to cover up. Why? Because sin wants to often hide. But when we hide, whether we knew it or not, this becomes a prison. Jesus comes to the captives, not to condemn them for doing things that now hold them hostage, but to free them. Jesus sees people spiritually "incarcerated" because of things they did in their past; He knows that they are being held hostage to their sins and to their regrets. Yet, He comes to liberate them, not judge and scold them.

Perhaps as a Christian, you realize that there is still a place in lockdown that needs deliverance. There is an area of your heart where you feel captive to something you did or to something that happened to you and you cannot get free. This is oppression. Jesus is not only Lord and King, but He will always be SAVIOR! We cannot allow the enemy any more footing to exploit a lie. Every time you keep pressing rewind on the areas you have been freed from, you have just handcuffed your soul.

Remember, the enemy is called the Prince of Lies. Often the voice of our past tells us "You haven't changed," "You're hopeless," and "What's the use?" These are lies, because Jesus came to set captives free. Did you do something wrong? Maybe you did. And true, you cannot change the past itself, but Jesus can free you from the consequences of the past. Jesus comes to change our reaction to our past failures and transgressions. He gives hope where there was no hope. Though we are likely to fail again, we are given courage to get up trusting in His forgiveness, defeating the enemy!

## Day 40

# Born to Bloom

*"Most assuredly, I say to you, unless a grain of wheat falls into the ground and dies, it remains alone; but if it dies, it produces much grain."* (John 12:24)

One of the biggest spiritual illnesses impacting mankind is… SELFISHNESS. It has become so active, and yet for many so common that we seldom see the true intent of it. Selfishness has an overall objective, and you may have thought that the main goal of it was self. Well there is more to its workings than just that. In fact, what selfishness does more than anything is prevent us from producing what we were designed for. You must understand selfishness is not the purpose of God. Since that is the case, the working of selfishness offers nothing but sickness, barrenness, disease, impotence, and destruction.

When God created the Seed Principle, He instilled for everything to "Produce after its own kind." In other words, God wanted everything that He created to produce the way He intended. Within any seed is the life of the thing that it represents. You and I are the Seeds of God, created to bear fruit (life) the way He meant to thrive.

God did not create you just so you could live and die for your "self." God has not endowed you with gifts and resources just for you to hoard them and die with them. Your life is a seed waiting to be planted. And your God-given talents, gifts and resources are also seeds waiting to be planted. But notice in our text, even the "grain of wheat (a seed) must go into the ground and die." Until we are willing to die to self and pursue life beyond "SELF," we will never bloom towards great fruitfulness. The evidence that you are dying to selfishness is that you are "producing much grain" (John 12:24).

Yet some believe that all the gain in one's life is the result of the Seed Principle. Sadly, that is not the case. Jesus broadened our understanding on this when He said, "If anyone would come after me, let him deny himself and take up his cross daily and follow me" (Luke 9:23). Following the Seed of the Father (which is Jesus) is to deny myself and take up my cross, which is to crucify anything that alters the manifestation to produce after His own kind. In other words, you were born to bloom!

## Day 41

# The Expose of Perception

*"And why do you look at the speck in your brother's eye, but do not perceive the plank in your own eye?"* (Luke 6:41)

Perception is a powerful thing. So many of our actions are determined by how we perceive things to be. How we perceive is based on what we think what we hear or what we see. Yet, our perception of events, words, and people can be entirely wrong. Why? Most perceive by their natural senses only. The natural mind is not only limited, but it is also a byproduct of distortion since the fall of man. In addition, the Bible shares, "The natural man does not receive the things of the Spirit of God, for they are foolishness to him; nor can he know them, because they are spiritually discerned" (I Corinthians 2:14). In other words, the perception of the natural mind has the capacity to miss the reality because it lacks God! Until our minds are completely renewed, then our perception is primed for distortion.

No wonder the Bible says, "And do not be conformed to this world, but be transformed by the renewing of your mind, that you may prove what is that good and acceptable and perfect will of God" (Romans 12:2). Often, we miss truth and fall into error because we do not believe that our minds need to be renewed. The Holy Spirit reveals the contrary. In addition, when we push away the continual transformation of the spiritual mind, then we learn to function and live primarily on the natural mind or the carnal mind.

Perception, by definition, means we receive something from the outside (hearing, seeing, feeling etc.), and it passes from our senses through our minds and gets into our hearts. Once it enters the heart, it becomes something that has now become significant to us. Discernment is revealed by the Spirit of truth, and when it enters the heart and becomes core, we operate through the will of God. The Holy Spirit delivers revelation and causes renewal of the mind. While on the flip-side, carnal perception causes our minds and hearts to be defiled, tainted, hardened, and fallow. That is why the Bible states, "Your word I have hidden in my heart, that I might not sin against You" (Psalms 119:11).

The natural mind operates on our own conclusions, and it lacks the agent needed to deliver true confirmation because it is laced with the flesh. The Bible shares, "It is the Spirit who gives life; the flesh profits nothing" (John. 6:63). If our perception is operating primarily on the natural mind, understand that it will affect how we think, how we act, and how we even determine life. It will cause us to respond to people in a certain way. It will cause us to judge, become critical, and have eyes that only perceive things the way we claim to see them and not how they really are. The reason we so often experience mistaken perception is that is we do not see through the eyes of God but through carnal eyes, and thus we judge carnally. Our passage reads, "And why do you look at the speck in your brother's eye, but do not perceive the plank in your own eye?" It reveals that we struggle to see the truth and shape a truth about others.

## Day 42

# THE RECONCILIATION FACTOR

*"If therefore you are presenting your offering at the altar, and there remember that your brother has something against you, leave your offering there before the altar, and go your way; first be reconciled to your brother, and then come and present your offering."* (Matthew 5:24)

If you know someone who is carrying unresolved anger toward you or someone else, Jesus tells us we are not to just simply ignore their condition. In fact, He plainly tells us He expects us to do something about it. Jesus requires us to leave our offering, exit the "church service," and do what we can to reconcile with our offended brother. To the Son of God, reconciliation is far more important than fulfilling a Sunday routine!

Reconciliation is to settle or resolve conflict, disagreements, division, and anything that separates the fusion of God's people together. Unfortunately, it is treated as if it is option in the church. How often have we witnessed where someone has been offended by another, whether it is a wife or a husband who may offend each other, or a friend who refuses to settle a matter?

The Lord knows that if we do not engage in some process toward healing, our offended brother will transfer his anger to others. Thus, Hebrews 12:14,15 says, "Pursue peace with all men… See to it that no one comes short of the grace of God; that no root of bitterness springing up causes trouble, and by it many are defiled." One angry person not only jeopardizes their own soul, but their root of bitterness can spread and "many can be defiled."

This is not a little thing to the Lord. Bitterness is a tool that Satan uses to break down marriages, destroy families, splinter churches, and wreck communities. You say, "How could one person's anger cause all that?" One person's anger would not, but picture a community of several thousand in which that one angry person is multiplied by fifty carrying unresolved rage. As a result, the fifty angry people infect, perhaps, up to 300 people with bitterness. Then, add to that number an equal amount the next month, when a different crop of angry people arises, a "fresh" fifty, each with their own angry offense, each who spread their bitterness to several hundred people.

The Lord wants us to reverse this curse. In fact, He calls us not only to go to the one who, for whatever reason, may be offended by us, but He desires we become ministers of reconciliation who inspire others to promote healing in relationships.

## Day 43

# I AM THE KINGDOM

*"Thy kingdom come, Thy will be done!" (Matthew 6:10)*

This is part of one the most famous passages in the Bible known as "The Lord's Prayer." Most likely, this is the most stated and most repeated prayer of all time, but may I expose a reality that may have been overlooked from this prayer? This prayer is Heaven's "Pledge of Allegiance." This prayer is a faith-decree that is God's will, through our living union with Christ, and should be accomplished today on earth. Where is the room for compromise in those words?

Jesus is saying that, with divine power, abounding joy and unwavering mercy, God's Will is being destined to be fulfilled on earth just "as it is in heaven!" We call it *The Lord's Prayer*, yet more appropriately, it might be called the *"Kingdom Prayer,"* for it is something Jesus gave to ignite fire in the hearts of His followers. This prayer is revolutionary.

The Lord's Prayer is not a weak, pleading prayer. Yes, there is a time for pleading with God, but this is a prophetic prayer. This prayer is about the release of the Kingdom's power! We already know it is the "Father's good pleasure" to give us His kingdom (Luke 12:32 NKJV). Jesus is not instructing us to beg for a blessing or two, He is commanding us to call forth God's kingdom to rule on earth, in our own very lives and in our own circumstances.

**This is a prayer of authority.** *The Son of God wants us to pray like we were created to bring Heaven to earth.* This prayer is about alignment with the will of God regarding the Kingdom. This prayer is centered towards those that have their spiritual eyes in tune with the vision of God. This prayer is about the dominion of God's presence on earth. When Jesus shared, "Thy kingdom come, thy will be done," He was sharing a prayer of proclamation! He was announcing His intentional plan that was to come through us.

**This is a prayer of agreement.** When we agree with the will and Word of God, then the presence of God increases in the spiritual realm, proportionally displacing the influence of hell on earth. When we embrace the reality that the kingdom has come with power then we are able to expect miracles, healings, and the pouring of God's grace. When there is a vacancy of the will of the kingdom's power, then we witness those who struggle with clear distinction of carnality. We observe those that settle with the territory in their lives that they were never promised from God, such as brokenness, bitterness, and barrenness. We must agree with the will of God so that we can see the realization of what Christ prayed for which is "Thy kingdom come; thy will be done."

## Day 44

# Our Place of Peace

*"Be anxious for nothing, but in everything by prayer and supplication with thanksgiving let your requests be made known to God. And the **peace** of God, which surpasses all comprehension, will guard your hearts and your minds in Christ Jesus."* (Philippians. 4:6-7)

Our scripture states that there is "a peace that surpasses all comprehension." In other words, this peace is beyond our conclusions, our equations, and our understanding. Many perceive peace as a place where there is a lack of problems or tension, but godly peace is not determined by the right circumstances falling in place. Godly peace is not a spiritual ticket in which God gives us to avoid the issues of the day. The Lord never wanted us to simply possess a man-made peace based on having no problems. His intention is to shelter us in His very own peace—the imperturbable peace of God. The peace of God is a deep calm that connects with the thought processes of the

Almighty. He is never anxious, always in command, and never without a remedy. He sees the end from the beginning and views the needs of man from the position of unlimited resources and capabilities. He perceives the needs of His children.

The peace He gives is not only *from* Him, it is an extension of Him—it is the very substance of His peace. No wonder Jesus said, "Peace I leave with you; My peace I give to you; not as the world gives do, I give to you. Do not let your heart be troubled, nor let it be fearful" (John 14:27). This peace is not determined on the outcomes or the input of those around me. It is not revealed because of a movement of mankind, or a rally in the community. This peace is God himself. It is this divine fabric that He says will "guard [our] hearts and... minds in Christ Jesus." If my heart is guarded, then it is protected by PEACE.

The voice of God (His Word) regarding peace reveals that there exists a place of refuge for those in the family of God. It is a realm guarded by God's very own peace where we can abide. As we enter this realm of trust, the Bible states, "That the God of peace will CRUSH Satan under our feet" (Romans. 16:20). When we dwell in God's special Place of Peace, it becomes an environment where Satan becomes like a bug under our boot. Therefore, the Lord commands us to "Let the peace of Christ rule in your hearts, to which indeed you were called in one body: and be thankful" (Colossians 3:15).

When peace RULES our hearts, then peace has saturated the confines of our hearts and seeks to leave no space where we can potentially allow circumstances or worriedness to navigate our hearts. Today, open your mind to a fresh/new word about the True Peace of God. It is not manifested by the actions of the world. It is not determined by avoiding trials and tribulations, it is an operation of the heart that is not based on certain conditions to claim it. This peace is originated from the nature of God. This peace is in the unification with the Lord. This is Our Place of Peace!

## Day 45

# "TEMPTATION ISLAND"

*"Let no one say when he is tempted, 'I am tempted by God;' for God cannot be tempted by evil, nor does He Himself tempt anyone. But each one is tempted when he is drawn away by his own desires and enticed. Then, when desire has conceived, it gives birth to sin; and sin, when it is full-grown, brings forth death."* (James 1:13-15)

When you think of a deserted island, what typically comes to mind? For me, I initially consider that I may be all alone, that no one is here to monitor, watch, or witness whatever is acted out on this island. An island mentality requires ISOLATION. I remember some years ago a song entitled "No Man Is an Island." The lyrics talked about how the island scenario for many is a place where we separate ourselves from being seen or being exposed. But the Bible reveals in Ephesians 5:11-13 "to expose every deed being done in the dark." Often though when we have the island position, we hide what we have been doing on the island. Remember the story *Lord of the Flies*? Here are these boys shipwrecked on this island without guidance, instruction, and order. These young boys shifted from how they normally lived and normally functioned while they operated on this island. On the island, they pursued… POWER and PLEASURE.

Temptation Island is a place today where many slowly and methodically gravitate towards stimulating the movement to push the button for the invitation of the FLESH. Whether we knew it or not, wisdom's great opponent is… WORLDLY LUST. It has a sales pitch that is connected to working on our senses to give in to our fleshly impulses. It showers us with baited pleasures that tantalize and urge us to move us just a little closer to Temptation Island.

On Temptation Island, you are so hidden that no one can see or know what you have allowed to cover your heart. Most do not even hesitate for consideration or contemplation that what Temptation Island is really hoping to accomplish is to captivate your heart. In truth, temptation wants to alter your heart towards being influenced so much that you stay on an isolated place away from God (which is Temptation Island).

So, let us go deeper with the objective of Temptation Island. Overall, it is designed to keep you separated from God. Remember when Jesus was tempted (Matthew Chapter 4), He was all alone and hungry. We must understand though that it was not an accident that the enemy tempted Him with food. Why is this? Because as a human, he was connected to the fleshly domain. Even though this was the case, Jesus resisted the temptation of the enemy by stating in Matthew Chapter 4, "Man shall not live by bread alone but by every word that proceeds out of the mouth of God." In other words, it is impossible to live without the SUBSTANCE of the Word!

Temptation's intent is that we give it room to become one of our basic consumption choices to be digested into our overall being. Jesus revealed to us that even if we are vulnerable to temptation, we must dwell on what brings real LIFE. Often though, temptation comes when we are so-called "vulnerable." In other words, we are weak, wounded, and susceptible to being inclined to traveling to a place where we consider "maybe my pain will go away if I pursue this." Temptation… Tantalizes. Temptation… Pleases. Temptation… Ends! The goal of temptation is to attract, with the intent to distract, to ATTACK!!! Notice that in our text, the Bible states that "everyone is tempted by their own desires." The emphasis is "He is drawn away by his own desires." In other words, temptation is a hook, an allurement, a bait to sway us towards something or someone that grows to the point that we act on it.

Temptation tricks us to rationalize and to justify that whatever we are seeking is legit. The Bible tells us that temptation is common to mankind (I Corinthians 10:13). In fact, even Jesus was tempted but did not sin. The trick about temptation is to conclude you have no other course but to feed into it. When we do this, we are in essence saying we are trapped on TEMPTATION ISLAND! One of my colleagues shared with me that Satan wants to isolate, to insulate, to be able to annihilate. Today, get off the island. Learn that when we are tempted like Jesus, we prove where we are in the heart. Today, discover that you were never created to live on… TEMPTATION ISLAND!

## Day 46

# "My Personal Trainer"

*"A pupil is not above his teacher; but everyone, after he has been fully trained, will be like his teacher"* (Luke 6:40)

Spending most of my adult life being concerned about the conditioning of my body, I have concluded that when my physical preparation is a daily systematic rhythm, there is an outcome that will enrich my body. In time, I feel it, I see it, and I know that my body has been developed. In the spiritual life, we should be able to assess spiritual development. In the spiritual, we should be able to witness an enhancement.

Spiritual training can come in an array of ways, but at the core of all spiritual progress is a heart that is serious about transformation. At this very moment, you can begin accelerated training simply by picking up the Word of God and asking the Holy Spirit to teach you. Remember, Jesus said, "The Helper, the Holy Spirit, whom the Father will send in My name, He will

TEACH you all things, and bring to your remembrance all that I said to you" (John 14:26).

The Holy Spirit according to the scriptures is our "Guide," our "Counselor, "and our "Comforter" (John 15:26). In other words, the Holy Spirit is our instructional guide in the impartation, and the transformation in the development to be in shaped in the likeness of the Lord. We so often want the Lord to save us and heal us, but what about TRAIN US?

The Bible states, "Physical training is good, but training for godliness is much better, promising benefits in this life and in the life to come" (I Timothy 4:8). In other words, spiritual exercise has benefits that are insurmountable! Exercising in the spiritual causes one's life to truly run with endurance. This spiritual workout removes the weight of the flesh. This is GOD'S GYM! Here we "remove every weight, and the sin which so easily besets us, and run with patience the race that is set before us" (Hebrew 12:1).

God desires that we enter a spiritual protocol where we follow the lead of our SUPERNATURAL GUIDE, the Holy Spirit. Most physical trainers require a change in almost everything we engage in when it comes to our body. The reason why is because the trainer is taking us on a journey where our bodies are being reshaped. In the spiritual, the Holy Spirit is taking us on a place, whereas the trainer, He is REMAKING the people of God into the true image of God.

This requires TRAINING!

## Day 47

# ROOTED AND GROUNDED

*"That Christ may dwell in your hearts through faith; that you, being rooted and grounded in love."* (Ephesians 3:17)

When I think of ROOTS or being GROUNDED, I think of stability. To think that one of the keys of obtaining personal strength lies in being stable in love, seems like just another message about the need of love, but upon further investigation, you will understand that establishing any kind of root system requires a few elements.

First, strong roots mean having a strong hydration system. Over and over the Word of God communicates spiritually the need to stay close where water resides. For instance, the Bible shares to "be like a tree planted by the rivers of water, that brings forth its fruit in its season, whose leaf also shall not whiter; and whatever he does shall prosper" (Psalms 1:3). Notice that the first thing the Psalmist highlights was to be planted by rivers of water! In other words, the water represents an ENVIRONMENT.

God wants His word (His Spirit) to saturate our lives to STABILIZE our lives! Too often for many, the principle to dwell where we are feeding off the Word as a source of life seems to be too religious and too demanding. But even a farmer or a gardener realizes that without ample amounts of nourishment for vegetation, the plant will cease to grow properly.

For some, they have learned to adjust to drought conditions in the spiritual life. In other words, they have become settled in having dryness, brittleness, and withered places throughout the totality of life. No wonder the Bible states that we "be rooted and grounded in love," because, God is LOVE! It is impossible to truly have love rooted and grounded without GOD.

Love is the nature of God. Love is in the makeup of God. Love is in the order of God, but it must be woven and embedded in your root system. Here is the thing; when something is rooted in your life, it is hard to pull you away from it! When something is rooted, it has staying power. When something is rooted, it plans to live!

Slowly and surely over time because of neglecting the need of our spiritual operation of being nourished (which is the created order of God to have His Word water our lives to have stabilization), we transition into something other than the created expectation, which leads us to having a perverted love, or as some state, "A problem with love." No wonder Jesus stated in Mark 4:17, "Since they have no root, they last only a short time." Our ROOT system determines what we are made of. Our roots dictate the kind of blooming to be released from our lives. I have concluded that whatever is growing or living from our lives is a direct result of what is in the ROOTS!

## Day 48

# SOUR MILK

*"For God doth know that in the day ye eat thereof, then your eyes shall be opened, and ye shall be as gods, knowing good and evil."* (Genesis 3:5)

Years ago, when I was in elementary school, we used to receive a carton of milk at lunch. I remember on one occasion when I discovered that my milk was soured. I immediately shared with my friends, "Man, my milk is sour!" Then each of my friends wanted to get a sniff for themselves. They wanted to smell the unpleasant odor of the milk. The milk went from one person to the next, with all my friends wanting to get their own individual whiff of the sour milk.

Every person that smelled the milk agreed that it had gone bad, but that did not stop the next person from wanting to smell the same rotten milk. Who would voluntarily want to interrupt the delicious taste of their lunch with a rotten odor? Most of the people at my lunch table wanted to expand their understanding and experiences to include the misery of sour milk.

When God told Adam and his wife, "But of the tree of the knowledge of good and evil, thou shalt not eat of it: for in the day that thou eatest thereof thou shalt surely die" (Genesis 2:17), He was saying don't open yourself up to what has already been presented as ROTTEN!

God had shared His spoken Word as a statement of truth, but Adam's family had to sniff anyway. Everyday God gives us His spoken word for protection, provision, and purpose, but many unfortunately keep sniffing what we already know is unpleasant according to God.

In fact, we follow this pattern of operation each time we choose to be defensive rather than be a peacemaker, when our thoughts dwell on fault finding instead of finding forgiveness in our hearts. Yet, for many, we justify the sniff over and over and rationalize that it is acceptable, not realizing that every time we open our spiritual nostrils to the foul and contaminated, we are then becoming prone to give it freedom and room to operate as a norm when all along it was SOURED.

## Day 49

# "For The Seekers"

*"Seek, and you will find."* (Matthew 7:7b)

It is not hard to recognize someone that has spent time and energy with knowing about our current affairs in the world. They are normally reading and reviewing insight from newspapers to listening to worldwide news on social media. In addition, it is not hard for someone to standout who professes to be a fan of a local sports franchise. He normally knows not only all the players, but he knows the statistics of the entire sport.

Likewise, people can tell when an individual has spent extended time seeking God. You may ask how, and the answer lies in how they navigate across the waves of life with Him and in the calmness of their hearts to have this trust with God despite their circumstances. There is a constant radiance exuding from their souls that is attracted towards seeking the Spirit of God.

Remember when Jesus said, "The kingdom of heaven is like a merchant seeking beautiful pearls, who when he had found one pearl of great price, went and sold all that he had and bought it" (Matthew 13:45-46). Isn't it interesting that people in general SEEK what they want? This merchant sought pearls of great wealth, and the application for us as it relates to God is, do we truly see Him as GREAT? Do you see him as a worthy investment? This merchant was so sure of his price that he sold everything for it!

To SEEK and FIND God leads to everything accessible to you. The Bible states in James 4:8, "Draw near to God, and He will draw near to you." Often because we are a people that expect immediate results, when we draw near to God, we immediately desire for something to transpire instantly, not realizing that what God is after is the PURSUIT for Him and not what He PROVIDES.

The love for God is a constant pursuit that seeks to get closer and closer to His presence. Every time we even consider the thought of a greater connection with God, it ignites a transformation within ourselves. Whether we knew it or not, when we abandon the idea that life revolves around what works for us, but rather what happens when we seek the Lord, we will witness (like the merchant) something that is worth more than anything we have and can obtain!

We may miss from the story of the merchant that he was willing to pay a price to have what he sought. The Bible states, "He sold all that he had and bought the pearl" (Matthew 13:46). All that he had means that he let nothing interfere in the investment that he deemed as the greatest of all. Often people nickel and dime their seeking of the Lord, not realizing that the Lord is also seeking for the true SEEKERS of Himself!

The Bible shares, "The hour is coming, and now is, when the true worshippers will worship, the Father in spirit and in truth; for the Father is SEEKING such to worship Him" (John 4:23). Did you ever consider that the Lord is also seeking? He is seeking for those that are seeking for Him. If you are wondering what the key is to alter everything, well it lies in… what we SEEK!

## Day 50

# "THE FIG LEAF APPROACH"

*"Then the eyes of both were opened, and they knew that they were naked; and they sewed fig leaves together and made themselves coverings."* (Genesis 3:7)

Sometimes it is too hard to come out of hiding and admit we have something we need to get taken care of! We hide instead, not willing to face up to it. We act this way with God as well. We say things like, "Well, I know I need to get right with God, but I need to get some things under control first." We tell ourselves, "I just don't know how to make it right again." So, we hide ourselves from God. We can pretend He is not there or act as though we will fix ourselves back up when we can and then present ourselves to Jesus, as though we could ever hope to fix ourselves in the first place. But it is so hard it seems to get down on our knees and admit we need help. So, we choose to hide because it is "easier."

I am going to compare us to someone in the Bible, and His name was Adam. In Genesis (the very first book of the Bible), we find the picture of a man with the same problem. I want you to imagine yourself in his position. You are in the Garden of Eden. All is well. The lion is cuddling up to the lamb ready for a nap. The vines are growing nice size grapes. When boom… you make a huge mistake! You just ate the wrong fruit. Guilt rushes into your mind as you and your mate try desperately to cover yourselves up. Knowing your naked is one thing, but now… here comes God. You are standing there naked and ashamed. You just did something He told you not to do. The guilt is written all over your face as you hear the voice of God calling to you. His voice is pleasant as always. The two of you have talked many times before around this same time of day. God has always been your friend. But now you have done something He told you would cause you to die. You betrayed God Himself! Think about it, how would you feel?

Chapter 3 and verse 8 of Genesis says, "And they heard the sound of the LORD God walking in the garden in the cool of the day, and Adam and his wife hid themselves from the presence of the LORD God among the trees of the garden." This is where it all begins. Adam hid from God because he could not face up to what was happening. He thought, "If I hide here and cover myself up before He sees me… then he won't know, and I can pretend everything is fine." It is not a funny matter when we attempt to hide our shortcomings and guilt filled moments by hoping we can just hide it or run from it. How many times have you had to come to the realization that what you are running away from is still going to be there when you run out of breath? The thing is, no matter how many fig leaves Adam attempted to use to hide, he would still be naked before God. In my life, I can look back where I have done my best to find leaves to cover my mess, to cover my faults, my wrongs, and my sins.

The Fig Leave Approach is sought out on so many levels because to truly face your own inadequacies is a sign of spiritual maturity. The Bible shares in I Corinthians 13:11, "When I was a child, I spoke as a child, I understood as a child, I thought as a child: but when I became a man, I put away childish things." Running, avoiding, and evading are all signs of immaturity, covering your inner self by placing the attention on something else other than what is needing a breakthrough from the FIG LEAF APPROACH. Lord help us to grow up and toss the FIG LEAVES!

## Day 51

# DISCOVERING THE REAL LIFE

When we hear the word "life," most of us consider mainly the physical condition of life, meaning a living organism. But the truth of the matter is that unlike a tree or a fish, man operates on a different level. Yes, we are all connected to the physical, but there is something uniquely wired into man that makes him unlike anything else. Most of us know that when God created man, unlike everything else created, He created him in His likeness; He created man in His image. But just what does that mean?

Let us break down some content. First off, there are three words that breakdown the word "life" that we witness every day. First, Bios—Biological or natural life. It describes plant and animal life. This even encompasses our earthly body. Like every living creature, we have biology to us, meaning the study of all living creatures. Then there is Psyche—which is the soul life. This also speaks of natural life and is often referred to as a manner of life. This encompasses the totality of the soul. Lastly, there is Zoe—the life of God, Eternal Life. This life encompasses the Spirit. The Zoe life is really the Divine life. The reason being is because this is life with God. It is really a walk with God. Review everything Jesus ever said, and you will notice an intentional move on His part to connect us to the same pattern of Himself and the father. He prayed that we would be ONE as He and the Father are one.

Often when we here of eternal life, most of us zoom right to HEAVEN. But pause and consider, isn't this life really a realm where we walk with Him, live with Him, abide with Him? Isn't this life just a stage of the eternal life? Eternal life began the moment you accepted Christ. Eternal life is not just a Heaven experience, it is a now experience! Eternal life is NOW.

John 17:3 says, "And this is life eternal, that they might know thee the only true God, and Jesus Christ, whom thou hast sent." Wow! Eternal life is not being in heaven but about becoming ALIVE in Christ! The Bible states that eternal life knows the one true God and Jesus Christ! This word "know" is about establishing a relationship. In fact, when someone knows something, they are really telling you how much of a relationship they have with it. Therefore, Jesus said in John 14:6, "I am the way, the truth, and the life." He was not saying "I will lead you to the way," or "I will lead you towards the truth or the life," but that He was the Way, the Truth, and the Life! The thing is to notice the sequence— First Jesus states He is the WAY. Meaning He is the course, the map to travel on. The way is about directions. The Way is about destination. The truth is about the reality, the certainty of God, the Word of God, and the voice of God is the truth of God. If we follow the Way and believe the Truth, it will always open us to the LIFE. This Zoe life, this Divine life, is the REAL LIFE.

## Day 52

# SOUL FOOD

*"And Jesus said unto them, I am the bread of life: he that cometh to me shall never hunger; and he that believeth on me shall never thirst."* (John 6:35)

With my wife being the most phenomenal Master Chef and Baker in my opinion, I have had the privilege of experiencing on my taste buds what appears straight from ABOVE! I know I may sound biased, but because I have personally eaten more than a few bites of her delicious creations throughout our marriage, I have concluded that our spiritual lives are remarkably similar. Here is why. Jesus says, "I am the bread of life, he who comes to me shall not hunger and he who believes in me shall not thirst." That is powerful.

To think that the Lord desires for us to consume His PRESENCE to the point that we discover that we end up FULLY SATISFIED may sound unbelievable, but remember Jesus also said, "I am the TRUTH." The truth of the matter is that many of us have not sat at the table of Jesus long enough to know the TOTAL EXEPRENICE of the Bread of Life. The purpose of the Bread is to give us an EVERLASTING LIFE. Do not get tripped up or think that this life means only the afterlife, it means this one as well!

Maybe we have missed the RESULT of having a FULL LIFE because we have digested too much spiritual junk food. In other words, we have spiritually consumed selfishness, depression, anxiety, and fear, which seems to be on our MENU. I challenge you today to walk into the Lord's CUISINE and uncover the TRUTH about your created APPETITE.

## Day 53

# Having a Stronghold?

Many people who pursue to change their lives from a world that seems to gravitate and feed on personal stimulation (meaning lusts, addictions, and uncontrolled desires) have discovered that the road sometimes, and perhaps for some even often, leads them right back to the place they assumed they had conquered. Some label this as a RELAPSE. But the truth of the matter is something still lingers in us that was never actually eradicated.

This operation exposes that we are still attached to something that has never truly been REMOVED. This is not a relapse, but a STRONGHOLD. A stronghold is a place where your thinking has become sympathetic to something that has adverse effects. It is a place where justification and rationalization reign supreme. It is a place where we flip-flop with what has position and power over our choices and our convictions. A stronghold is a place where the intent is to get you stuck on the FLESH.

We tell ourselves, "This activity won't hurt anyone but me." That is really a stronghold! We say, "Nobody will ever find out." But that is still a stronghold. We even say, "God will forgive me of this act," not knowing this is still a stronghold. The Bible shares, "As a man thinks in his heart, so is he" (Proverbs 23:7). In other words, you are what you think you are!

John Piper said, "Sin is what we do when we are not completely satisfied in God." This is the reason so many succumb back to our previous dangerous thoughts. John Calvin conveys this truth when he says, "The evil in our desire often is not in what we want but that we want too much." If there remains a passion and a mental hook that craves for activation in our lives, we still are operating with a stronghold. You may have a good day, even a good week or month, but if it returns like it never left, that is because it never really did. It was just dormant, waiting for you to release it!

To effectively tear down a stronghold, our minds must be saturated with the presence of God. Let us look at II Corinthians again. It reads, "Take captive every thought to make it obedient to Christ." Notice that the text states "every thought." One little thought can be the catalyst the enemy could use to release damage. No wonder the Bible shares, "Give no opportunity to the devil" (Ephesians 4:27). The enemy is focused on pushing us to exalt anything to a level that it fights for position of preeminence in our lives. He wants anything to "exalts itself" in our thought life that it gets placed in what I call "The Stuck Mode" in our minds. The reason why is to prevent us from unlocking the truth about ourselves. When the truth sets us free it is supposed to set us free indeed! So, ask yourself, are you really having a relapse or is this a STRONGHOLD?

*Day 54*

# "The Case on Gossip"

*"A perverse man spreads strife, and a slanderer separates intimate friends."* (Proverbs 16:28)

Did you ever consider that GOSSIP is a seed from Hell? Think about it. Timothy wrote, "Men will be lovers of self, lovers of money, boastful, arrogant, revilers, disobedient to parents, ungrateful, unholy, unloving, irreconcilable, **malicious gossips**" (2 Timothy 3:2-3), and the list goes on. During this list of what would be seen in the last days, the apostle includes "malicious gossips."

Gossip today has taken on an acceptable appeal in our current generation. It is accepted as casual, typical, and as regular conversation. This "malicious gossip" concept has become a norm even in politics, leadership, and in corporations. We see it so approved in social media that it has taken on a way of life.

Yet the Bible connects "malicious gossip" to the devil. In the New Testament, the Greek word *diabolos*, which is translated "devil," is translated impersonally elsewhere as a "false accuser" or a "slanderer." A slanderer is one that promotes doubt, worry, disapproval, and complaint, and one who sabotages. This is what the devil does! Perhaps you know people who always have something negative to say about others, who always bring negative information about people into their conversations. I pray that the Holy Spirit will reveal to us how "malicious gossip" is kin to the nature of Satan himself.

The Scriptures say that we will be justified or condemned by our words. Yes, our words even those spoken in secret with a spouse or friend about others are used by God to measure our obedience to His will. James writes, "If anyone does not stumble in what he says, he is a perfect man" (James 3:2). Words have power. Scripture reveals that "death and life are in the power of the tongue" (Proverbs. 18:21). Our words, expressed as a confession of faith, bring us into salvation, but words without faith can lead us and others with us into destruction and heartache.

James 3:8 warns, "The tongue… is a restless evil… full of deadly poison." "The tongue," he says, "is a fire, the very world of iniquity" (v. 6). And James reveals a most profound thought, "The tongue… sets on fire the course of our life and is set on fire by hell" (v. 6). The enemy gains access to our world, to destroy all that is good and holy in it, through our tongues. The very course of our life, the direction and quality of our earthly existence, is "set on fire by hell" through the words we speak. If we talk negatively about someone or maliciously gossip, the destructive fire of hell itself is released through our words. Lord, help us to understand the power of our words!

## Day 55

# "What Do You Produce?"

*"Beware of false prophets, who come to you in sheep's clothing, but inwardly they are ravenous wolves. You will know them by their fruits. Do men gather grapes from thorn bushes or figs from thistles? Even so, every good tree bears good fruit, but a bad tree bears bad fruit. A good tree cannot bear bad fruit, nor can a bad tree bear good fruit. Every tree that does not bear good fruit is cut down and thrown into the fire. Therefore by their fruits you will know them."* (Matthew 7:15-20)

The Bible says, "You don't pick grapes from a thorn bush." A thorn bush has what? Thorns! And thorns hurt. They poke you, cut you, and scratch you. None of us like getting pricked by a thorn. Sometimes in life we meet those that impact our lives much like a thorn. They cut us, poke at us, and even wound us. What we fail to realize though is thorns are the byproduct of what is growing from a source. A thorn bush produces thorns. The dilemma is that some that are in situations do not realize what may be happening in terms of prosperity has everything to do with the source they are connected too. Some of us do not like what we are producing. We fail to reflect on a reality made by Jesus and that is…"You are known by your fruit."

You may not like what you are producing, but ask yourself, what can you do to alter and change the outcome? Jesus said, "I am the Vine and you are the branches" (John 15:1). In other words, He is the source! The determining factor that verifies if we are in fact a product of the Vine is that the same benefits seen in the Vine are also seen in us.

We are supposed to be bearing the fruit of joy, peace, love, and our obedience for God. But some are experiencing the bearing of thorns and not realizing that thorns hurt our closeness, our connection, and our commitment! Some have gotten so used to bearing thorns that they say, "Well that's just me." You mean it is you to cut, poke, and hurt? So, what does that produce? Not fruit. Our scripture says, "That a healthy tree produces healthy fruit, and an unhealthy tree produces unhealthy fruit." When a tree is unhealthy then its fruit will be as well. In other words, if it is sick or diseased, then it will reveal what is being produced from your life! Fruit from a tree is the evidence of what kind of condition the tree is in. In other words, if we claim that we are the byproduct of a good tree and what we are producing is not reflective of that, then we must conclude that this is the result of our relationship to the Vine (Jesus).

Today, I want you to be fruit examiner. Because if the fruit is unhealthy, then something from the tree is the result of that. If anger, bitterness, resentment, unforgiveness, or even the critical spirit is seen in what comes from you or out of you, then it is time to examine what you produce. Jesus said, "Every tree that does not produce good fruit is chopped down and thrown into the fire." You may ask why it will be chopped down. Because it is not doing what it was designed to do. God wanted us as His people to produce after His kind. If his spirit, his ways, and his glory are not coming out of our lives, then Christ is saying I rather not see it grow. You may say that is a bold statement, but this is a theme throughout the message of Jesus.

It was Jesus who said, "Why call me Lord, Lord, and do not the things that I say?" In other words, do not give lip service when who you are is not being seen in your producing. Verse 20 says, "The way to identify a tree or a person is by the kind of fruit that is produced." In other words, we can examine who we are by the stuff that is coming out of our lives. So, what are you producing?

## Day 56

# "Your Authentic Identity"

*"The first man, Adam, became a living soul. The last Adam became a life-giving spirit."* (1 Corinthians 15:45)

Did you know that the name "Adam" meant man? In addition, his origin and creation are a representative of mankind. In our text, not only are there two specific Adams but there are two distinct species of man. The first species according to the truth of God's word was a being that established a sinful nature. His mind, which was carnal or natural, sought to satisfy the pleasures of the flesh.

The second species according to the Word of God is a "life-giving spirit." The Bible states in John 4:24 that "God is spirit," clearly verifying that He is divine. In addition, the rest of that text states that "those who worship God must worship Him in spirit and truth." In other words, our connection and spiritual rapport with God is woven through the Spirit.

Many though have created an identity that is strictly implanted in the first species of man, not realizing that even the first man was offered the identity of the life-giving spirit. Dwelling where our lives are centered on the life-giving spirit is not only a desire, but it is a statement of the truth of our origin. The spirit centered man has thoughts, dreams, and aspirations that connect with the Spirit and not with the natural man. In other words, attaining the glory of the natural for personal primary benefits only.

Today we witness across the globe what I call the "Great Divide." This falls into race, culture, social status, and color, where mankind suffers with being disconnected and separated from our authentic identity.

From God's perspective, He sees us either by being controlled by what the soul desires or by what the spirit desires. The first species loves to receive from the natural (the world), and the second species loves to receive from the second Adam… Christ!

Think about it, the first Adam unfortunately left us with question marks above our heads. The second Adam gave us answers! Questions without answers promote doubt, depression, and delusion. The second Adam, namely Jesus, said, "I come to give life." This is the absolute fullness of our identity. This promotes peace, prosperity, and purpose! This is the answer to our true origin.

## Day 57

# "The See-Through Man"

*"Jesus said: You make yourselves look righteous to other people. God knows your hearts. The things considered of great value by people are worth nothing in God's sight."*
(Luke 16:15)

There was a group in the time of Jesus called the Pharisees. They were the religious leaders of Israel. The Pharisees were the leaders of the synagogues. They were the most studious of the law, the most meticulous in interpreting the law and applying the law, the most relentless in giving attention to the law, and the most eager to observe the ceremonies and the rituals that indicated that they were worshipping the true God. The problem with all that is that they did all this but… Did not have a relationship with GOD! Rituals and routines have everything to do with form and truly little to do with FAITH. They have nothing to do with the relationship the Lord truly desires. Today many have claim that they know God because they know about Him, yet do they truly know Him?

In the time of Jesus, men loved Religion more than they loved a RELATIONSHIP with the Lord. Today, there is a similarity to some degree; men love their churches more than they love Christ! In our text, Jesus makes it clear that people make themselves look righteous to be viewed by others. But the Bible states, "God knows your heart." It is amazing that many people travel to a Sunday routine hiding from the world the condition of their hearts by portraying all is well on the outside.

Jesus basically stated, "This is no value to me." Here is a question for you: Why do we place such a standard on how we look before PEOPLE but seldom consider how we look before GOD? Perhaps because "we love the praise from men rather than praise from God" (John 12:43). There is nothing wrong with wanting some healthy praise, but when it becomes exclusive to only you, then... "We have a problem!"

The Pharisees loved the attention. They loved the attraction. They loved the adoration, not realizing that when a person has this much focused on oneself this is really a form of worship. I call it the triple AAAs. When we seek only to have the Attention, the Attraction, and the Adoration, we are worshipping ourselves! Worship was designed to give the AAAs to God. God can see through whatever has the preeminence in our lives.

It is also worth noting that when we place ALL the ATTENTION on ourselves, we miss that this holds no value to God. There are so many things that people deem as great, but push pause for a second and ask what is great to God? Ready for the answer? Here it is: "You shall love the Lord your God with all your heart, and with all your soul, and with all your strength, and with all your mind; and your neighbor as yourself" (Luke 10:27). This was considered the Greatest Commandment by Jesus because the greatest thing is to know Him to the degree that He can SEE all the way THROUGH ME!

## Day 58

# "FIGHT"

*"For the weapons of our warfare are not of the flesh but have divine power to destroy strongholds."* (II Corinthians 10:4)

Throughout the Word of God, there is a theme that is focused on God's people battling, fighting, and in being in what I call "war mode." In fact, we reference passages like, "Fight the good fight of faith" (I Timothy 6:12). Also, "Put on the whole armor of God" (Ephesians 5:10). How about, "You must endure hardship as a good soldier of Jesus Christ" (II Timothy 2:3). These scriptures and others highlight a reality about the spiritual life, and that is every day we should be BATTLE READY!

You see, Jesus was always aware that He lived in a WAR ZONE, no matter what He was doing, whether He was laughing with sinners or driving out demons, whether He was healing the sick or training followers. Beneath the surface of His outer activities, the "war mode switch" in Jesus' mind was always on.

For some, when we think of war, we consider it as something we should avoid. We conclude that it involves casualties, chaos, and consequences that devastate the innocent. But when I speak of war, I want you to expand your spiritual mind and consider it from a much deeper perspective. Such as, if your child were very seriously sick, wouldn't you fight that illness with every medical benefit at your disposal? Spiritually, should we not display the same force?

For some reason or another, we have taken things like depression, doubt, division, and discouragement as items that can have territory in our hearts and souls. We have allowed the progression of these things that cause us to eventually want to give up. Often people have said, "I can't take it no more!" By saying this, we give access to the things that want dominion in our lives! Words like "victory" and "overcome" in the Word of God give us the impression that it is in God's nature to be a victor and to be an overcomer. We must be willing to FIGHT!

What is interesting about warfare in any capacity is that to truly fight you must know how to fight! As a former boxer and a wrestler, I discovered that it was not always who was the biggest, or the strongest, but who was EQUIPPED for the fight. The Bible teaches us that God wants every believer equipped with the ingredients that reveal His character, His commitment, and His cause (Ephesians 4:12-16). It is sort of like having a "spiritual BACK-PACK." Meaning, like a backpack, we can use what we need from God as we face the conditions of this life.

Before you vocalize possibly a word of quitting or giving up on whatever it is you must face, I want you to know that God wants you to come to His fitness program starting today and learn to fortify from His nature the skills to FIGHT!

## Day 59

# "Stormproof"

*"If the foundations are destroyed, what can the righteous do?"* (Psalms 11:3)

Just as there are foundations that are dug and laid for buildings, so there are spiritual foundations upon which we can build a stable spiritual life. If our foundations are destroyed, or if we try to build our lives upon an incomplete foundation, to that degree we compromise our ability to stand during life's storms.

I have known many people who would visibly try to convince everyone but God that they were connected to Him. They perceived that church attendance and helping with church events would suffice in building a spiritual foundation.

Others pass through a challenge that reveals what kind of foundation was truly set in their lives. Outwardly they portrayed consistency and commitment, yet inwardly their spiritual lives were unstable. As soon as difficulties arose, they fell apart. Why?

As "together" as they may have seemed, they had something missing from their inner foundation. They crumbled during the storm. Jesus put it this way, "Everyone who comes to Me and hears My words and acts on them, I will show you whom he is like: he is like a man building a house, who dug deep and laid a foundation on the rock; and when a flood occurred, the torrent burst against that house and could not shake it, because it had been well built" (Luke 6: 47-48).

The question is not "if" a storm is coming, but "when." Storms are a part of life. Everyone will experience them. Life has a way of going from a calm and peaceful spiritual condition to suddenly turning turbulent or adversarial. The only way one's house can stand during these times is if it is well built. This house that Jesus is referring to is really our lives. In building the spiritual house (your life), we must build on the right foundation for the structure (your life) to stand when storms come. The thing is any building contractor will tell you that long before any area of the foundation is built, it must follow the specifications of the blueprints that have been created. There is work required before breaking ground on the foundation.

This work is necessary in following the approved layouts where the intent of the creator is to follow what has been mandated by the instructions. Jesus also stated, "But the one who has heard and has not acted accordingly, is like a man who built a house on the ground without any foundation; and the torrent burst against it and immediately it collapsed, and the ruin of that house was great" (Luke 6:49). To Jesus, building without a foundation is a certifiable way of witnessing a great crash. How do you know for sure what kind of foundation you have? By how you handle and manage the outcome of storms. To the one who has built his or her life on the ROCK, when they are facing the strong winds of this world or when they are dealing with the downpour of personal damage, they still STAND, not because of themselves, but because of the foundation that is on the ROCK!

*Day 60*

# "No More Repeats of the Old Nature"

Often, I witness and observe many people who suffer from a REPEAT of patterns of despair, depression, and division. They are repeatedly frustrated with self-pity, anger, immoral thoughts, or fleshly lusts. Deep down they conclude that these thoughts will not go away on their own. Yet, ideas and feelings keep promoting and whispering within, "Press REPEAT."

We must always keep in mind that "it is not in man to direct his own steps" (Jeremiah 10:23). In other words, to get through what many are facing and being impacted with every day, we must journey towards the realm where only God brings a complete conversion.

Every person who desires to stop the repeat of the old nature must embrace that our minds must be renewed through repentance and the knowledge of God's Word. In other words, if I continue to hear in my mind that my present life, and potentially my future life, has doubts, destruction, and disbelief of a new life, understand that this is not a word God has spoken but a word that has taken significant roots in your heart.

I would like to pause for a second to identify that for some who think that the path is truly renewed within, we must understand that the Devil is in the business to cause us to remember and recall what our personal old nature was.

This is accomplished by what is currently on your thoughts. Remember when Jesus stated, "Now when the unclean spirit goes out of a man, it passes through waterless places seeking rest, and does not find it. Then it says, 'I will return to my house from which I came'" (Matthew 12:43-44).

Jesus explains that even if you have had a genuine deliverance from the hand of God, a time may still come when that "unclean spirit" seeks to return to the "house from which" it came from. The house it seeks to reenter is the darkness created in your soul by your pre-repentant thought-life. In other words, it seeks to REPEAT what you thought was removed by reconnecting to your thoughts.

You may ask how this becomes a reality, and it happens when the unclean spirit comes lurking for wiggle room in your own thoughts. Jesus warns that if the unclean spirit returns and finds your soul unguarded, it brings "seven other spirits more wicked than itself" (Matthew 12:45).

The enemy loves to plants seeds in our thoughts. Often, we see it as if it is our own thoughts, but the truth is it was masquerading as our own thoughts only so it can be reintroduced as the REPEAT of our lives!

## Day 61

# "CHRIST IN YOU"

*"Christ in you is the hope of glory."* (Colossians 1:27)

What if I told you that you were meant to be the representation of something great, would you believe me? The truth of the matter is that through the course and map of the Lord, every child of God in His fold is to be something that stands out! Our text states, "Christ in you is the hope of glory." Consider in your spirit today that with Christ in you, there is something glorious reigning in you.

In fact, when Christ reigns in you, then there is a KING in you. If the king reigns in you, then what reigns in you is provision, protection, and power. Think about it. When something is in the capacity of providing glory then it is magnificent, significant, and honorable. There is a king in every child of God that is waiting to reveal His splendor through YOU!

When Christ reigns in YOU as King, He offers His dominion, His authority, and His influence!

Christ in YOU is the hope of glory. This means in you is the expectation of something wonderful. Hope is divine. Hope is eternal. Hope is supernatural. In the natural capacity, hope is only WISHFUL THINKING. We hear comments like, "I hope things change for me," and "I hope I get that house," but this is not the hope of the Word of God. The reason being is because God's hope involves God's expectations. In other words, there is something God has in mind through his will that involves ME!

Christ in YOU is the hope of glory, meaning God has an intention of using you for His GLORY! That means you are in the VISION of God. That means you are in the purpose of God. Every day as you exist before this world, always keep in mind that there is a glory at work that reigns in you because of the CHRIST in YOU!

## Day 62

# The Perfecter of Faith

*"Looking unto Jesus the author and finisher of our faith."*
(Hebrew 12:2a)

Our scripture states that Christ is not only the author of our faith, but he is the perfecter of it as well. Meaning Christ not only created the script for your faith, but He also desires to see that faith perfected. This faith is not determined by just following some religious doctrine or system; this faith is identified through the application of living it out loud. This faith is way beyond amassing a gob of facts and statistics. It is a working reality seen in how we navigate through personal storms.

Christ desires that we obtain a trust in Him that can withstand and overcome the frequent storms of life. This is the kind of faith that brings the reality of Heaven to earth. Faith, therefore, is more than head knowledge; it is our ability to unlock not only the strength of God but the MIGHT of God, which is the realm of the authority of God where all joint heirs have the privilege to access. The result is that no matter what we face outwardly, inwardly we stand secure. And no matter what the world looks like outwardly, it has the potential to be transformed by our faith, as Hebrews 11 makes it PERFECTLY clear.

For some, their core faith is established on what they see in and around their lives. But the Bible states, "Walk by faith, and not by sight." Think about it. No matter where you are walking, you have need of a guide. In other words, even walking by faith requires that we look at God. When we walk by sight, we desire to see where everything in our lives falls into place. Walking by sight is a lifestyle condition where we allow the physical world (what we see or control) to shape us and direct us as we travel in life. When we walk by faith, the controls and spiritual GPS is in the Lord's hands.

Too often, I think, we desire a Savior who, after assuring us of eternal life, leaves us alone until our next crisis. We want Him to comfort us but never confront us; we desire Him to heal us but not inhabit us. We want the Holy Spirit to help us obtain the "American dream," yet what about obtaining the dream of God which is man living in the image of Christ? When the Lord perfects faith, He accommodates and redeems the conflicts that storm against our souls, turning them into a classroom for the perfection of our faith!

Life is the classroom where we perfect our faith. Yet many fold and buckle when confronted with travesty and tension, not knowing that perhaps God has set up for you and me to encounter face to face with an obstacle that intensifies our walk by faith. Remember it was Jesus who stated, "All things are possible to him who believes" (Matthew 19:26). How does that apply to perfecting faith? Well, for starters every situation we meet has a result established by God. Meaning, even if I face calamity and confusion, the Lord has an outcome, and I just must believe it! That is the perfection of FAITH!

## Day 63

# KEYS TO THE KINGDOM

> *"And I also say to you that you are Peter, and on this rock, I will build My church, and the gates of Hades shall not prevail against it. And I will give you the keys of the kingdom of heaven, and whatever you bind on earth will be bound in heaven, and whatever you loose on earth will be loosed in heaven."* (Matthew 16:18-19)

Having, in my opinion, too many keys on my key chain, I must remind myself that all these keys represent that I have AUTHORITY into a variety of entrances. Today as a child of God, many are walking and living not knowing that Christ has given us ACCESS into certain domains because we have authorization.

Right at this moment, I have keys to my office, keys to my car, and keys to my house. Keys speak of ownership. Each of my keys gives me the ability to lock and unlock something. My keys give me power and control over the things that they are for me. For instance, I may own my car, but without the keys I am powerless to use it. I want you to understand that Jesus has given each of us a set of keys, and one of those keys unlocks the very gates of hell. YOU OWN HELL.

Think about it, gates deal with containment and control. The powers of hell want you and me to stay on lock down from the freedoms that await us in the Lord. Notice that Jesus said, "The gates of hell shall not prevail." In other words, this is a strategy. This is a plan meant to manipulate the church. Not a building, not an organization, but the PEOPLE.

The word "church" in Greek is Ecclesia. This means the called out of the world by the blood of Christ or the salvation of Christ. Hell's plot is to keep God's people from knowing how to unlock the Power of the Kingdom.

Gates are barriers, but once you possess the mechanism to unlock that gate, you now enter territory that at one time you could not. We possess the keys of the Kingdom; in other words, WE HAVE AUTHORITY.

Nothing that the enemy of my soul throws at me will deter me, slow me down, or cause me to give up, because I possess the keys of authority. The power of heaven binds what I bind, and the power of heaven will lose what I loose.

When we cannot unlock what we already have authority over, it is because we are ignorant of the KEYS!

Remember on one occasion where the scripture records, "And they were astonished at his doctrine: for he taught them as one that had authority, and not as the scribes" (Mark 1:22). Jesus possesses ALL AUTHORITY! He said, "All authority has been given unto me on heaven and earth" (Matthew 28:18). He has the Authority to command the wind and waves, the Authority to heal diseases, and the Authority to open blinded eyes. This is the authority that is made available to us!

So how do we access it? When I was a kid, my parents owned their own business, and they sold a variety of things. Often, I would tell my dad when I needed something from the business, and I would ask if I could use the business credit. This was due mainly because I was his son. As heirs and joint heirs of the King, we are related to the Father to occupy territory, because the King already owns it! When I was a child in this role, I assumed this was the natural order of things. In the Kingdom, it is the supernatural order for us to walk into what we already have access into. We must simply believe that God has given us the keys!

## Day 64

# BEWARE OF DOGS

*"Beware of dogs, beware of evil workers, beware of the concision."* (Philippians 3:2)

When I was seven years old, my Mom on occasion would allow the next-door neighbor to be my babysitter until she was back from handling errands. As a child, every time I would go over, I was blown away to witness this elderly woman bake homemade butter biscuits for her massive Rottweiler named Tiger. I could not believe that he would have a table setting with three gigantic biscuits smothered in butter and jelly. But one day I had enough of Tiger getting those delicious biscuits when I was not given one, so I attempted to get me a few without him watching. But before I could reach back with the biscuits I had clenched in my hands, Tiger had other plans and clamped down on my arm with his powerful jaws. I learned a valuable lesson about dogs that day, and that is a dog will always be a dog!

The dogs in the time of Jesus were not quite what we think of today. We are not talking about Lassie or Benji. For instance, dogs were not the nice, domesticated puppies many of us have at home. In fact, no one kept dogs as pets then. The dogs of Jesus' day were wild, feeding on garbage and roadkill. The Bible states in Isaiah 56:11 that certain men are like "greedy dogs which can never have enough." In other words, dogs have an insatiable appetite. They never get full! They always want more. They have a lustful pursuit where the on button is always pressed. I am not referring to just the kind of lust that may be identified in the sexual manner. This lust is a craving that cannot be satisfied. The Bible even shares in Proverbs 26:11 that a "dog will return to his own vomit as a fool returns to folly." Basically, clarifying that dogs have actions where the outcome leads to the devouring of anything.

We claim that dogs are man's best friend, but the dogs that the Bible is referring to is not Rover or Spot. These dogs attempt to consume our souls to create and cause destruction. These dogs have no respect for sacred things or that which is holy No wonder Jesus shares, "Give not that which is holy unto the dogs, neither cast ye your pearls before swine, lest they trample them under their feet, and turn again and rend you" (Matthew 7:6).

Ask yourself if you have given something holy to the dogs. In other words, have you given something holy that has been discredited, disrespected, and dishonored? What we fail to recognize about the dogs the Bible is referring to is that they tend to mess things up. These dogs reject your word, your character, and your position. Like Tiger the Rottweiler, they care nothing about the you that God sees! Their only concern is themselves. We miss the fact that there are dogs among us every day trying to mutilate everything we present or proclaim. It is time to stop feeding the dogs around your life that want to follow you home. God wants us to beware of the dogs!

## Day 65

# For His Pleasure

*"Thou art worthy, O Lord, to receive glory and honor and power: for thou hast created all things, and **for thy pleasure** they are and were created."* (Revelation 4:11)

Let us settle the issue—we were created not only by God, but for Him as well. The key to lasting happiness and real pleasure in this world is not found in seeking gratification, but in pleasing God. And while the Lord desires that we enjoy His gifts and the people to whom we are joined, He wants us to know that we were created first for His pleasure.

As a child and young man before His ministry began, Jesus was just a carpenter's son. Yet, before His public ministry began before there were any miracles or multitudes, there was a quality in Christ that, even as a carpenter, swelled the heart of God with pleasure. From His youth, the compelling vision of Christ's life extended far beyond merely becoming another good man. Even His sinless life to the Law, as magnificent as this was, existed far beyond Christ's highest goal. The all-consuming desire of Jesus Christ was to give pleasure to His Father.

Think about this, could Jesus have heard a more wondrous sound than that which He heard at His baptism in the Jordan? At the sound of the Father's voice, the heavens opened and the river of God's pleasure flowed down to His Son: "Thou art My Beloved Son, in Thee I am well-pleased" (Mark 1:11; see also Luke 2:52).

Remember, Jesus was still a "lay person" when the Father spoke to Him. In other words, He had not yet entered His public ministry. Friends, my breath is taken away as I consider this reality—it was Jesus' life as a tradesman, a blue-collar worker, which increased the Father's bliss.

Jesus did not need miracles or great sermons to touch the Father's heart. While accomplishing common, everyday tasks, Jesus touched the heart of God.

Likewise, to give pleasure to God is the purpose of our existence as well. Jesus' ability to please the Father while working a secular job tells us God is looking for something deeper than theological degrees and correct doctrine. He is looking for our sustained and focused love. And in this, we also can please Him. Whether we are housewives, secretaries, or auto mechanics, in God's eyes, true ministry is not in what we do but in what we become to Him!

## Day 66

# BREAK THE CYCLE

*"Ye have compassed this mountain long enough: turn you northward."* (Deuteronomy 2:3)

Why did it take the Israelites 40 years to make an eleven-day journey? You know the story how that Hebrew people walked in the wilderness for 40 years, and when you survey the territory where they traveled, you begin to realize they were only an arm throw away from the Promised Land.

So, for forty years they struggled with no possession because of their position. Today as people of God we too struggle with what we possess because of where we are positioned. Like the Israelites, we have walked too long in places where God expected something new; do not get me wrong, for many we need the training time in the wilderness, so thank the Lord for the training territory! But it is one thing to go through our own wilderness experience for training, and another just to go around and around, and around.

The definition of a cycle is to repeat the same thing. It is to witness the same action over and over. I don't think I'm wrong in stating that some of us have been watching spiritual reruns in our lives where we keep witnessing the same outcomes, the same results, and the same stuff that we thought we walked past yesterday! Look here; today is a declaration day to BREAK the CYCLE. Some of us are having current cycles of fear, others struggle with continuing circles of a broken heart, and then there are those who deal with constant circles of the flesh. I mean it keeps showing up and showing up where we keep dealing with it over and over.

You must understand the true nature of a cycle. A true cycle is where you're first maintaining a place that seems stable enough. I mean, it appears to be established, it appears to be rooted, but it is not!

The reason God told the Israelites to "turn you northward" was to break from the cycle of circling this land. And just before entering the Promised Land, He wanted to make sure that this rotating would be shattered forever by sending them to a town called Gilgal, which means the turning of a wheel, or rolling, or should I say... A CYCLE.

It was here that God would take away the reproach of Egypt from them. This place represented all their wilderness wanderings, their endless circles, their ceaseless activity, and their unprofitable ceremonies that were void of God's power. Breaking any cycle requires first the ability to trust God. Second, it requires surrendering to the will of God, for you see our own personal cycles are really designed by ourselves. We are responsible for cycles! Third, I must follow the lead or direction of God that enables me to stop what has been cycling in my life.

## Day 67

# BABY FOOD

Recently I observed a mother feeding her child baby food. Most of us have some recollection of Gerber, right? Well, she was doing her best to feed her child and at the same time consume what looked like a Granola bar. Unfortunately, she had a problem, and that was the baby wanted what Mom was munching on and not the taste of her baby food. In the spiritual life, we encounter the same situation where those who are still in need of baby food are more stimulated with what is accessible for the more mature, not realizing that we change our spiritual appetite when we change our stage of personal growth spiritually. Case in point, in I Corinthians Chapter 3, the writer Paul shares to his audience (the people of the city called Corinth) that they were babies and they could not handle more mature main dishes, "However, brothers and sisters, I could not talk to you as to spiritual people, but [only] as to worldly people [dominated by human nature], mere infants [in the new life] in Christ!" (I Corinthians 3:1 NAB).

The Apostle Paul could recognize where they were in their spiritual growth cycle by what was dominating in their lives. Either it was the Holy Spirit (divine nature) or the human nature (or worldly nature). Paul basically said, "We couldn't have a conversation like I wanted to because of your current state spiritually!" Often, I see people attempting on so many levels to extend themselves in serving a spiritual meal that is only meant for the mature to those who are still needing BABY FOOD.

The question is, how do you know when someone still needs baby food? Well, the people of Corinth gave us a legitimate example. First, this is what Paul discovered, "I fed you with milk, not solid food; for you were not yet able to receive it. Even now you are still not ready" (I Corinthians 3:2 NAB). Paul knew that they could not consume what he called "solid food." In other words, spiritually they were not operating where the solid food would impact in a healthy way for them. He makes it plain that he has tried and tried to feed them spiritual meat, and the results were still the same… they needed BABY FOOD.

Next, he states how he knew they were infants only needing baby food. "You are still worldly [controlled by ordinary impulses, the sinful capacity]. For as long as there is jealousy and strife and discord among you, are you not unspiritual, and are you not walking like ordinary men [unchanged by faith]?" (I Corinthians 3:3). Who would have ever thought that jealousy, strife, and discord were signs of still being a BABY spiritually? These traits prevent and block any real growth. Why is that? Because they operate in the flesh. When we are feeding or living off the flesh, our appetites are adjusted to responding and interacting by the flesh. In fact, the flesh has an insatiable appetite, meaning it is always hungry for the flesh!

Case in point: I love ice cream. It is so good to me all the time, but for my body to have what it needs to operate, it is not so good all the time. The flesh wants us to consume what it wants all the time. Notice also when we are consumed by the flesh, the Apostle Paul stated, "We are still worldly," Meaning we are controlled by our fleshly impulses. If there is a consistent appetite for the flesh, we will struggle and become stagnate in the Spirit. Recently while mentoring a young man struggling in school, I observed the traits—jealously, strife, and discord. I realized that whenever there is jealousy, strife, and discord operating in a person, it is due primarily because of what the flesh is starving for. All three are really a byproduct of the SELFISH nature.

To crucify the flesh from within us, we must digest from the Spirit (The Word of God) and allow our souls to surrender to the will of God. The flesh, unfortunately, is only concerned with achieving its own will's agenda. That is why we must do as the Bible states, "Die daily" (I Corinthians 15:31). This DAILY death sentence is a spiritual movement of refusing to feed the appetites of the flesh by feeding our spirits with the word. Therefore, the Bible shares in I Peter 2:2, "As newborn babes desire the sincere milk of the word that you may grow thereby," because as we consume spiritual baby food, we also adjust our spiritual operation to only desire what benefits our true godly nature and not snack to propitiate the passions for the flesh.

# Day 68

# "THE SPIRITUAL CUISINE"

*"Jesus said to them, 'I am the bread of life. He who comes to Me shall never hunger, and he who believes in Me shall never thirst.'"* (John 6:35)

The Bible uses the word *bread* to mean "that which is taken into the body and provides nourishment." Unfortunately, many do not consider the spiritual life is always active, and there is a need to keep it fueled and to keep the spiritual palate maintained.

Since this is a reality whether we knew it or not, many are feeding into their lives spiritual junk-food This is the kind of substance that has an adverse effect on our spiritual operation. From this biblical example, there are two types of bread mentioned in the Bible, which are Leavened Bread and Unleavened Bread.

Leavened Bread symbolizes the corruption of sin. The Bible states in I Corinthians 5:8, "Therefore let us keep the feast, not with old leaven, neither with the leaven of malice and wickedness;

but with the unleavened bread of sincerity and truth." Leavened Bread is spiritual JUNK FOOD! Everyday something is looking to get tasted in the spirit whether it comes from God or not. No wonder the Bible shares, "Taste the Lord and see that He is good" (Psalms 34:8). For many, their spiritual taste buds have become adjusted to acquiring the substance that is fueled with MALICE and WICKEDNESS. Sounds bazaar? Reflect for a moment on just what malice has in it. The ingredients consist of resentment, bitterness, animosity, and spitefulness to name a few. Let us not leave off what is added into wickedness, from depravity, viciousness, degradation, decline, debasement, to disgrace.

The consumption of spiritual junk food is such a function in our society that many have adapted to its application in their lives as if it is good eating. The problem is we can never change authentically what we eat spiritually as a lifestyle until we embrace the truth (that's Unleavened Bread). For instance, Jesus said in the Lord's Prayer for kingdom living, "Give us this day our daily bread" (Matthew 6:11). Your daily bread is having nourishment for your life DAILY! Yet we have more people who are just satisfied with EATING once a week, or every now and then. Little do we realize that when there is a minimization of DAILY BREAD, our spiritual palates have been satisfied with an alternative substitute. I always thought it was interesting that certain physical foods are recognized as bad for my health and well-being, yet we never consider that spiritually something wants me to CONSUME to the degree that it has side effects on how I function. In other words, it impacts how I exist. Remember Jesus said, "I am the bread of life. He who comes to me shall never hunger, and he who believes in me shall never thirst." There is a spiritual cuisine that comes from Jesus that if I truly consume what it offers, it creates an appetite for nothing else. Now that's good eating!

*Day 69*

# "FAKE FRUIT" (PART 1)

*"Another parable He put forth to them, saying: 'The kingdom of heaven is like a man who sowed good seed in his field; but while men slept, his enemy came and sowed tares among the wheat and went his way. But when the grain had sprouted and produced a crop, then the tares also appeared. So the servants of the owner came and said to him, 'Sir, did you not sow good seed in your field? How then does it have tares?' He said to them, 'An enemy has done this.' The servants said to him, 'Do you want us then to go and gather them up?' But he said, 'No, lest while you gather up the tares you also uproot the wheat with them. Let both grow together until the harvest and at the time of harvest I will say to the reapers, 'First gather together the tares and bind them in bundles to burn them but gather the wheat into my barn.''"*
(Matthew 13:24-30)

H ere is a word we do not hear that much of everyday… "TARES." This in a nutshell means that even though what may look like wheat, and appears to be wheat, upon further investigation when you look a little deeper you realize it is… NOT. It is counterfeit. Jesus makes the point in this text that it is hard to tell the difference between what the REAL wheat is and what is not.

This passage and many others point out something that Jesus wanted us to capture. For instance, let's capture the parable about the ten virgins in Matthew 25:1-13. Here we find that there was a difference between the five virgins that had lamps with oil and the five that had lamps without oil. From the surface, you would hardly know. Think about the parable of the dragnet (Matthew 13:47-50) that brings in all sorts of fish, only to discover once the net is brought to shore that there is a distinct difference between the healthy fish and those that were not.

What are tares? They are just weeds. They look like wheat, but it is difficult to tell the difference with the naked eye. However, when the time comes for the wheat to bear its fruit and be harvested, the harvester will always recognize that the evidence of whether it's wheat or tares by what comes out in the harvest. In our journey of development, there is a season where we prove what is growing. The season of harvest is the season of bearing FRUIT! And the truth about tares is, "Tares produce NO FRUIT!" (Matthew 13:26-29).

Jesus said it this way, "By your FRUIT you are known." In other words, fruit is the evidence. Seeing fruit in one's life is to know that fruit is the result of what has been growing within. Some claim and confess that they are legit with having LORDSHIP with Jesus, but the confirmation of that is to witness the FRUIT. The Bible shares "that the fruit of the Spirit is **love**, **joy**, **peace**, forbearance, kindness, goodness, faithfulness, gentleness and self-control" (Galatians 5:22). This is the fruit that should be growing from our lives!

## Day 70

# "FAKE FRUIT"
# (PART II)

*"Another parable He put forth to them, saying: 'The kingdom of heaven is like a man who sowed good seed in his field; but while men slept, his enemy came and sowed tares among the wheat and went his way. But when the grain had sprouted and produced a crop, then the tares also appeared. So the servants of the owner came and said to him, 'Sir, did you not sow good seed in your field? How then does it have tares?' He said to them, 'An enemy has done this.' The servants said to him, 'Do you want us then to go and gather them up?' But he said, 'No, lest while you gather up the tares you also uproot the wheat with them. Let both grow together until the harvest and at the time of harvest I will say to the reapers, 'First gather together the tares and bind them in bundles to burn them but gather the wheat into my barn.'"*
(Matthew 13:24-30)

I remember as a child when I would visit my grandmother it always fascinated me that she would have a bowl of FAKE FRUIT on the living room table. I mean there were bananas, grapes, apples etc., and they all looked legit, but they were FAKE. Because I was not a shy kid to ask things, I asked my grandmother what was the point of having FAKE FRUIT in a bowl? She said because "IT LOOKED GOOD."

Today, be a fruit inspector of your life! Gage the condition of the fruit that is blossoming from your life. Make sure that after observation it is not FAKE FRUIT. The interesting revelation about this text is that the enemy and the devil are one in the same, and verse 25 states, "An enemy has done this and sown the tares among the wheat." The devil loves to counterfeit the truth. He (the devil) is a liar from the beginning, and he loves to deceive. Ultimately, he wants to damage the work of God. He wants to infiltrate counterfeit into that which is authentic. What greater deception could there be than for the devil to make people believe that they are saved, and they are in the kingdom of God, when in fact they are not?

Is this not what Jesus meant when He stated, "Not everyone who says to Me, 'Lord, Lord,' shall enter the kingdom of heaven, but he who does the will of My Father in heaven. Many will say to Me in that day, 'Lord, Lord, have we not prophesied in Your name, cast out demons in Your name, and done many wonders in Your name?' And then I will declare to them, 'I never knew you; depart from Me, you who practice lawlessness!'" (Matthew 7:21-23). If you look at Chapter 13 of Matthew again, it indicates that there are some tell-tale signs of the difference between wheat and tares. Look at verse 27: "The servants of the owner came and said to him, 'Sir, did you not sow good seed in your field? How then does it have tares?'" They thought the seed that he sowed was contaminated in some way with tare seeds. So, it appeared that the servants of the owner of the field recognized some differences as these two plants grew up. The truth is GOOD SEED will always bear GOOD FRUIT!

*Day 71*

# "FLAWED"

For too long many have portrayed the life and the walk of Christ as something that is essentially flawless. But the truth of the matter is that throughout the journey of God's people, we have all been FLAWED!

Think about it. Elijah was suicidal, Joseph was abused, Job went bankrupt, Moses had a speech problem, Gideon was full of fear, Samson was a womanizer, Rahab was a prostitute, and the Samaritan woman at the well was divorced. If you had not figured it out yet, God uses people that are flawed. Christianity is not reserved for the "WORTHY," nor does God limit himself to the spiritually pious. The simple truth is we are all battered, bruised beggars at the doorstep of God's mercy. Romans 3:23 shares, *"For all have sinned and fall short of the glory of God." The ministry of Jesus was focused on this reality… sin flaws mankind!*

We live in a world that has fallen to sin, and as a result, everyone is guilty of something. No one is perfect. Yet one of the great wonders of the Gospel is that God uses imperfect people to spread His glory. Since mankind first took their step outside

Eden, God has been calling the broken, the faithless, and the poor in spirit to do great things in His name. If you were to take a simple sample of God's Word, you won't get far without witnessing that the will of God is to redeem the brokenhearted, lift the downtrodden, bring sight to those blinded by this world, and to bring deliverance to those that are caught in some type of captivity. Jesus came as the ultimate example of perfection to restore that which is imperfect. As His people, our transformation into His image is mainly a confirmation of the one who died for sin that is reigning and existing in our lives.

When we pursue Christlikeness, it is not to boast, brag, or be bigshots. But on the contrary, it is to reveal the true nature of the personal remodeling and restructuring that Christ has done in one's life. True conversion is a work on the inner man. When we fake and falsify who we really are beneath the exterior, we attempt to hide our brokenness and our true selves, not realizing that God not only knows the truth of our hearts, but the fruit of hearts as well. Let us stop the nonsense of trying to create a fallacy of who we are and understand "**there is none righteous**, no, not one" (Romans 3:10). In other words, no one can escape that without the sacrifice of Jesus, we would not have righteousness. True righteousness is not obtained through our works or our portrayal to those around us, but it is verified through the CROSS!

So, every day because we wrestle (fight and live) against the flesh, the flesh must face an ending by being crucified to the cross. Jesus said, "Then he said to them all: 'Whoever wants to be my disciple must deny themselves and take *up* their *cross* daily and follow me'" (Luke 9:23). NO ONE IS FLAWLESS! But when we admit (confess) that we are flawed and that we need His Forgiveness and Restoration, we activate the divine order of God where we tap into GRACE and MERCY!

## Day 72

# POISON

*"Looking carefully lest anyone fall short of the grace of God; lest any root of bitterness springing up cause trouble, and by this many become defiled."* (Hebrews 12:15)

Webster defines poison as a substance that can cause an illness or a death. Most things that contain poison in it have a label or a warning on the material containing the poison. Most people, who immediately observe the warning sign, take great consideration and safety when poison is involved in handling certain chemicals or products. The interesting parallel with the spiritual life is that every day, whether we knew it or not, we are faced with personally allowing a poison that impacts our souls. There are many poisons that invade the soul such as discouragement, envy, greed, selfishness, pride, fear, perversion, and bitterness. What we have failed to register in our minds is that these poisons are a legitimate contamination to what the Lord envisioned to flow within our hearts! Such as, "Peace that surpasses all understanding" (Philippians 4:7) and joy that fills our souls to capacity!

The Bible highlights the importance of the removal of toxins of the soul when we read, "Get rid of all bitterness, rage, and anger, brawling and slander, along with every form of malice" (Ephesians 4:31). To remove something that is ruining our lives, we must become acquainted with the truth. The Bible also states, "When you know the truth, the truth will make you free" (John 8:32). When we understand that the "knowing" of a thing reveals the establishment of a relationship with that thing, what we therefore have is a connection with something or someone because of what we "know." So, if that is the case, if what we "know" is POISONIOUS, then it becomes the thing we tend to reveal and expose because it is the thing we are connected too.

Bitterness may be one of the most dangerous and divisive poisons we face. It will eat away the vitality of your spiritual life until your personal testimony seems like trash. Bitterness is the cancer of the soul, wanting to transfer to different levels not only to the carrier but to impact others as well. The problem with bitterness is that you cannot hide it, nor contain it. No wonder the Bible states, "Lest any root of bitterness springing up trouble you, and thereby many are defiled" (Hebrews 12:15). It spreads like a plague until it affects everyone around you.

Some are so saturated with bitterness that they fail to recognize that it is oozing out of their souls with every relationship that they become twisted, turned, and torn. Many martial couples exhibit bitterness as if it is a natural environment. Some are so filled with bitterness that nothing good is seen in how they see others. I remember my grandmother telling me as a child, "Your heart will always tell on you!" Meaning, whatever spiritual germ that has invaded your heart will seek to control your heart! Today, I encourage you to know the truth about the condition of your heart. Examine throughout the confines of your life what needs to be removed because it could be POISON.

## Day 73

# AN EXPOSE OF THE THREE TEMPERATURES OF PEOPLE (COLD, HOT, AND LUKEWARM)

### The Expose of COLD LOVE (Part I)

*"Because lawlessness is increased, most people's love will grow cold."* (Matthew 24:12)

What if I told you to check the spiritual temperature you possess; would you know it? It is quite shocking that the Lord has three specific categories or conditions where all of us must equate where we stand. Jesus made several remarks about these temperatures of people throughout the scriptures. In fact, He shares this in Matthew 24:12, "Because lawlessness is increased, most people's LOVE will grow cold." Jesus spoke these words and others in the text that is widely known for speaking about the future, or the prophecy of that which is to come. He uncovers what the Cold characteristics look like when He said in verse 10, "And then shall many be offended, and shall betray one another, and shall hate one another." Here we see what is known as a Seed of Offense that has been planted and has also activated betrayal and hate.

Interesting enough, the word "offense" means a TRAP. It typically involves someone who feels that someone has stated something about them or has done something where they feel they have been offended. In marriage, when a spouse refuses to speak to his or her partner because of something they said or did for long periods of time, this is the spirit of offense. Whenever the famous words "DON'T TALK TO ME" are being used, then someone is wrestling with the spirit of offense. The reason it resembles a trap is because it engulfs your ability to move forward, to forgive, to flow! This is one characteristic of the COLD CONDITION.

Verse 11 states, "And many false prophets shall rise and shall deceive many." In this future state, there will be an increase of false prophets or imitation leaders. In other words, there will be an abundance of spokesman representing God, but they will not be authentic. The key element that always proves if there is falsity is the gradual movement away from TRUTH. The challenge though is the rest of the text states that these false leaders will "deceive many." Deception can only be achieved if it is meshed in with some truth. Think about it. Even Adam and Eve knew the truth communicated from God, but when the serpent asked them what God had said, he got them to consider an option to what they already knew. This is the meat of deception. It operates where we have some truth, but that truth is challenged by our own desires. In fact, deception and temptation go hand in hand. You cannot be tempted by anything that you do not already have a desire for.

## Day 74

# An Expose of the Three Temperatures of People (Cold, Hot, and Lukewarm)

### The Expose of COLD LOVE (Part II)

*"Because lawlessness is increased, most people's love will grow cold."* (Matthew 24:12)

Now that we have some insight on the COLD characteristics, let us now look overall at what comes out of this condition of "COLD LOVE." Meaning, when it comes to recognizing any kind of love in this condition, it lacks unity, availability, vulnerability, hospitality, forbearance, and forgiveness.

This cold love is a demonic stronghold. In our generation, cold love is becoming increasingly more common. It shuts down the power of prayer and disables the flow of healing and outreach. In fact, where there is persistent and hardened area of un-forgiveness in a person, then the demonic world (known in Matthew 18:34 as "torturers") has unhindered access.

The Scriptures warn that even a little root of bitterness springing up in a person's life can defile many (see Hebrews 12:15). Bitterness is unfulfilled revenge. Another's thoughtlessness or cruelty may have wounded us deeply. It is inevitable that, in a world of increasing harshness and cruelty, we will at some point be hurt. But if we fail to react with love and forgiveness, if we retain in our spirit the debt the offender owes, we then become participants of the spirit of offense that will rob our hearts of our capacity to love. Gradually, we will become a member of most of the end-time Christians whose love is growing cold.

To leave the COLD condition, we must be willing to repent and forgive the one who hurt us. Whether we knew it or not, painful experiences are allowed by God to teach us how to love our enemies. Remember, it was Jesus who stated, "Love your enemies."

If we still have unforgiveness toward someone, we have failed this test. Fortunately, it was just a test, not a final exam. We need to thank God for the opportunity to grow in divine love. Thank Him that your whole life is not being swallowed up in bitterness and resentment. Millions of souls are swept off into eternal judgment every day without the hope of escaping from embitterment. But you and I have been given God's answer for your pain, which is His love!

# An Expose of the Three Temperatures of People (Cold, Hot, and Lukewarm)

## The Expose of LUKEWARM LOVE

*"So then because you are lukewarm, and neither cold nor hot, I will spit you out of my mouth."* (Revelation 3:16)

As we continue to share on the three temperatures of people, we now approach a temperature where there is a completely different observation. This temperature according to the Lord is so non-appealing that the scriptures declare that He will "spit it out His mouth." Reflect for a moment when you spit something out of your mouth. Typically, it is something that is horrible, distasteful, and for many of us, we want something else in our mouths to take away the taste.

So, what was it that brought these believers to a place of LUKEW a.m. Well, before Jesus said they were lukewarm, He said is in verse 15, "I know your WORKS." This is referring to their loyalty, dedication, and pursuit to please the Lord. We know this because the Lord emphasizes that He knew their works, and throughout the Word of God, works deals with our actions or activity specifically as it pleases the Lord not ourselves. What we must also take into consideration is that James said, "Show me your faith without your works, and I will show you my faith by my works" (James 2:18). Our faith is always connected to our activity in the Lord. To go further, our choices, decisions, and what we place as valuable is recognizable in our faith. The reason being is because faith is backed up by what you do with it.

Have you ever taken a sip of lukewarm water? Usually, lukewarm is not a good temperature. We like our drinks either hot or cold, and lukewarm is sickening. We want hot showers and cold refreshing drinks. You never hear anyone say, "I am burning up; I would love a nice glass of lukewarm water." You never hear anyone say, "I am tired and aching, I would love to take a lukewarm bath." The picture of lukewarm is a picture of something that has no use at all.

So, this lukewarmness makes Jesus sick to His stomach, mainly because there is no spiritual benefit for the Kingdom, so He will spit them out. The Greek word for lukewarm means "to vomit," which is even worse than to spit. If a person who claims to love the Lord can determine no spiritual benefit, the Bible states in II Corinthians 13:5, "Examine yourselves as to whether you are in the faith." In other words, God desires that you have spiritual check-ups to gage your faith outcome. These believers from this Bible passage were from a town called Laodicea, where for the most part they were more focused on material things, wealth, pleasure, or just self. We know this is the case because in verse 17, Jesus shares that they say, "I am rich, and have become wealthy and have need of nothing, and do not know you are wretched, miserable, poor, blind, and naked." Even though they had stuff, Jesus gave an overall operation where their lives appeared empty and ineffective. Jesus advises us to BUY FROM HIM (verse 18).

In other words, make an investment where we intentionally go out of our way to obtain the things that please the will of God. This was a warning to these believers who were losing their created intent in the Lord. When we focus on being lukewarm, we are just going through the motions; like warm water, it is in the middle. It is neither cold or hot. We have lost our passion, pursuit, and the pleasing of the Lord and replaced it with facsimile that looks the part, but the faith with works always gives it away!

## Day 76

# An Expose of the Three Temperatures of People (Cold, Hot, and Lukewarm)

### The Expose of HOT LOVE

*"I would thou wert... hot."* (Revelation 3:15b)

Many times over, the Lord reveals His desire for us to be hot or on fire for Him. This temperature describes our zeal, our pursuit, and our love to please the Lord. Hot water is known as temperature that helps with impurities, soothing, and wellness to overall life.

Water in scripture is used with incredible imagery. There are over 600 references to water. It is used in three main ways: as a cosmic force only God can control, as a source of life, and as a cleansing agent. Water is highly significant in the life of the ancient world because of the scarcity of its supply. In our text, the people of Laodicea were known as lukewarm, in which the Lord said, "He would spew (or spit) out his mouth." As I already stated, lukewarm represents non-committed, going through the motions, and lacking an authentic relationship that is moved by the voice of God. So, what does it mean to be hot spiritually? It is to "Love the Lord your God with all your heart and with all your soul and with all your mind and with all your strength" (Mark 12:30). When I love the Lord to the capacity He designed and designated for me then I am functioning where I am on fire for the Lord.

When James says, "But be ye doers of the word, and not hearers only, deceiving your own selves" (James 1:22), the emphasis is to make the Word of God active in one's life. When we are "doers," we are moving for the Lord, maturing in Christlikeness, and maximizing the power of the Kingdom. Doing the Word of God has an outcome. The Bible states, "My words shall return void (or empty)." The temperature of being hot for the Lord is dependent on not only how close you are to the Lord, but what you are willing to change, confess, and claim for His name.

The equivalent of being HOT in the Lord is to be on FIRE for the Lord. II Timothy 1:6 says, "Stir up the Gift of God." Other versions state, "Fan into flame the gift of God" (English Standard version) and "Kindle afresh the gift of God" (The Message Bible). Finally, the life application says for verse 6, "Stir into flame," giving us the impression that this fanning or stirring is something we must participate in doing so that we can keep the FLAME of God at a level where it does not impact the gifts that we were given by God.

Today, ask the question about the condition of your fire. Do we at times find ourselves being concerned over our own spiritual temperature, as well as the temperature of our circle of influence? As Ambassadors of Christ, we must continually STOKE THE FURNANCE! We must make sure that we are intentionally keeping the temperature at a level where God's intensity can burn what needs to be eradicated from our lives and where His fire can purify us, cleanse us, and modify our lives. His Heat causes an increase in what is evidently full in our lives… the Holy Spirit. The Bible says, "Be filled in the Holy Spirit." When we are overflowing in the Spirit, our temperature is reflective of the outpouring of the nature of God. The Bible says, "Our God is a consuming fire" (Hebrews 12:29). Today, where is your temperature?

## Day 77

# Laying Aside Unresolved Conflict

*"See to it that no one comes short of the grace of God; that no root of bitterness springing up causes trouble, and by it many are defiled."* (Hebrews 12:15)

Unresolved conflict means that someone in any relationship is unwilling to accept a barrier that is preventing the movement of resolution or reconciliation. The Bible states, "And God has given us this task of reconciling people to him. For God was in Christ, reconciling the world to himself, no longer counting people's sins against them. And he gave us this wonderful message of reconciliation" (II Corinthians 5:18-19).

Reconciliation is the ministry of every believer. No matter in marriage, family, our neighbors, or at our church, God wants us to reconcile. To reconcile means the assurance of forgiveness, the availability to now bear FRUIT, and lastly, the acknowledgement by reconciling that you are an Ambassador of

Christ. An ambassador is one that has a position that has been given authority that reflects the one who is in authority, which is Christ the KING. It is the expectation of God that conflict be resolved.

For a couple going through periods of unresolved conflict means there is a breakdown to deal with differences and a refusal at times to accept what another may add or share with the other party. Often when unresolved conflict continues for a long haul, it manifests into disrespect and a defensive spirit that blocks the opportunity to reach what the Bible shares, which is, "Come let us reason together" (Isaiah 1:18).

For many who walk into unresolved conflict, as a typical norm we witness that it is emotionally fueled and is recognized with a behavior where one party is unwilling to consider the other's comments. For healthy dialogue to be introduced, there must be the ability to be approachable. For some when going through conflict, anything that is said directly to them personally causes an immediate wall of separation. This is a sign of spiritual/emotional immaturity.

When it is hard to hear then it is difficult to accept what someone has to say. Those who can hear what others communicate, also recognize when a person is speaking from a position of hurt, pain, and frustration. We must be able to look not only through our lenses but through theirs! For the most part, when someone shares something that is linked to some unresolved conflict from a broken or a beaten up past we may notice a defensive justification or a placing of blame towards the other person without taking any ownership at all to any of what is at work that is causing the conflict. When we retaliate, we are doing the exact opposite of what the spirit encourages us to do.

"Not returning evil for evil or insult for insult but giving a blessing instead; for you were called for the very purpose that you might inherit a blessing" (I Peter 3:9). For many who live with unresolved conflict, they tend to not deal with it, overlook it, minimize it, or just move on. This unfortunately becomes a heavy weight over time where the load is not reduced or vanquished but is keep in the crevices of the heart.

The keys to have resolution are (1.) "Let us therefore make every effort to do what leads to peace and to mutual edification" (Romans 14:19). In other words, our goal is to have an outcome that eventual builds up and not tear down. If we witness destruction in dialogue, then we must assess that someone is not considering how to build. (2.) "Do not be overcome by evil but overcome evil with good" (Romans 12:21). Often when evil arises like anger, rage, bitterness, being callous, or even condescending another, this bears fruit that ends up being evil. (3.) "The way of a fool seems right to him, but a wise man listens to advice" (Proverbs 12:15). When we refuse to hear or be open or transparent about our situation, we are proving that we have taken on the role of foolish behavior, which is really refusing to consider what is shared. If you are going through unresolved situations, I pray today that God will break the yokes of conflict and establish the promotion of reconciliation.

## Day 78

# DRIVING Through DISAPPOINTMENT

I heard a story some time ago about the device that the adversary uses more as an aggressive effective tool than any other. It is called DISAPPOINTMENT. The story starts with one of his demonic lieutenants stating, "Sir what weapon do we have to use against their power of the Christ?" "We have tried pleasure, power, possessions, and even philosophy. Yet, they seem to STAND!" The General (Satan) of the demonic force states, "There is however one specific weapon that has worked time and time again and that is to have them confront DISAPPOINTMENT."

Disappointment is not just some dejected emotion but a chasm of disappointment that can disconnect our hearts from faith. I have personally witnessed many who were along the path of God, heading towards His intended direction, only to meet some form of disappointment that became so paralyzing that they succumbed to it, whether it is a disappointment in a relationship, or the disappointment over a decision, or perhaps the disappointment that slowly disintegrates the foundation of faith where eventually the spirit of unbelief creeps in. The Bible states, "Hope deferred makes the heart sick." When one is disappointed, they are cut off from their appointment with destiny. Their appointed breakthrough remains in the heart of God, but the individual is so isolated by unbelief that for some there is no breaking through. It is here, even during disappointment, that the righteous must learn to live by faith!

When facing great disappointments, some decide to decrease their faith and increase their doubts and fears, which is the main objective of disappointment. On one occasion when Jesus was sharing with His disciples something that would test the fabric of their faith, they stated to Him, "Increase our faith" (Luke 17:5). They had enough spiritual sense to realize the only way to drive through what they were facing would require intensified faith. Often though, when we are challenged with a powerful play of disappointment, we immediately lose courage, commitment, and even care to move forward. But the Bible states, "The just shall live by faith" (Habakkuk 2:4). In other words, faith is essential for breakthroughs even during devastation.

When the just live by faith, it is their source for thriving (Faith)! No wonder the Bible shares, "Faith is the victory that overcomes the world" (I John 5:4). To overcome anything, one will have to face it and eventually overcome it. But the will of God is that whatever we encounter from this world, face it with FAITH! In fact, the intention and outcome prophesied by the Spirit is that we will witness VICTORY. Here is what I want you to ask yourself today—are you carrying any level of disappointment in your heart? Because if you are, it is a weapon against you and not for you. As a soldier of Christ, our objective is to gain territory. That includes the territory of your heart.

Do not settle for portions and pockets of your heart being taken captive by having years of unresolved disappointment. I encourage you to BUILD UP your FAITH and keep driving right through your disappointments.

## Day 79

# "PHASES OF THE HEART" (PART I)

*"The troubles of my heart are enlarged: O bring thou me out of my distresses."* (Psalms 25:17)

Today across the globe, one of the things that has become synonymous with most is that we have encountered a broken heart. Our scripture of emphasis may even be the state of some as they read God's insight on the matters of the HEART.

The question most desire to be answered is how do we walk through the pain and debris of a heart that has been shattered?

Here is the proof that God restores hearts: "Wait on the LORD: be of good courage, and he shall strengthen thine heart: wait, I say, on the LORD" (Psalms 27:14). Waiting on the Lord is a place that relies on the follow through of the Lord. It is a pause with expectation.

For whatever reason, we have become a people that no matter what we face in the heart, our inability to wait has been reduced to almost becoming non-existent. I remember my grandparents talking about the Great Depression. It was a time where the people of our nation did not trust in man, the government, or the system; they trusted in the arrival of an on-time God.

Waiting has everything to do with what I entitle: "STAY TUNED!" It is an anticipation of the provisions of God. Wait a second (no pun intended), think about all the times we have acted irrational in the heart because of what the heart was going through. We refused to wait or hesitate. We acted on impulse. In fact, many missed that behind the scenes while our hearts are going through pieces of our hearts being fragmented off, we are vulnerable to latch on to anything that will take away the PAIN.

But notice that the text stated, "Wait on the LORD: be of good courage, and he shall strengthen thine heart: wait, I say, on the LORD." The Lord knows we must WAIT for what He has already been decided on that He will deliver, and that is STRENGTH to the heart!

Many though, because of the instability of our hearts, are susceptible to opening themselves up to outside influences that do not REPAIR the heart but give a false impression of repair. Today, if you are going through any kind of breaking of the heart, I challenge you to trust the voice of God and rely on an unchanging hand of deliverance!

## Day 80

# "PHASES OF THE HEART" (PART II)

Did you know that soil in the Bible is a representative of our hearts? The Bible states in Psalms 119:11, "I have hidden your word in my heart that I might not sin against you." When the word is hidden in our hearts, it is planted in our hearts.

The challenge though is God is called the "Vine-dresser" in John 15:1, which means "Gardener." If he is the gardener, then He is concerned about our soil (or our hearts) because that is where he puts His SEED. That soil is your heart. God is always trying to prick our hearts, turn our hearts, and move our hearts so he can penetrate our hearts with His SEED.

The Bible states, "The seed is the word" (Luke 8:11).

The Bible states that "God is not the author of confusion" (I Corinthians 14:33). Typically, an author uses words to incline our hearts. Satan's agenda is to keep the chosen from the SEED of GOD or should I say, the Word of God. Why? Because "thy word is TRUTH" (John 17:17). It is only when the TRUTH makes you free indeed that you can truly thrive!

The adversary or the evil one has been in the business of delivering a false word since the beginning of man's existence. He told Adam and Eve that if they ate of the fruit, "they would not die" (Genesis 3:4). Not only was this a lie/deception, but it was a new word. The wrong word.

The devil loves to spread false seed to those that are trying to find their way, find their purpose, and find their identity. Typically, he introduces this false word when we are vulnerable, weak, insecure, and unstable. That is why the Bible shares in Matthew 13:19 that the "Wicked one comes and snatches away what was sown in his heart." Whether we knew it not, when we hear the Word of God, that is the first step of the word being planted in us, but this is where we are susceptible to be invaded and introduced with a false word, because we have just touched the surface of allowing the word (or seed) to GROW. So, we face doubt, which is unbelief, and whether we knew it or not, unbelief is a seed looking for a place to be planted.

You heard the phrase "a seed of doubt." All knowledge, no matter its origin, is seeds looking for somewhere to be planted. The problem is it is not the seed of God but some other seed looking for somewhere to be planted. Meaning it may not be seed from the True Gardener. We must know today what is trying to infiltrate our hearts. We must know what is trying to be planted in our lives.

## Day 81

# "PHASES OF THE HEART" (PART III)

> *"Thus, saith the Lord; Cursed be the man that trusteth in man, and maketh flesh his arm, and whose heart departeth from the Lord. For he shall be like the heat in the desert and shall not see when good cometh; but shall inhabit the parched places in the wilderness, in a salt land and not inhabited."*
> (Jeremiah 17:5-6)

Reflect for a moment on what the prophet is sharing from this perspective, "If you trust in man or make the flesh your source of strength your heart is disconnected from God." In other words, you take stock in the preeminence of yourself, or seeing yourself as the God of your own life.

Did you know that the biggest idol we worship today is the same one we have struggled with for thousands of years? That is… OURSELVES. The prophet stated, "If your heart is in this condition it's like you are in the desert, and when good comes along you don't even embrace it." In other words, you are never satisfied. We have seen people like this. They are never satisfied in relationships, never satisfied with appetites from pleasure, never satisfied in life, or never satisfied at work. Why? Because this is a condition of the heart.

When does our hearts depart from the Lord? The Bible states here, "When man trusts in man and makes the flesh his strength." In other words, there is a departure from God. It is like a voyage where we discover new desires connived and controlled from within ourselves. When the flesh is our strength, then we function off our own circumstances, situations, and events!

When the flesh is our strength then we operate off what we can control and contain. This is called the carnal life. The Bible states in Romans 8:8, "Those who are in the flesh cannot please the Lord." It also adds, "To be carnally minded is death, but to be spiritually minded is life and peace" (Romans 8:6). The carnal MIND means my thoughts, desires, and intents have been shaped by a seed that produces what the Bible calls DEATH.

Often, when we hear the word "death," we think of only the end of our physical existence, but death means the removal of having life, spiritual and emotional, such as peace, hope, love, joy, contentment, stability, and security. But when we allow God's word to penetrate to the depths of our hearts and become more than just surface dwellers, we witness the transformation that God designed for His SEED, and that was life, and life abundantly (John 10:10)!

*Day 82*

# "PHASES OF THE HEART" (PART IV)

*"And he said, So is the kingdom of God, as if a man should cast seed into the ground; And should sleep, and rise night and day, and the seed should spring and grow up, he knoweth not how. For the earth bringeth forth fruit of herself; first the blade, then the ear, after that the full corn in the ear. But when the fruit is brought forth, immediately he putteth in the sickle, because the harvest is come."* (Mark 4:26-29)

The Bible states in the Word of God that soil represents the hearts of men. In fact, in Matthew 13: 38 it says, "The field (the soil) is the world." He also states that "he who sows the good SEED is the Son of Man" (Matthew 13:37). The seed is the Word of God (Luke 8:11), and the Lord wants His seed scattered all over our hearts (soil). In fact, those who are recipients of the SEED have a fulfillment as carriers of the SEED, and that is to spread it! The Bible says: "The good seeds are the sons of the kingdom" (Matthew 13:38). In other words, we who have become mature or have grown as seeds have a responsibility to deliver His Word to the hearts that the Lord has placed along the territory He purposed along the path of our lives!

Notice that Jesus desires that we SCATTER His SEED. When something is scattered, its intent is to influence everywhere it goes. You and I are agents of influence. Our objective, like a farmer who scatters seed, is to witness the manifestation of a seed doing what it was designed to do!

When God scatters you to meet all kinds of people who live and exist in an array of situations, His goal is to scatter the seed through YOU. As the family of God, we are sowing SEED everywhere God wants us to touch, which are the hearts of the world. If the Word is the SEED and Jesus is the Word, then you are a representative of the WORD. That is why we are called Ambassadors because ambassadors are spokesman of the nation they are under authority of. Ambassadors speak on behalf of the nation that they represent. The Bible states we are a "Holy nation" (I Peter 2:9). Ambassadors are responsible for the territory they have been given the authority to operate in. The Bible says "all authority has been given to Me (Jesus)" (Matthew 28:18) and that we are joint heirs of that authority (Romans 8:17).

As joint heirs of His authority, as Ambassadors, we are the SEED of Jesus to those God has placed in our lives. Remember in our text about the man who was a farmer and the Bible states that after he scattered the seed, he went to bed that night, and when he woke up that morning, he was stunned to discover that something had happened? What had transpired was when he woke up, the SEED had brought forth fruit! God always has a HARVEST in mind for all His seed that is scattered. God knows what the expectation or outcome will be once seed impacts hearts, and that is it will change or manifest into His design!

## Day 83

# The Believing Heart

*"But God be thanked, that ye were the servants of sin, but ye have obeyed from the heart that form of doctrine which was delivered you."* (Romans 6:17)

Your heart has been created with an utterly amazing capability. Your heart has been given the capacity to believe, and most wonderfully, to believe in God. It is in the heart that faith springs up, dwells, and works (Acts 15:9). It is unbelief in the heart that draws men away from God (Hebrews 3:12).

God speaks to our hearts because in our hearts lies the center of our spiritual purpose. No wonder God shared that "He seeks a man after His own heart" (I Samuel 13:14). The heart is the core of man. So, God speaks to hearts that are open and accessible to His voice. Remember when Jesus stated that His sheep know His voice? A believing heart is open to the WORD of God. This kind of heart heeds and knows when He speaks.

Romans 10:17 states, "Now faith comes by hearing and hearing by the word of God." God builds faith in the heart through our receiving, believing, and obeying the Word of God. To truly follow the Lord, there must be a word spoken to our hearts that creates a BELIEF. It's interesting that today more and more I bump into people that claim and advocate that they believe in the Lord, but there seems to be a reduction in the listening department that causes us to follow the Shepherd, meaning Jesus. If we believe in God, then that belief is verified by the knowing of the voice of Jesus. It was Jesus who said, "My sheep know my VOICE" (John 10:27).

The Bible states, "Even the winds obey Him" (Matthew 8:27). How is that you ask? The winds know the voice of Jesus. We believe whatever we follow or obey. Some are confused that even our behavior and actions are connected to what we believe. Take for instance the person who is afraid of getting close to another for the sake of going through distrust, discouragement, and disconnection again. This is a belief, and this belief is obeying what has already been written on their hearts.

What we believe makes us, molds us, and moves us! So, for some, when the heart believes that it will encounter loss and lack and not love, it is a condition of belief that has impacted the heart. I implore you today to inventory what you believe, because what you believe is shaping your heart. Therefore, in our text of focus, the scripture states, "You obeyed from the heart that form of doctrine which was delivered to you." That form of doctrine is the voice of God or the voice of the Shepherd Jesus. The Lord desires to change the landscape of what we believe in our hearts by speaking to us His TRUTH.

## Day 84

# "TRAPPED"

*"Do not remember the former things, Nor consider the things of old. Behold, I will do a new thing, now it shall spring forth; Shall you not know it? I will even make a road in the wilderness and rivers in the desert."* (Isaiah 48:18-19)

Why a title like TRAPPED? Because so many are just that. They are trapped in the past, trapped in their failures, trapped in baggage they just cannot unload! Some attempt to push it down, suppress it, and compress it, only to discover that what you BUILD UP will eventually BLOW UP. I call it the B.U.B.Us. When we are trapped emotionally, many do not realize that it is hardwired to our operation spiritually. Here is why… the soul of man is really that part of man that houses his thoughts, feelings, anxiety, frustration, bitterness, resentment, depression, and stress.

In Greek, the word soul is "Psyche," which today we have derived into Psychology, which is really the study of the mind or our thinking. When our souls are trapped or contained in places that were never part of God's plan, we end up dealing with the aftermath of having a trapped SOUL. Your soul may be trapped on a hurt you just cannot let go of. Perhaps, you just cannot forgive someone to the degree that you truly wish the worst, instead of the best. This is not uncommon. Sure, we say, "I'm over it," but many of us are really TRAPPED.

Our text emphasizes first that we "Do not remember the former things." That is your broken past, your hurts, your flops, and mishaps, and let us go further, it is YOUR SIN. My pastor shared recently, "YOU ARE NOT YOUR SIN." But many cannot free themselves because sin is released from the one who died for it. True repentance is the willingness to lay our sin sick souls before the savior of sin. It is the MOVE to change from where you have existed, it is to bear fruit showing that the change is REAL, and it is to resemble the NATURE of God instead of the nature of sin.

The Message Bible interprets our text in a powerful way by saying, "Forget about what's happened; don't keep going over old history." If someone is in a vicious cycle of reruns and repeats that has everything to do with their PAST, then it still can keep them TRAPPED. But as we continue with the text, the word says, "Behold, I will do a new thing, now it shall spring forth; Shall you not know it?" God gives us a bold, powerful movement of something different about our old past by stating He plans on doing "a new thing."

Think about it. Some of us are so wrapped around our past that we hold the past as the culprit and the criminal as to why we are the way we are. But God has an intent to make something new! The Bible shares, "As a man thinks in his heart so is he." So, whatever has captured our minds to stay and be stuck on the past makes us who we are. But all that can be altered if we can embrace the reality of God's intent for us to have a NEW THING!

How does one allow the Lord to do a new thing? Here is the answer—by believing! "Therefore, I tell you, whatever you ask in prayer, believe that you have received it, and it will be yours" (Mark 11:24). No wonder God said in our text, "Shall you not know it?" God expects His word to deliver change to those that believe! Jesus said in Mark 5:36, "Do not fear, only believe." For many our fears come from our past, but Jesus wants us to be open to new thing by BELIEVING! Lastly, for many, we expect that this new thing will happen in a new place, and sometimes it will, but God reveals in His word that "I will even make a road in the wilderness and rivers in the desert." In other words, God does not have to take you somewhere different to become NEW!

He will work where you are currently. The wilderness is an example of being isolated, barren, and lacking. Rivers in the desert demonstrates that God can provide this change in a place that has been dry and parched (which could be our lives). But God can make rivers appear, revealing that God can bring something fresh and flourishing wherever you are. God wants to wash away everything that has held you trapped and send it straight down the river. Today, I pray for anyone that has been stuck, paralyzed, or on a Ferris wheel spiritually and emotionally where they keep dealing with thoughts, feelings, and even the outcomes because of how they think that keeps them going around and around. This is not the will God. He came to present a NEW THING. He came to unlock us from being TRAPPED!

## Day 85

# Is it Possible?

## A Testimony of C.J. Jackson

*"What is impossible with men is possible with God."* (Luke 18:27)

I am constantly surprised and bewildered, and honestly sometimes even dismayed, at how people who claim to love God and claim to have accepted Jesus Christ as their personal savior and even testify of the moving of the Holy Spirit in their lives, live so far beneath their privilege as children of the King.

Many of us have been in church longer than we have been in anything else, and yet while we excel and achieve and grow and enhance in other areas of our lives, we keep flunking out of Spiritual Development 101. We are seemingly hooked on holy happy meals and addicted to spiritual junk food. So much so that whenever an attempt is made to wean us off the bottle so that we can be introduced to a real robust spiritual meal, we rebel and must be given a pacifier to suck on. So, I would like to share some on spiritually living below the POSSIBILITES of God.

In April of 2016, I was diagnosed with fourth stage cancer. When I first found out, to say I didn't pause would be an understatement, but the God in me said, "What is impossible with men is possible with God." This spoke to my spirit that this encounter would not only breathe more life into me, but it would produce that God is a deliverer of His WORD! The paralyzing truth is that there were more so-called believers that spoke doubt, despair, and death over what I was facing than what I ever expected! Even some that were close to me were so captured by the current onslaught of cancer, that they could not see the Christ having the ability to use this for His glory.

What I realized as I walked this part of my life out was "Where is the FAITH?" I mean we claim and testify as believers that we have faith, but when faith is challenged, we discover what we really have. The Bible says in Hebrews 11:6, "Without faith it is impossible to please God." Everything that we encounter requires faith. How do I know this? Because the Bible says, "The just shall LIVE by faith." If faith is a living ingredient to our spiritual existence, then it must be tested to prove that it is faith. You must LIVE IT!

Did you know that everything that God offers you comes through faith? SALVALTION comes by faith—Rom. 10:9 says, "That if you confess with your mouth, 'Jesus is Lord,' and believe in your heart that God raised him from the dead, you will be saved." HEALING comes by faith—Acts 3:16 says, "By faith in the name of Jesus, this man whom you see and know was made strong. It is Jesus' name and the faith that comes through him that has given this complete healing to him, as you can all see." BAPTISM comes by faith—Colossians 2:12 says, "Having been buried with him in baptism and raised with him through your faith in the power of God, who raised him from the dead." FINANCIAL blessings come by faith—2 Kings 22:7 says, "But they need not account for the money entrusted to them, because they are acting faithfully."

Now the Bible says, "we walk by faith and not by sight," but do we really believe that? Do we really know what that means? It means you act and LIVE based on what you believe. For example, if I feel like I am not going to have a good day, then I speak what I believe is going to manifest, and that is I am not going to have a good day. If I feel that I would never be anything in life, then guess what, I will never be anything in life. But the devil is a liar! Because my Bible tells me, "Greater is He that is in me, then he that is in the world" (I John 4:4), and that I'm more than a conqueror, I am the head, and not the tail, I am above and not beneath, I am the lender and not the borrower, and you shall have what you say, if you believe and just have faith!

The Bible says in Romans 10:17 "faith cometh." This word (cometh) in the Greek language it is a continuing verb that means "Faith" is continuing to grow, based upon your use of it. God has given everyone a measure of faith, but if you do not use your faith, you cannot develop your faith! If you cannot believe God to heal your headache, why would you believe God to heal cancer? But still some say, "IS IT POSSIBLE?

## Day 86

# "Superheroes and Sober-mindedness"

*"Young men likewise exhort to be sober minded."* (Titus 2:6)

Recently while hanging out at the park, I noticed a group of kids planning what they called the Superhero game. The game involved every kid picking out their favorite hero and then fighting crime. The problem though was that every kid wanted to be Spider-man! Before this game could even begin, the kids would argue on who would be Spider-man for what seemed like forever. Finally, I decided to intervene (since I love superheroes) and gave the kids some other characters that they could be like Batman, Ironman, Antman, and Superman. What I realized as I gave the kids alternatives for heroes is that as they were arguing over who would be Spiderman, they lacked the one thing that distinguishes heroes from villains, and that is Superheroes always sacrifice. The kids in the park refused to budge an inch on giving in on being Spiderman.

Today, as the family of God, we witness the inability to give in on so many fronts. Whether it is letting someone go before you in the grocery store line or helping someone even though you know they may not be grateful. The scriptures add this, "For I say, through the grace given to me, to everyone who is among you, not to think of himself more highly than he ought to think, but to think soberly, as God has dealt to each one a measure of faith" (Romans 12:3-4). It appears that the Apostle Paul knew in the Spirit that we would deal with pride, arrogance, and selfishness in the Body of Christ. Notice that in the text it uses the word "think" three times. Each time he highlights something of importance that connects with true heroes.

The Lord desires that we not think of ourselves more than someone else. In other words, do not be HIGH-MINDED, and go beyond yourself. The third time the word "think" is used is when the text adds, "Think soberly," also known as being sober-minded. I Peter 5:8 says, "Be sober-minded; be watchful. Your adversary the devil prowls around like a roaring lion, seeking someone to devour." To be sober-minded is to be composed and not to be carried away with your own feelings. It is to pay attention to your own actions and of those around you.

Did you know the devil preys on thoughts? I Corinthians 15:34 reads in the King James Version, "Wake up from your drunken stupor." When we lack the ability to be sober-minded or walk in righteousness, it is like we are so intoxicated with pride and self-justification that we push our own agenda. The kids playing the Superhero game were so preoccupied in pursing their own needs to be Spiderman that they missed that their own actions were emulating the identity of division and destruction. When we push to the point to address what is being motivated from within ourselves with a selfish mind and not the sober mind, we have just displayed the same actions as those kids in the park. Today, become a superhero in Christ by possessing a SOBER MIND.

## Day 87

# THE COST

*"And whosoever doth not bear His cross, and come after me, cannot be my disciple. For which of you, intending to build a tower, does not sit down first, and count the cost, whether he have enough to finish it?"* (Luke 14:27-28)

I remember as a child every summer I would spend time with my uncle who lived in the Mojave Desert. The reason I wish to draw attention to this time is because of my first encounter mountain climbing with my uncle up what was known as Galileo Hill. It was enormous for me at 13 years old. My uncle told me what to bring along for the hike. He told me to bring an ample supply of water and snacks, but for whatever reason, I just thought it was no big deal, so I refused not only to dress appropriately for the hike, but I was not prepared with adequate snacks and water.

So, as we ventured up the hill at first, I thought it was a breeze, but remember, this is the Mojave Desert, and after the sun rises in the summer, the temperatures can hit extremes as high as 120 degrees! So here I am soaked and wet from sweat and lacking the necessary supplies to accomplish this trip. Boy did I ever learn to count the cost!

No one should ever totally commit into anything if they do not at first count the cost and are unwilling to pay the price. For no one can make a total commitment until he or she knows what that commitment entails. Until we truly embrace the real nature of Christ, and the quest to be discipled, then it manifests by what we discover in Christ. Discipleship to Jesus is a pressing into the deeper life in the Spirit, where many still lack that depth. When Jesus tells us to "bear the cross," He is describing the cost and asking if we are willing to pay this price. Bearing the cross is not what most have been led to believe. It is not accepting sickness or suffering as a cross, nor is it seeing how much pain we can handle. In fact, our pains and afflictions have already been addressed by Christ on the cross!

Bearing the cross is not dealing with a cheating husband or an alcoholic spouse, or even the losses of loved ones. It's not losing your job that have worked for years or having to deal with an obnoxious boss. So now that it is out of the way, what exactly is bearing your cross? First, the cross does not mean one thing for Jesus Christ and an entirely different thing for us. In the time of Jesus, the cross meant one specific thing—"DEATH." He deliberately chose to die. For us as well, it is a path we must deliberately chose. Sounds off or weird? Here's the point, Galatians 2:20 says, "I have been crucified with Christ and I no longer live, but Christ lives in me. The life I now live in the body, I live by faith in the Son of God, who loved me and gave himself for me." The bearing of the cross leads to places where there is the willingness to give up your life and replace it with His life. But you may say, "That's hard." Jesus knew the cost it would require, and that is why He said we must "DIE DAILY" (Luke 9:23).

This dying daily is a constant operation of dying to self and a living for the SAVIOR. As we constantly die to ourselves, we ignite more of Him! The way into a deeper life in Christ is a crucified life. This crucified life is a life of the crucifixion of "SELF." It is a complete life of living entirely in Christ. In other words, the cost is giving up our wills and our ways for His. And for all of us that requires a death. No wonder the Bible says, "Now if we have died with Christ, we believe that we shall also live with Him" (Romans 6:8). This death or crucifying of ourselves leads to a place or plane where we operate exclusively in His POWER. No wonder the Bible says, "I can do all things IN CHRIST." When we pursue the quest of getting deeper in Christ, it requires the payment of giving up our will for the exchange of being able to DO ALL THINGS! Now think about, isn't that worth THE COST?

## Day 88

# The Good Shepherd

*"Be thou diligent to know the state of thy flocks and look well to thy herds."* (Proverbs 27:23)

The pursuit of Jesus was always about the protection, the purpose, and the prosperity of the FLOCK. Jesus knew He was the Good Shepherd. In fact, He stated in John 10:11, "The thief comes only to steal and kill and destroy. I have come that they may have life and have it in all its fullness. I am the good shepherd. The good shepherd lays down His life for his sheep." Jesus knew the only way to make us the REDEEMED was to give His life for us as the good shepherd. The interesting parallel with Jesus being a shepherd is that shepherds understand that for the sheep to truly live, they need the SHEPHERD. Many Christians miss that there are some key components that are established when the Lord is the good shepherd.

1. **The Good Shepherd Leads.** If we are avoiding or evading the leadership of the direction that the Lord has paved, we miss our purpose. Jesus said, "I am the WAY," meaning He is the direction for DESTINY. Many are attempting to find purpose and destiny outside of the created order of God. When we exclude or dismiss the Lord from having the role of leading us completely, then we miss what His intentions and goals are for in this life and the life after!
2. **The Good Shepherd Provides.** Not only is the Lord "The Bread of Life," which is the substance of life, but He provides the BREAD himself. So many are unaware that there is an enemy that is clearly attacking what you CONSUME that interferes with your spiritual development. Our enemy is not just attacking you but hoping to prevent the BREAD of LIFE from impacting YOU. The nourishment of God is His WORD. The Bible says, "When your words came, I ate them; they were my joy and my heart's delight, for I bear your name, LORD God Almighty" (Jeremiah 15:16).
3. **The Good Shepherd Protects.** Remember, Jesus said that eventually "The thief comes to steal, kill, and destroy, but I come that you might have life, and have it abundantly" (John 10:10). He protects us by giving us LIFE and removing everything that has been taken like hope and love. He prevents killing. In other words, He prevents the nullifying a thing from its function. When something is KILLED, it is no longer able to function in its designed role. Lastly, He protects against being destroyed, meaning dealing with annihilation. When

something is annihilated, it is eliminated and erased from meaningful purpose.
4. **The Good Shepherd KNOWS.** The reality about any shepherd is that he knows his sheep down to each specific one. Jesus said, "I am the good Shepherd; and I know my sheep and am known by mine" (John 10:14). In other words, there is a connection and closeness that is realized by not only the Shepherd but by the FLOCK. The flock know the Shepherd too. The Bible adds, "They will hear my VOICE, and there will be ONE FLOCK and ONE SHEPHERD" (John 10:16). The voice of the ONE Shepherd is His Word, and the ONE Shepherd is Jesus! Not only do they KNOW His voice, but the Bible shares in John 10:27 that "My sheep hear my voice, and I know them, and they FOLLOW ME."

So, ask yourself today, are you truly witnessing the benefits of the Good Shepherd leading your life? Is the Good Shepherd providing for you in your life? How about having the protection of the Good Shepherd? Finally, do you KNOW Him like He knows you? Because if we do, His expectation is that we follow where He leads!

## Day 89

# GOD SEES THE BEST

*"This Man, if He were a prophet, would know who and what manner of woman this is who is touching Him, for she is a sinner."* (Luke 7:39)

Right this second, I want you to stop and reflect on how God can see you. God sees a lot of value in you, so much that He sent His Son for you! In the mind of God, you are special and valuable! God sees glorious things in you, and He knows full well what you are capable of. In 1 Samuel 16: 7, it is written, "... For the Lord does not see as man sees; for man looks at the outward appearance, but the Lord looks at the heart." And so, when God looks at you, He sees the best in you. He sees what others do not or refuse to see in you. Many people live in bondage to feelings of rejection and do not even realize it. It causes us to believe lies about ourselves and project hurtful emotions on others. It also undermines our relationships with God.

I know from experience that rejection hurts, and I really do not mind being vulnerable and admitting I resented being rejected too. I prayed about it. I thought maybe God would answer me quickly and I would know just what to do about it. But God's answer would come in God's time and not mine. However, I am reminded that Jesus Himself also experienced rejection in his hometown at a point where He was not expecting it. As a result, He did not question who He was. He did not defend Himself. He did not even deny the hurt that He experienced.

And He did experience some personal pain, but He went right on to the next villages telling them of God's love. There are several steps we usually go through before we realize that God views us differently than those around us. Remember the woman who anointed the feet of Jesus with oil in Luke 7:36-48? This woman approached Jesus in an open setting, a banquet, and it appears that even though people may have thought negatively about her, through Jesus, she realized that she was loved, and she learned how to not care about what they thought.

People get tripped up even though they believe that God is seeing the best in them, and the reason being is because they venture to where what others deem as the best instead of God. In fact, many may care more about what others say than what God said or done. I know that I will receive some disagreement, but allow me to explain. Yes, you should be concerned about your reputation but not when people criticize you falsely. When they lie on you and disrespect you, this should not be something that dominates your mind. If you are constantly one who worries what others think of you, I would like to help you reverse those unpleasant thoughts. No matter what it is that you obsess about, if it is trying to look good for complete strangers, listening to rumors, or getting into a negative cycle, there is a way out. The late Bishop G. E. Patterson once said, "I had to be delivered twice in my life, first I was delivered from sin, and then I was delivered from people."

When we are concerned about the negativity coming from other people, we need to do several things to overcome this. We should first stop overthinking, although this may sound a bit harsh, but you are not the most important person in the world, at least not to everybody. Most of the time, when you think you are being judged, you probably are not. It is just too hard to judge every single person you meet, analyzing their flaws and imperfections like they are here to test you are trying to grade you. This is exhausting! If you could only see the you that God SEES. God's perception of me is beyond my flaws, my failures, and what was considered as my fault. I encourage you today to start trusting the voice of God at His Word as it relates to what He sees in YOU!

## Day 90

# "DISTRACTED!"

We live in a time with more distractions in life than ever before! Some of us have become so accustomed to distractions that when there is a place of calmness and absolute quietness, that by itself is literally a distraction. In other words, we need NOISE!

From social media, Alexa, Siri, the Internet, games, music, etc., there are those who find it weird to exist without something always distracting them. Whether we know it or not, we are being bombarded with all kinds of voices and messages that are attempting to influence us and alter us by what we open ourselves up to. Even our ability to listen to another has been hindered by the distractions that have become synonymous with life. Think about it. Listening intently has become a huge endeavor for children, students, and even adults because we have become so attached to having distractions as a functioning apparatus in our lives.

Even for many who take on the title of Attention Deficit Disorder, we have been saturated in environments where there was no attention toward them or their issues, and now they pursue looking for substitutes in life that will give them what they long for as a need, and that is… ATTENTION. There is a saying, "Knowledge speaks, but wisdom listens." If we want to be wise and listen, then who we listen to is vital. Shouldn't that voice be the voice of all knowledge, the same voice who spoke all that we know into existence? Then He personally sent His Son to speak and demonstrate His compassion and love for us in the flesh.

Followed by the Holy Spirit to be that indwelling voice that guides us, God has had a lot to say about man's entire existence. He is still speaking to us today, but we must take care in who has our ear. As stated before, listening to the wrong voice can be disastrous. After all, when the first family (Adam's family) lived in perfection, Eve let one lie voice distraction to her and not the truth of who created it all for them. Then Adam let a distracted wife divert him from the very one he walked in the garden with, the one voice he could trust (casting doubt on that truth).

Today we have a variety of voices screaming for our attention from every possible direction and device. How do we cut through the thousands of distractions and focus on the one true voice of wisdom? John 10:27 says, "My sheep listen to my voice; I know them, and they follow me." Isn't it interesting that the expectation of the Great Shepherd Jesus is that His sheep know His voice? Having spent some time on the farm with my grandfather, I learned that to capture the animals' attention, you would have to know them or have had a relationship of reliability with them. They knew that my grandfather fed them, provided for them, spent time with them, and grazed them. When you spend insurmountable times on whatever you relate to you, do you know that you are developing a relationship with that thing? In addition, you begin to move in that direction for substance, safety, and even security. But this is what the Great Shepherd envisioned for the flock of God.

Think about this: If Adam and Eve listened to the wrong voice when there were only two voices speaking, then what do we do with all the voices speaking in an array of ways? We are doused with all kinds of voices that are looking for ways to lead us, guide us, and persuade us. But you can always make out the voice of the one you have the closest relationship with. I am often asked, how do you hear God's voice? Here is the answer: You spend time with Him (The Lord). It is that simple! Here is the kicker: wherever I do not have the Lord focused as the apple of my eye (Proverbs 7:2) it will cause vulnerability to consider others that will position themselves for my attention. All this is an attempt to DISTRACT.

## Day 91

# LEARNING TO LIVE IN HIS PRESENCE

*"And He said to me, 'Son of man, feed your belly, and fill your stomach with this scroll that I give you.' So, I ate, and it was in my mouth like honey in sweetness. Then He said to me: 'Son of man, go to the house of Israel and speak with My words to them.'"* (Ezekiel 3:3-4)

One thing I personally realize at this stage of my journey with God is that I keep discovering MORE! Now mind you, this does not happen automatically. It is not an overnight manifestation either. It is a constant seeking of His presence by opening our spirit to His and allowing Him to pour His power, His protection, and His purpose right into us. To truly embrace Him, we must seek His glory constantly. Why you ask? Well, it is due, because most of all our lives we have been consumed with seeking other things. Think about it. Even in our everyday operation, we deal with the hustle and bustle of life, trying to take care of families and loved ones, and plain dealing with life. But even during all that, the Lord desires that we seek Him more than anything else!

Jesus warned, "How can you believe, when you receive glory from one another, and you do not seek the glory that is from the one and only God?" (John 5:44). The Lord requires that we seek Him above all else. Today though, many have created a seeking of church service and not a personal seeking of Christ the Savior! Others are more in tune to revealing some kind of outward display before men to impress men. But the Bible says, "The outward man perishes but the inward man is renewed day by day." In other words, there is hunger that is created for the seeking of the Lord that is independent of wondering what others are looking at. This is the inward operation of the Spirit that is accomplished by seeking His presence.

No wonder the Bible states in our text, "'Son of man, feed your belly, and fill your stomach with this scroll that I give you.' So, I ate, and it was in my mouth like honey in sweetness." While Ezekiel was alone, the Lord poured in His word (His presence). Whether we know it or not, His word confirms His presence. He speaks through His word. He saves through His word. He stabilizes us through His word. He secures us through His word, and He makes us significant through His word!

We must seek the Lord's presence until we finally have found Him. This is not a thing we do only at church; it is what we do in LIFE! It is a consumption of the Lord that thrives in a place that we personally develop in your own time of worship, in our own time of receiving His word, and in our own time from witnessing His wonders through the Spirit. It is only when we stay in His presence that we are prepared to proclaim and propel His will to others. Therefore, after Ezekiel ate of the word, He was told, "Son of man, go to the house of Israel and speak with My words to them." If spiritually you seem stagnant in your faith walk, I implore you to change what you truly pursue.

## Day 92

# THE FUTILE GROUND

*"While a large crowd was gathering, and people were coming to Jesus from town after town, he told this parable: 'A farmer went out to sow his seed. As he was scattering the seed, some fell along the path; it was trampled on, and the birds of the air ate it up.'"* (Luke 8:4-5)

*"This is the meaning of the parable: The SEED is the WORD of God. Those along the path are the ones who hear, and then the devil comes and takes away the word from their hearts, so that they may not believe and be saved."* (Luke 8:11-12)

The Parable of the Sower represents one of the most powerful and yet applicable sharings of Jesus. I know many have heard the text shared from many spiritual teachers, but I would like for you to consider that the seeds that fell on the ground represent people who are of the futile ground. In other words, this ground represented being unproductive and unfulfilling.

This is the ground that ends up being hollow and ineffective. The example that Jesus uses about GROUNDS in this text is really about PEOPLE! Spiritually, we are all some kind SOIL. The challenge though is that many are unaware of their soil condition, not realizing that soil management is really HEART management. The soil is the representation of the heart.

While Jesus was sharing this parable to the masses, He encountered a lot of people that had gathered and crowded around Him. They felt good about Him and felt good about themselves, and even followed Him from town to town. Crowds were impressed with Jesus, but please understand that Jesus was not impressed by their attendance, their attention, and their adulation, because they were coming for all the WRONG REASONS. Therefore, He specifically shared the parable about the ground. He wanted them to know what kind of soil (heart) can bear much fruit.

Our text in Luke describes and emphasizes that the seed was trampled upon before the birds feed on it. In other words, this ground had not only been the result of heavy foot traffic but because the seed could not be established in the ground, the birds came in and swooped up the seed. What is the application of this as it relates to the Futile Ground? Well, a lot of people come to church for information but not for intake. They are in the house but not in fellowship. They are interested, but not inspired. They do not comprehend the Word of God, have no conviction in their heart, and are not converted in their soul. So, the seed (the Word of God) becomes trampled and becomes bird food (ate up by the enemy).

Before many reach the point of believing the word (the seed) to cause change in their lives, the devil takes away the word (the seed) from their heart. The devil influences believers more than those who do not believe. The reason being is because He knows what happens when the soil is right for growth and expansion spiritually. So, he attempts to overpower those whose soil is still being impacted by the debris from this world.

The seeds that have been trampled down and munched by the birds have truly little signs of life and no chance to survive. In addition, the possibility of cultivation becomes pointless. Therefore, Jesus emphasizes that we become the GOOD GROUND (Matthew 13:23). The devil does not want unbelievers to belong to Christ, to believe in Christ, or to be like Christ. He wants them to be called a Christian but bear no FRUIT. Today, do not be fooled just because you believe in God! Determine how far the Word of God (the seed) gets into your HEART.

## Day 93

# THE GREATER PLACE

*"From everyone who has been given much, much will be demanded; and from the one who has been entrusted with much, much more will be asked."* (Luke 12:48)

Have you noticed that when we approach the last day of the year, many are looking forward to a wonderful filled new year of happiness, excitement, and comfort? Here is something to consider for those that claim the Lord as Christ, "That to whom much is given much is required." In other words, when God has allowed us to operate in places, positions, and even in roles with people, we are put in these scenarios to reveal what He has given and that is MUCH! Sometimes, we are so preoccupied with just living according to our so-called daily operation that we miss what the Arranger, Orchestrator, and Operator has designed specifically for us to do with what He calls MUCH.

What we must understand is that much is relative to each his own. Whatever God has given you is much. We must stop viewing our situation as lacking, little, and lousy. God has done and is doing so much in an array of ways! The adversary wants to drop seeds in your mind to get you see not MUCH but what is insignificant in you.

When God gave His Son, He gave us MUCH! In fact, He gave us the greatest gift, the most precious gift. The gift of the Son offers us everything that was against us that has now been nailed to the cross (Colossians 2:13-14). When the Father gave us Jesus, He gave us the ability to be a new CREATION. The Bible says that the objective was that old things would be forever removed and replaced with new things (II Corinthians 5:17). Wow! That is MUCH!

Do not allow the voices from the enemy to speak a word to you that shrinks and places the King of Kings and Lord of Lords in a place that is not considered MUCH. Despite whatever you are currently walking out, you must comprehend that this path is nothing new. Many before us, and even many who currently walk this path, realize that this journey requires that no matter what we have we still have MUCH. It is not based on possessions, power, positions, and even pleasure. It is based on the supernatural understanding that despite whatever or whoever you are or what you have, God wants and desires that you seize the opportunity with every chance to see that you have been given much!

The Bible says, "He entrusted us," meaning He deposited something in us. He made an investment in us. What did the Lord invest in us? His SON! The Bible says, "Guard the good deposit that was entrusted to you—guard it with the help of the Holy Spirit who lives in us" (II Timothy 1:14). There is a deposit of God stored inside everyone that has activated an intimate relationship with the Lord. He did MUCH in YOU!

The Bible shares, "But we have this treasure in earthen vessels, that the excellency of the power may be of God, and not of us" (II Corinthians 4:7). So, we are searching for the GREATER PLACE not realizing that we already possess it in Christ.

## Day 94

# CHECK YOUR ATTITUDE

I have often stated that God is not nearly as concerned with what we are going through as He is with our RESPONSE to what we go through, In all that He designs or allows us to experience, His chief concern is that our ATTITUDES become consistent with those of His Son, Jesus Christ. It does not amaze me that people base their attitude on what they are confronted with. In other words, if someone comes at us in a harsh, heavy, or hellish manner, then we will establish a responsive attitude to combat or confront what we have to face. The challenge is we still struggle with the responsibility of attitude. We want to blame the boss, the cashier, and the driver next to us as the reason why we display ACTIONS that uncover what lies at the core of our own attitudes.

Webster says that an attitude is a way of thinking, but let us go further with the concept that it is an issue of the HEART. Mainly because the scriptures say, "Out of the mouth the HEART SPEAKS" (Luke 6:45). Think about that. Your attitude is really about a position of the heart. When I think about a position, I think of AUTHORITY. Reflect for a moment that on any sports team there are several so-called positions. Everyone on a team realizes that they must first not only know their own position, but they must respect the position of everyone else. If for whatever reason any player decides to shift out of his position and venture into his fellow players position, the team becomes vulnerable to invasions.

When we disrespect our own position, we may cause someone else to settle for existing out of position. True leaders understand that to become a great leader you must VALUE PEOPLE. This is a foundation of our own attitudes. When we value people, it is not based on what position they are in but rather the position that we are in. Value is about seeing the good, the great, and the grand in others even when they do not see it in themselves!

Many people refuse, resist, and rebel those where their positions are off. It could be your manager, your mom, or even Mr. Jones next door. When we miss that our attitudes are about being or staying in position even if the response from others is unbecoming or unsettling, we receive a supernatural outcome that is not based on how people respond but based on what God said. Here is what happens when we stay in position; it works in conjunction with the Will of God. The Bible says, "When a man's ways please the Lord, He makes even his enemies to be a peace with him" (Proverbs 16:7). The challenge is many people have still taken on the approach that their abusive, aggressive, and argumentative attitude is the result of someone else. This is the result of having the wrong attitude about ourselves. Real Attitude adjustment work is an internal job where we must evaluate the FRUIT that is blossoming from our lives.

Jesus said, "You are known by your FRUIT" (Matthew 7:16). Your fruit is the evidence of what is coming out of your life. No matter what approach another may have with you, you are still responsible for what is manifesting from your life! That is how we CHECK OUR ATTITUDES.

## Day 95

# "Dressed Like a Wolf"

Jesus calls false prophets "wolves in sheep's clothing" (Matthew 7:15). In other words, false faith knows how to dress, impress, and even express what has the potential to entice! Think about it. A wolf has one major goal: "Self-Perseveration." The wolf is concerned only about his well-being. He will do whatever to get his ends accomplished. The true nature of a wolf who hide's his true intentions is one who camouflages his outer self to mask his inner desires.

Even in the illustrations by Jesus, it is apparent that wolves love to hang around sheep. Jesus even stated, "My sheep know my voice, I know them, and they follow me" (John 10:27). Where here is the challenge, how do you determine the difference between what is dressed like a wolf and what is legit? Here is the answer, Jesus said, "By your FRUIT you are known." All fruit is a representation of what is the evidence of what is being identified from one's life.

No wonder Jesus told us, "Go; behold, I send you out as lambs in the midst of wolves" (Luke 10:3). Jesus gave us instructions of what we would encounter as we propel forward for His Kingdom, and that is we would come face to face with WOLVES. The problem is for a wolf to be in your midst and in mine, he must have gotten close enough to give his undercover approach. Too often as soldiers of Christ, we have not become fruit examiners. We assume based on titles, roles, and facilities that things must be on the up and up. When Jesus was walking the earth, He personally encountered men who He called "Brood of Vipers" (Matthew 12:34). These men were so-called church leaders. They were scribes, leaders of the law, and men that hung around the temple, but deep down their true nature was hidden. Wolves say one thing and live entirely another way. Wolves can share even the WORD of God but struggle to personally apply it.

Wolves love to hang around sheep, not to comfort, care, or counsel sheep. Wolves hang around sheep to consume them. In other words, they bring doubt, depression, destruction, division, and delusion. After that revelation about wolves, one can see that wolves are not restricted by locations, places, and areas that we have even deemed as those where we should see peace, hope, and love. Remember, wolves love sheep, so their intentions are to infiltrate the people of God! What better place to find the people of God then in churches?

Wolves dress as messengers, servants, and spokesmen of God when all along they are WOLVES! We know this because Jesus said, "Many false prophets will rise up and deceive many" (Matthew 24:12). Undercover missions of wolves are to IMPRESS, IMITATE, and give false INSTRUCTION. The spirit of the wolf is one that goes after the wounded and the young sheep. They shy away from the strong and solid sheep. Wolves love to create friction, frustration, and fear. Wolves love to spread a word that promotes gossip and guilt, and brings grief. Here is the question for us today: Why would Jesus give us so much insight about WOLVES? Here is the answer: "I know that after my departure savage wolves will come in among you, not sparing the flock" (Acts 20:29).

As the unfolding of the final days are being lived out before our very eyes according to the scriptures, we must have a faith that looks out for the FLOCK! The flock is the Body of Christ, or the family of God! If we sit back and let the wolf ravage the flock, we are no different than the WOLF, because we did nothing to prevent what Christ warned us to confront. The next time we see gossip, hearsay, rumors, and innuendos, and witness debris that promotes the characteristics of the wolf, I pray that you represent the Great Shepherd and remove the fruit of the wolf.

# "PREPARED FOR PROSPERITY"
## (PART I)

There is some debate on the topic of "Prosperity." Does God really want His people to prosper or just barely get by? There are many critics of this so-called prosperity teaching, but what does the Word of God really say about this? John 10:10 states, "The thief comes only to steal and kill and destroy; I have come that they may have life and have it to the full." The context of John 10 speaks about eternal life, for Jesus spoke that He lays down his life for His sheep, and we know why he did that—for us to have LIFE! God permits things to happen to us for our character building for Christlikeness. The fullness of this abundant life should be our experience here on earth. We do not need abundance in heaven because its already there.

It is important to remember that the word "save" in Greek is the word "sozo," which literally means to heal, preserve, save, do well, and be (make) whole. It means deliverance in the present as well as in the future or in eternity, physical as well as spiritual. The word "abundance" in John 10:10 is "perissos," meaning exceeding some number or measure or rank or need. It also means superior, extraordinary, surpassing, and uncommon. When Jesus saved us, His intention was not only to save our souls, but also to save us from our present condition.

The enemy can only attack us in our ignorance. You may believe that prosperity is not for you, but why would you live below your God-given privileges? I asked God, "Lord, why are some of your children so doubtful or skeptic about prosperity?" Or they insist in living below the riches of your glory? The Holy Spirit whispered these thoughts in my heart, "You will be made rich in every way so that you can be generous on every occasion." "Now he who supplies SEED to the SOWER and bread for food will also supply and INCREASE your store of seed and will ENLARGE the harvest of your righteousness" (II Corinthians 9:10).

Let us break this text down. First, God is the one who supplies seed to the sower. God is the giver of seed, and He gives seed to sowers. So, lets pause for a second and ask a question. Are you a sower? Because if we want to witness what the word implies and that is the supplying of seed, we then must become sowers! This word supply means to continuously provide. For this to be the case, we then must be SOWING!

Second, sowers understand they do not eat all the seed. Therefore, the scripture states, "He who supplies seed to the sower and bread for food will also supply and increase your store of seed." We must not eat up all the investment. God is wanting to modify and magnify your store of seed. The Bible says He wants to not only supply it but increase it! "Don't eat it all!" Do not be GREEDY! When the body of Christ is full of GREED, then we cannot see legitimate NEEDS. This text also adds that "you will be made (what?) rich in every way (why?) so that you can be generous on every occasion." God desires that we become overtaken in the spirit of generosity, not just because it is Thanksgiving or Christmas, but because it is in you to do on every occasion. You were PREPARED for PROSPERITY.

## Day 97

# PREPARED FOR PROSPERITY
# (PART II)

There is a difference between riches and wealth. Riches means to enrich your value and quality, and wealth signifies ABUNDANCE. It deals with living out a legacy, which deals with living in an inheritance. The reason I am sharing this is to help us understand what God is about is… AN INHERITANCE. When we think of inheritance, we also think about our Birthright. In other words, something that was given because you are in the family. Folks, God is waiting to deliver His inheritance upon us!

Hebrews 6:7-12 says, "For the earth which drinketh in the rain that cometh oft upon it, and bringeth forth herbs meet for them by whom it is dressed, receiveth blessing from God: But that which beareth thorns and briers is rejected, and is nigh unto cursing; whose end is to be burned. But, beloved, we are persuaded better things of you, and things that accompany salvation." Again, salvation is more than just going to heaven, it provides salvation to all of life! Verse 10 says, "For God is not unrighteous to forget your work and labor of love, which ye have shewed toward his name, in that ye have ministered to the saints, and do minister."

Farmers do not eat all their investment. They do not have that kind of thinking. Farmers have learned to separate the seed so that they may plant again. The farmer knows that seeds play a major role in prosperity, and so does God. Prosperity does not happen by accident. Or I should say, harvest does not happen by accident. Do not eat everything God gives you! Why? Because God is in the harvest business and so are, we, Say this, "Today, I will no longer consume everything God gives me, but I will invest and expect a harvest."

When you plant your seed, have the spirit of expectation because all farmers expect harvest. What does that mean? Well, when I was in the 1st grade, my teacher let each student plant some seeds in a small cup. We watered the seeds, gave them sunlight, and waited for growth. We had an expectation. When God gives you the seed of His word and you have not planted it into anyone, do not expect a harvest. When God blesses you with possessions, property, opportunities, favor, or just anything that you possess outwardly or inwardly, all of it represents a seed where God is awaiting a harvest.

Many Christians say, "Oh, when I give, I don't expect anything in return." 2 Timothy 2:6 states, "The hardworking farmer should be the first to receive a share of the crops." Those of you who are seeking wisdom about biblical prosperity need to understand that it is not something you just find. No one can give it to you; you must create the desire within yourself. And be aware that when you receive something from God, He wants to multiply it. So, you need to sow it.

The Bible is not against prosperity, but against covetousness, greed, and trusting in wealth. Our hearts will always go where we put our seed. (money). Matthew 6:21 reads, "For where your treasure is, there your heart will be also." The Bible is teaching us to sow seeds or to give as an antidote (cure) to greed and materialism. How do we cure GREED? Give! Generosity is the key to prosperity. And the Lord has made it clear He wants us prosperous.

Psalms 23:1 says, "The Lord is my shepherd I shall not want." In other words, the Lord is my substance. He is my provider. Psalms 35:27 states, "Let the Lord be magnified, who takes pleasure in the prosperity of His servant." God's major reason for prospering us is not just to raise up our standard of living but also to raise up our standard of giving. The mindsets of the people who are in a poverty way of thinking consider that they are exempted when it comes to giving. Their position is "I am poor," and "Someone should help me." Acts 20:35 shares, "It is more blessed to give than to receive." There is no stipulation of how much you have or where you are. Today, embrace that PROSPERITY is God's intent for your life!

## Day 98

# "DON'T LET THE DEVIL DECIEVE YOU"

No matter how beautiful the world around us seems, remember there was a serpent lurking in Paradise itself. If Adam and Eve had possessed a WAR mode mentality, they never would have casually accepted the lies of Lucifer.

Likewise, today, we need to be wise and walk carefully for "the days are evil" (Ephesians 5:16). You see, Jesus was always aware that He lived in a war zone. No matter what He was doing—whether He was laughing with sinners or driving out demons, whether He was healing the sick or training followers—beneath the surface of His outer activities, the "war mode switch" in Jesus' mind was always "ON."

For you see, Satan fears VIRTUE. He is terrified of HUMILITY; He hates it. He sees a humble person and it sends chills down his back. His hair stands up when Christians kneel, for humility is the surrendering of a soul to God.

The devil trembles before the MEEK. Why you might ask? Because the Bible states, "Blessed are the meek, for they will inherit the earth" (Matthew 5:5). Meaning there is an inheritance that we receive from God Himself, right here on earth! Often, we do not extrapolate from the word that when God says we will inherit the earth that we will be positioned in a place of AUTHORITY.

The devil is a deceiver. His objective is to deceive, which is to manipulate the TRUTH. In other words, to get us to consider or reconsider other options as it relates God's purpose for you on the earth.

When we allow the devil to deceive us, we must be open to deception. How does someone become open to deception? It comes in the form of being tempted. The Bible says, "Each one is tempted when he is drawn away by his own desires and enticed" James 1:14). Yet the Lord knows this and adds in James 1:17, "Every good gift and every perfect gift is from above, and comes down from the Father of lights, with whom there is no variation or shadow of turning." In other words, when we have the Light of God, we have the illumination/knowledge of God. We also do not have any shifty and shady operating from God, which makes His Word dependable and reliable, and He is accountable to watch it perform. On the contrary, the devil is known for perception through deception. Therefore, our eyes are open (spiritual eyes) when we "know the truth it makes us free" (John 8:32).

When we possess the characteristics of the Lord, we now have power and provisions where once the devil had access, but now what stands in its place is the Lord, and Satan is terrified of Jesus Christ!

*Day 99*

# The Axiom of Humility

*"God opposes the proud but gives grace to the humble."*
(James 4:6)

One word that has fallen off the lips and lives of those in our generation today is humility. It is identified as a word describing the weak or the vulnerable. It is seen as a word announcing that one is thin-skinned or a sucker.

It is striking that when the Word of God shares on what to defend ourselves with when the devil comes knocking on our doors, the conclusion is to possess humility. In fact, James 4:7 reads, "So humble yourselves before God. Resist the devil, and he will flee from you." The key to confront the devil starts with humility.

Many may miss what HUMILITY is all about. Some think it is about groveling in front of others or showcasing a display that appears you are less than others around you. But the Word of God provides proof of what humility is truly all about. The Bible states in I Peter 5:5, "Clothe yourselves with humility toward one another, because God opposes the proud but gives grace to the humble." From the mind of God, when you are humble, you are free from pride and arrogance. In other words, you do not have to defend yourself when the truth is aimed directly at whatever needs attention in your life.

Let us face it, many of us want to immediately defend ourselves when we are trying to portray or hide something that may make us look differently than what we want. This is the place the devil hopes we are open towards. Godly humility is being comfortable in who you are in the Lord. No wonder the Bible states, "Do nothing out of selfish ambition or vain conceit, but in humility consider others better than yourselves" (Philippians 2:3). When we truly dress ourselves in humility, we have a life that needs God. Meaning, we live depending on the Lord. We need the help of God in every matter! Strive to let God into every crevice of your life. We pull the curtain that wants to stay closed because we know that we can truly be humble only by being real with God.

Therefore, to overcome the devil we need humility. To humble yourself is to refuse to defend your image—you are corrupt and full of sin in your old nature. Yet we have a new nature that has been created in the likeness of Christ (Ephesians 4:24), so we can agree with our adversary about the condition of our flesh. When Satan seeks to condemn you for impatience, your response should be, "Yes, in my flesh I am very impatient. But since I have been born again, Jesus is my righteousness, and through His blood I am forgiven and cleansed."

Turn again to God. Use the accusation as a reminder that you are not standing before an angry God but rather a THRONE of

GRACE, which enables you to boldly draw near to God for help (Hebrews 4:16). Satan is terrified of HUMILITY. The reason being is because humility is the surrendering of your soul to the Lord, and when you surrender to the Lord, you allow His supremacy to activate His full authority. When we struggle in being humble, we leave room from PRIDE, and this is where the devil keeps us from the throne of God. Do not let anything strive to keep you from His Great Grace. Be open to the axiom of humility!

## Day 100

# SILENCE YOUR ENEMIES WITH PRAISE

*"You have ordained PRAISE because of your enemies, to silence the foe and the avenger."* (Psalms 8:2)

Did you know that your praise binds the enemy? In fact, praise executes the WORD of judgement over the enemy (Psalms 149:6-8).

The reality is that God has ORDAINED PRAISE. In other words, God has established and fixed praise for a specific function. Not only does God love the praises of His people, but praise will impact those that are against us. Praise, therefore, is a weapon. It is a spiritual tool used for silencing those that are against the will of God.

Think about it. The scripture says, "Silence the foe and the avenger." That means anyone who opposes, oppresses, and is obnoxious about the life you have in Christ. To silence means to hold them speechless. It literally means to have them be quiet. Often our lives are impacted with negative noise. We are bombarded with being like a trash can, where people come and throw things at us that are loud, disrespectful, and hateful. Yet by allowing our spiritual nature to praise God, this unlocks a power that diffuses and distinguishes all those that would be confrontational.

How do you practice PRAISE? First, you must be a living vessel of God. It is like you are a cup, and when you are ready to pour what comes out of you, it is the presence of the Lord, not friction, or being fussy, or operating always with frustration. When these elements are normal operating tools to how we live then the enemy is unquestionably very LOUD. Remember that prayer is praise. Speaking the name of Jesus is praise. Surrendering to His will is praise.

The next time you struggle with any kind of enemy, whether its distraction, division, depression, or any kind of dysfunction, always be mindful that PRAISE activates the presence of God to work on your behalf!

## Day 101

# "I SEE CHRIST!"

*"Jesus said, 'He who has seen Me has seen the Father.'"* (John 14:9)

Have you ever considered that every time you deeply seek the Lord's involvement in your life or want Him to step into greater territory in your heart, you are getting more clarity to see Him? Every time we open the Word of the Truth (the Word of God) we are really looking into His presence, witnessing His power, and watching His purpose. Jesus is the image of the invisible Father (Hebrews 1:2-3). "In Him all the fullness of Deity dwells in bodily form" (Colossians 2:9). Jesus is God's form. He mirrored on earth those things He SAW His Father doing in Heaven; He echoed the WORDS the Father whispered to Him from eternity.

Unfortunately, many of us have reduced the Christ to a picture hung on the wall or a story that has passed down through the ages of time that is seen as folklore. Why? Because to truly know Jesus is an intimate reality and requires a thirst, a hunger, and a desire to peer into the SPIRIT RE a.m. Seeing in the Spirit is beyond natural eyes; it is removing the preventions that keep us from seeing His glory. If you truly desire to see God, then Christ's words are windows through which the pure in heart behold the Almighty (Matthew 5:8). Opening windows gives us not only access to the greater of the Lord but causes us to SEE Him in a much broader way. When the window of my heart is open, then I have given my heart the opportunity to have complete submersion in the depth of the Spirit. This thereby opens me to see beyond this world, because He said, "I am not of this world" (John 17:16).

When Jesus was born, it was foretold by the prophets of old that He would be called the Messiah, the Christ. He would be King, and the angels said on His birth that He would "take away the sins of the world" (John 1:29). Yet what we may miss is that His mother never had a SEED of a man to create her child, but the very SEED of God Himself. God immaculately placed His divine seed inside of the woman, and she bore a child that the powers at the time (Roman Empire) wanted Him dead (King Herod). The reason why... He represented CHANGE in what they saw. King Herod wanted no threat or force to interfere with who he was or what he had.

Today, many are "walking by sight and not by faith" (II Corinthians 5:7). Both require that we walk. To walk by faith, we must see in faith just like walking by sight. We walk in faith not in the natural or in the flesh but in the Spirit. When we walk by faith, we see through God. The teachings of Jesus Christ are not to be blended into the Bible as though He were one of the many voices used by God. He is the living revelation of God Himself, the sole expression of His invisible glory. When Christ speaks, we are listening to God unfiltered, unbiased, and unveiled. He said, "When you see me you see the Father!"

## Day 102

# "On the Shores of Strife"

*"For where envying and strife is, there is confusion and every evil work."* (James 3:16)

When we typically think about shores, we imagine wonderful, calm sandy beaches, with a gently wind blowing over our faces. We consider a warmth in the air that stimulates our bodies and causes us to relax and exhale. But in the spiritually/emotional lives of many, we live and exist where our lives emulate shores where there is conflict, obstructions, and constant friction. The Bible calls this place confusion. Yet the Bible also adds that "God is not the author of confusion" (I Corinthians 14:33). So, wherever there is confusion, its creator and originator are not the Lord.

Our text highlights that wherever there is envy and strife, there will be confusion. For many, we are so used to being on the shores of strife that is has become our norm. It has become our natural habitat, meaning we have it made it our system of survival. We have made it a place where it breathes all around us! The thing about strife is that it will not go away voluntarily. Strife must be faced. Strife must be confronted. The thing is many avoid it and walk away from it on eggshells whenever they encounter strife. Yet they continue to live in it. They put up with it and allow it to be on the shores they wake up to every day. Here is the thing—you will never correct what you are unwilling to confront!

On one occasion in the life of Jesus, He had to deal with one of His disciples wanting Him to be on the shores of STRIFE. It was his disciple Peter, and he communicated to the Lord what he considered the Lord was about to walk out on. Here Peter attempted to correct the Lord on this course. The Bible shares, "Then Peter took him, and began to rebuke him, saying, be it far from thee, Lord: this shall not be unto thee" (Matthew 16:22). Suddenly, the gentle and kind Jesus revealed a nature of steel. Meaning He was unmovable in fulfilling the will of His Father. He was unshakable in His stance before the shores of strife. This was revealed because of what He stated to Peter. "He turned and said to Peter, get thee behind me, Satan: you are an offence unto me: for you are not concerned about the things of God, but of men" (Matthew 16:23). Jesus had frozen Peter in his tracks. To call Peter who was His disciple and friend "Satan" was something. But what we may miss in this exchange of words is not so much Him calling him Satan, but what characteristics reflected the nature of the evil one to Jesus, and that trait was him getting in the WAY of God.

Did you ever consider that getting in the way of God's will is considered STRIFE? We must consider that all strife gets in the way of God. Strife is just another word for being rebellious or resistant. It is a contentious spirit, meaning someone who always or most of the time must RESIST what is set. But this was the Son of God. The one who came to fulfill the law. He came to fulfill the prophecy of His coming as King. And because Jesus told Peter the truth about what that entailed, including giving Himself up to be crucified, Peter refused to accept that and decided to give Jesus an alternate route, not caring or realizing that this was not the will of God.

The application for us today is that we will confront those who have an alternate way in which they see life through Christ. They do not see life through the will of the Lord. They struggle with it, refuse it, and resist it, yet they offer what they call their input. Little do they know this input puts a blockage into their position to follow the author and finisher of their faith (Hebrews 12:2). When confronted with any type of strife, we must resemble the Lord and realize that this is not the will of God. When we are presented with any kind of strife, meaning an obstacle, it must be overcome, because it's in the way of pleasing the Lord of those who love the Lord with all their heart, and all soul, and all their mind (Mark 12:30). We must prove where we live by refusing to live on the Shores of STRIFE.

## Day 103

# BE CONSIDERATE

*"We who are strong must be considerate of those who are sensitive about things like this. We must not just please ourselves. We should help others do what is right and build them up in the Lord. For even Christ did not live to please himself. As the Scriptures say, 'The insults of those who insult you, O God, have fallen on me.'"* (Romans 15:1-3)

As Christians, we have responsibilities. Some are to God, some are for us, and some are for others. A mature child of God realizes all three responsibilities. The question is are you weak, or are you strong in the consideration of those three areas?

For the sake of the discussion, let us say you are strong. The divine duty of the strong is to consider the needs of all believers. If we are strong in the Lord, we must meet the needs of those who may be weak.

Our focal passage recognizes that there are those who are strong and there are those who are weak. But let us be real and honest and realize that sometimes the so-called alleged "strong" will look down on the weak. And, as a result, division, disunity, and discouragement has occupied territory of both the STRONG and WEAK!

The Bibles states in Galatians 6:2, "Bear one another's burdens, and so fulfill the law of Christ." If you consider yourself not to be among the weak, you should be CAREFUL so as not to be condescending, and you must bear the infirmities and SHORTCOMINGS of the weak.

We all have our infirmities, but the weak are more likely to suffer more than others. We must consider that about the weak and not put them down. We must encourage them and support them, and despite their infirmities and shortcomings, give them what has made us strong in the Lord and in the POWER of His might (Ephesians 6:10). Through their shortcomings, the weak may choose to judge or even to censure us, or maybe even speak evil of us. Nonetheless, we should learn to be patient with them and carry the reflection of Christ where He loves us with no conditions. We must learn to bear their weaknesses and console them. We cannot distance ourselves from them because Jesus was always intentional with the weak.

He bore the weaknesses of even His disciples. We too must also bear the infirmities of our fellow believers by empathizing with them (realizing it could have been us), showing genuine concern for helping them, and ministering strength to them with the love of the Lord.

Whatever is heavy on their spirits should never become the least of our concerns. The Bible states in I Thessalonians 5:14, "And we urge you, brothers, admonish the idle, encourage the fainthearted, help the weak, be patient with them all." Our maturity in Christ is not about US! It is about the Christ in us using us for His glory. Our goal is not about the pleasing of ourselves. Rather, we must please God by being a blessing to others. This is what it means to BE CONSIDERATE.

## Day 104

# UNCONDITIONAL GIVING

> *"Jesus sat down opposite the place where the offerings were put and watched the crowd putting their money into the temple treasury. Many rich people threw in large amounts. But a poor widow came and put in two small copper coins, worth only a few cents. Calling his disciples to him, Jesus said, 'Truly I tell you; this poor widow has put more into the treasury than all the others. They all gave out of their wealth; but she, out of her poverty, put in everything-all she had to live on.'"* (Mark 12:41-44)

How many remember the story of the little drummer boy who was at the birth of Christ and realized to himself he had no gifts to bring before the new King, so he decided to play his drum like never before? This was his gift. Today, people spend thousands of dollars to experience giving. For many, the after-effects of Christmas leave many in financial burdens and debt, all for the sake of buying gifts. I do believe we can learn a lot from the Little Drummer Boy. He gave what he HAD.

He knew that others were bringing more elaborate gifts before the presence of Jesus, but He gave from the heart. From our text, later in the life of Jesus Christ, He talked about this woman who gave all she had. She witnessed as others gave of their gain or excess, but she gave out of her heart. It was not based on surplus or calling the news to release to the world what she was giving. Because the Bible shares the rich threw in large amounts.

I remember as a child my parents would get me one gift for Christmas, but the kids in my community had a grip of toys and gifts they would show off and throw around in my face, attempting to make me feel bad because my parents only gave me the one gift. But here is the thing, I knew my parents gave from the heart. Why? Because that is what I always saw. I knew my parents were limited in funds. I knew they were on a fixed budget. I was simply happy to have a gift!

Today, kids get upset if the gift does not measure up to their standards. They get all twisted if it is not the right color, look, or make. The question is why? It is called being UNGRATEFUL, meaning unappreciative of whatever is given as a gift. This woman gave what the Bible calls only a few cents. The amount did not matter to Jesus. What matters is the way the giver gives. The Bible states in II Corinthians 9:7, "Every man according as he purposed in his heart, so let him give; not grudgingly, or of necessity: for God loveth a cheerful giver."

True giving is a condition of the heart not of your pocket. Therefore, Jesus says this about this woman, "Truly I tell you; this poor widow has put more into the treasury than all the others. They all gave out of their wealth; but she, out of her poverty, put in everything—all she had to live on." This woman gave out of her poverty, meaning she did not let what she did not have stop her from giving! And Jesus said she put more into the treasury than all others. How is that possible when all these rich and wealthy people were putting in gobs and gobs of money? Because she gave unconditionally. It was not based on the pocket; it was based on the heart.

## Day 105

# "HOLY"

*"Because it is written, 'YOU SHALL BE HOLY, FOR I AM HOLY.'"* (I Peter 1:16)

Believe it or not, it was the intent of God that we embody His nature of holiness. In fact, the scripture of focus describes, "Be Holy for I am Holy." It is as if God purposed and prepared man to resemble what is a function of our existence to Him.

The Bible also states in II Timothy 3:1-5, "This know also, that in the last days perilous times shall come. For men shall be … having a form of godliness but denying the power thereof."

In other words, there is a fake operation that will be at work, but it will lack POWER. True Holiness is not only a correlation to God, but it is power! Think about it. Most people do not even consider that Holiness is a statement of power.

Have you ever met a truly holy man or woman? There is a power in their godliness. If, however, one has never known a Christ-like soul, it becomes quite easy to fake Christianity. Remember this always, being false is NATURAL to the human heart; it is with much effort that we become TRUE.

Unless we are reaching for spiritual maturity, our immaturity shapes our perceptions of God. Often, we position ourselves to make statements like, "The Lord really doesn't require all that godliness." When this happens, we have compromised the standards of His kingdom. Whether we knew it or not, the moment we stop obeying God is when we start faking Christianity.

True holiness is not found in a Bible class or in attending church for 10 years straight. It is an operation of transformation, restoration, and rebirth. No wonder the Apostle shares, "I have been crucified with Christ; and it is no longer I who live, but Christ lives in me; and the life which I now live in the flesh I live by faith in the Son of God, who loved me and delivered Himself up for me" (Galatians 2:20). True Holiness is attained by denying our will and in the end submitting to His.

Living with any level of a false life is a sign of needing more deliverance from immaturity. When we are immature, we spiritually portray what we want to be and not what God demands that we become.

As we mature spiritually, we begin to realize that the Spirit of Christ is within us, that the cross is more than a necklace or a statue, but that it stands upright before us, confronting us with what Christ already died for on the Cross. The Cross is our access to true holiness. But always remember, true holiness is an identifiable power. If Christ is within us, we should be living holy, powerful lives. If we are not holy or if there is not the power of godliness in our lives, let us not blame God. As it is written, "Let

God be found true, though every man be found a liar" (Romans 3:4). It is God's will that we face ourselves with the truth of His word as it relates to what He envisioned. He created you and me to be like Himself, which is to be HOLY!

## Day 106

# DANCE!

*"And David DANCED before the LORD with all his might; and David was girded with a linen ephod."* (II Samuel 6:14)

Have you ever been in a great mood and one of your favorite songs comes on the radio as you are driving, and before you know it, your head is moving and your shoulders are swaying to the beat?

Dancing has everything to do with connection. Think about it. When we hear certain songs, it causes us to respond with reflection. When many are filled with joy and intimacy from the Lord, there is a response to "Dance before the Lord!" Today, my objective is to encourage us to move significantly closer to the Lord and become more passionate in our relationship with Him.

In our text today, there is some dancing going on. David danced before the LORD as the ark of God was being brought to Jerusalem. He praised God for this momentous occasion. It was not because his favorite song just came on. He danced because of something the Lord had done.

The Scriptures teach us that King David was a man after God's own heart. Despite his many faults, and he did have many, what David always wanted to do most was to please God. David was not a perfect man, but he was a passionate man about his God.

He was passionate as he played the harp to soothe King Saul's temperament whenever an evil spirit plagued Saul. He was passionate about preserving the honor of God and Israel when he slew the Philistine Giant Goliath. He was passionate in his devotion to his friend Jonathan, Saul's son, and even though Saul tried to kill David, he remained passionate about honoring Saul as King of Israel. David was indeed a passionate man. He was passionate on the battlefield as he slew tens of thousands of the Philistine army. David was a passionate poet as he wrote over 100 psalms praising God in the good times and lamenting the bad times, but through it all, David honored God for being God.

What was the prompting that moved David to dance on this special occasion? David and most of Israel were excited because the ark of the Lord had finally been brought home to Jerusalem. The ark of the Lord was significant because it represented the very PRESENCE of God on earth. The ark of the Lord had been away from the heart of Israel, in Kirjathjearim, for twenty years. That is a long time to be in a spiritual DROUGHT! Twenty years is a long time to have the presence of the LORD away from your faith of community.

When God's presence has lost connection with you, it prompts the loss of spiritual FOCUS. When you do not witness God's presence, you begin to fear the people, the problems, and the pain more than you fear God. When God is no longer in your camp (heart), you will lose BATTLES. David, a man after God's own heart, knew the value of the ark of the Lord. David knew the value of God's presence. So shortly after David becomes King, he goes to get the ark of the Lord, and as he leads the processional of Israelites into Jerusalem, he DANCES before the Lord!

## Day 107

# "Moving Past Survive to THRIVE"

I am sure I am not the only one who has heard the saying, "I'm just surviving," which gives the impression that one is just getting by or just getting along. We may have missed that our created intent in God's new creation was not just to survive, but to THRIVE! When God released His GLORY of His SON, He also delivered what is called a NEW CREATION (II Corinthians 5:17). This new creation comes with ability to possess a Christ-like operation, a Christ-like mind, and possess the seal of the Holy Spirit. But for many, unless we GROW UP in Christ, we will find ourselves with having Christ but only surviving. It is like having a thoroughbred colt that one day could enter the Kentucky Derby, but because the colt had no specific training as to who he was, His outcome was impacted by it.

When Christ died on the CROSS, that death brought not only life to those that would embrace it, but it brought forth a life beyond our previous one. In fact, the text says, "Old things are done away behold all things are new." So, this new life creates a passage where we blast past the OLD THINGS.

The intent of Christ was to get us off the treadmill of rehashing the old man, which for many is a place we call "I can't," "It's hard," "It's too big!" Throughout the ministry of Christ, His mind revealed moving past where we have never ventured before. No wonder He said, "If you have the faith of a mustard seed, you could say to this mountain be moved, and it would move" (Mark 11:23). Jesus wanted His new creation to THRIVE. The term "old man" in the Bible is beyond our old faults and failures. It is way past our doubts and defeats. This term "old man" means the CARNAL MAN, or the sinful man. The challenge for most of us is we are totally unaware that the sinful man is really a lifestyle. Therefore, for many to walk in the land of thriving, they find it overwhelming, because the sin life is a life that flows in a place called survive.

Think about it. Sin is a condition that when traced all the way back to Adam and Eve, after sin was released, they lost something with God. His protection, His power, and His presence. They now were forced to deal with pain and problems, and instead of thriving, they learned to SURVIVE. Before the fall, they had the ability to THRIVE. Most people when they think of sin assume primarily that one has been bad or his or her conduct is unbecoming. That is true, but sin in the eyes of God is not following His Plan or His WORD. In fact, it is when we resist, rebel, and refuse to accept His Plan and pursue ours, the Bible says, "It is not in man to direct his own steps" (Jeremiah 10:23).

If man cannot direct his future, then our futures have been purposed by the creator. The reason Jesus became what is known as the second Adam (I Corinthians 15:45-47) is to set us back into the designated place He created, which is to have dominion (Genesis 1:26-28). When we walk in dominion, we live in power! So, our course is to unchain ourselves from the old man. Romans 6:6 says, "Knowing this, that our old self was crucified with Him, in order that our body of sin might be done away with, so that we would no longer be slaves to sin." When we crucify the old man, which is sin, we move past it to be FREE to THRIVE!

## Day 108

# "PURSUE PEACE... WITH ALL MEN"

In difficult moments, most of us vacate peace and we are more prone to react with retaliation, rebellion, and resistance.

You may ask why this is, and the reason is because PEACE is a part of the nature of God. It is not natural to operate in peace, its supernatural. Jesus is called the Prince of Peace because it is a part of His identity.

The thing is, we cannot manufacture peace without the presence of God. Without peace, we function in turmoil, friction, and animosity.

When there is no peace, then there is conflict. Therefore, the Bible shares, "Pursue peace will all men" (Hebrews 12:14), in other words, peace must be pursued.

Once we truly possess the peace of God and obtain it, we then can aggressively take the initiative to make things as they should be, which means we act on behalf Heaven's Son rather than allowing anger and division and separation to serve the pit of hell.

Often conflict is normal in our society. Many become so comfortable with conflict as an operating force that they expect it, anticipate it, and create it. In fact, a trauma induced situation throughout our society is happening on so many levels and in so many lives that a great many of those impacted by it do their best to avoid it on every turn.

The problem with that is this—conflict is inevitable in life. We cannot escape conflict, but we can PURSUE PEACE! Jesus never ran from conflict because He was PEACE. To offer peace in a conflicted world, you must personally possess it.

I have heard it said, "You are what you PURSUE!" As people of the Most High God, we reveal what pushes us and what pulls us in different directions. Yet Jesus said, "Peace I leave with you" (John 14:27). In other words, peace is already available. Peace is already accessible. Jesus left PEACE for us to establish restoration, revival, and renewal. There is no greater place where this is needed then in dealing with men.

## Day 109

# SELF-RIGHTEOUSNESS

In the time of Jesus, to those who were confident of their own righteousness and looked down on everybody else, Jesus told this parable, "Two men went up to the temple to pray, one a Pharisee and the other a tax collector. The Pharisee stood up and prayed about himself: 'God, I thank you that I am not like other men—robbers, evildoers, adulterers—or even like this tax collector. I fast twice a week and give a tenth of all I get.' But the tax collector stood at a distance. He would not even look up to heaven, but beat his breast and said, 'God, have mercy on me, a sinner.' I tell you that this man, rather than the other, went home justified before God. For everyone who exalts himself will be humbled, and he who humbles himself will be exalted" (Luke 18:10-15).

To be self-righteous is to view one's life through a personal set of lenses instead of viewing life through the lenses of God and His word. To be self-righteous is to view yourself as something better than the crowd. You criticize those that are broken, hurting, tripping, or maybe just LOST. Jesus made it plain when He said, "It is not the healthy who need a doctor, but the sick. I have not come to call the righteous, but sinners" (Mark 2:17).

Self-righteous individuals are often intolerant of the opinions and behaviors of others. They avoid and invade those that are controversial. They shy away from people, problems, and predicaments that push them to be seen as awkward with those that are different, difficult, and maybe just in the DARK.

The Lord called us to go into dark places, which means with people who are struggling, rejected, and abandoned. The Bible says, "Do all things without complaining and disputing, that you may become blameless and harmless, children of God without fault in the midst of crooked and perverse generation among whom you shine as LIGHTS in the world" (Philippians 2:14-15).

Being self-righteous can sneak in and be so subtle. When we complain about how people live, act, talk, or just exist, remember Jesus said while dying on the cross, "Father forgive them for they know not what they do" (Luke 23:34). In other words, He knew they needed the TRUTH. Not to just be told the truth, but for someone to live in the TRUTH. That is why we must STAND-OUT and SHINE!

Sure, we may say, "I'm not self-righteous," but every time we struggle with going where God has called us to go into the whole world (Mark 16:15), which includes the challenging, chaotic, or perhaps the even corrupt, we must ask God to help us to humble ourselves.

## Day 110

# "TURNING FAILURES INTO FULFILLMENT"

*"And Moses said unto God, Who am I, that I should go unto Pharaoh, and that I should bring forth the children of Israel out of Egypt?"* (Exodus 3:11)

Did you know before Moses became the man that followed God, he was a man that was being shaped and molded by the Egyptian school system? The Bible states in Acts 7:22, Moses had grown to be a "man of power in words and deeds." Whether we knew it or not, Moses was a significant leader of the Egyptian way of life and leadership. Yet when He was confronted with God to take on the mantle of leadership to serve God now at the ripe age of 80 years old, he responded to God with, "Please, Lord, I have never been eloquent, neither recently nor in time past, nor since You have spoken to Your servant; for I am slow of speech and slow of tongue" (Exodus 4:10). Come on Moses! What do you mean you have never been eloquent? Have you ever met someone who said something like "NEVER" even though you knew it was in their past? Whenever words like these are released from someone, they are telling you that their PAST was so devasting and difficult that all they can remember is FAILURE.

Moses was a successful man in the life as a Prince of Egypt. Yet now at the age of 80 years old, all he could see in himself was someone who couldn't speak correctly, had a problem with confidence apparently, and saw himself in what appears to be a depressed state. Think for a moment that God did not come to Moses when he was riding high as the prince in Egypt, but he came to him in the condition where he thought of himself as insignificant.

I can only imagine the very word "EGYPT" most likely made Moses numb. I mean, he did run and flee from this nation because he was hunted as a murderer (Exodus 2:12). He was an outcast. I am sure deep down as he ran from everything that was connected to his life, he dealt with rejection, abandonment, and a lost identity. Then He encountered God who asked him to return to the place where all that came from! Moses feared returning to the place of his humiliation. Yet God had not called him to be a part of His PAST, but to move into the role of his FUTURE, now as a servant of God.

To be a servant, one does not need be eloquent, but obedient. Have you ever considered that God has His own timing to reveal His specific will towards your life? The Lord waited until Moses was in this specific place to use him for His glory. Some of us are trying to move God when all along He is waiting on us to become pliable, useable, and willing to surrender to His purpose. Do not let your failures, weaknesses, and the PAST keep you from stepping into what God has appointed over your life. Age, time, and location has nothing to do with what God can do! Moses was 80 years old, separated by Egypt by many years, and a father, a husband, and a Shepherd just trying to cope and survive. But God's will was to go way beyond just surviving. Moses was just getting by. I hear people say this all the time, "I'm just surviving," or "I'm just making it." Moses was not in a place of PURPOSE but a place of POVERTY. The spirit of poverty is not about money but about a mindset. It means in your mind you see lack, emptiness, and struggle. It does not matter at this moment where you are. What matters is who you have encountered that can alter how you see your FAILURES and turn them into His FULFILLMENT.

## Day 111

# "WALK THIS WAY"

*"Therefore I, the prisoner of the Lord, implore you to walk in a manner worthy of the calling with which you have been called, with all humility and gentleness, with patience, showing tolerance for one another in love, being diligent to preserve the unity of the Spirit in the bond of peace."*
(Ephesians 4:1-3)

When we consider what walking is, we typically view it as simply taking one step, then another, then another… but walking in the Bible deals with LIVING. The term "living" defines your character and your conduct. In fact, the writer went on to add that this worthy walk be one "with all humility and gentleness, with patience, showing tolerance for one another, and being diligent to preserve the unity of the Spirit in the bond of peace." This special impartation of the Word exposes the urging from the Spirit of God to live in such a way that it is worthy of your calling (your vocation/assignment). In other words, walk appropriately to what God has purposed for your life!

Ever since my military days, I have been told that I have a walk that is distinguishable. In other words, it stands out. Whether I am with a group or being seen from a distance, friends and family have told me that my walk gives me away. Spiritually, we must embrace the truth of how we live and conclude that it will always connect us with what we are rooted in and established with. So, how is your walk? The word for "worthy" is the word "axios" in Greek. It refers to the intrinsic value of something. The Lord desired a walk that had a VALUE to it. In the Third Millennium Bible, our text reads like this, "In light of all this, here's what I want you to do. While I am locked up here, a prisoner for the Master, I want you to get out there and walk—better yet, run on the road God called you to travel!" What a powerful illustration of what kind of walk the Lord truly desires! The plan for our walk with Him is to excel and reach places where we can witness an intensity.

One of things we witness when we walk in Christ is that in time, we pick up speed, progress, and tenacity in this walk. Notice that the Bible shares, "Walk with humility, gentleness, and patience, showing tolerance for one another in love." When we walk His way, there is an intended outcome where we witness the fruit of the Father. Walking out humility, gentleness, and patience, and showing tolerance for another in love is developed in the Spirit.

Here is the deal, a lot of people have been walking in regret, rebellion, and resistance to the will of God. Every time we live (or walk) in rage, revenge, and walk in pride, we build an inner operation that reveals itself in our outer existence among the world. Who we claim to be is really being seen by how we WALK IT OUT! I heard a story about a young man who was determined to win the affection of a lady who refused to even talk to him anymore. He decided that the way to her heart was through the mail, so he began writing her love letters. He wrote a love letter every day to this lady. Six or seven times a week she got a love letter from him. When she did not respond, he increased his output to three notes every twenty-four hours. In all, he wrote her more than seven hundred letters. Guess what? She wound up marrying the postman. This man penned his love through letters, but never showed it; however, the postman did. We must learn to walk out the image of Christ. Today I encourage you to WALK THIS WAY!

*Day 112*

# 20 Feet Tall

*"Then the people shouted when the horns were blown. As soon as the people heard the horn and shouted a great war cry, the wall fell flat. After that, the people went up into the city, each one straight ahead, and they captured the city."*
(Joshua 6:20)

Have you ever faced an obstacle that seemed overwhelming and unsurmountable? For some of us, we face walls in life that come in all forms such as cancer, marital upheaval, job loss, money woes, and even death in the family. These are some of the most significant walls, but for others, their walls vary from personal confusion, conflict, and chaos. In our story, we have who are known as the children of Israel. Otherwise known as the Israelites. They were God's promised people. But as a promised people, they were required to trust the promise keeper, which was Jehovah God. As His people, they were given instructions to face a people that were surrounded by walls that were over

20 feet tall. Some experts say exceedingly over 26 feet! Yet God had planned for His people to not only face this great wall but believe in His word on the method that would be required to unfold His will.

Listen to what Jehovah tells Joshua, "You and your fighting men are to march around the city. March around it once each day for six days. Carry the ark of the covenant with you. Seven priests should walk ahead of it and blow their horns. On the seventh day you should march around the city SEVEN times. Then give a long sound on the HORNS and have EVERYONE SHOUT with a great war cry. And the WALLS will FALL down FLAT!" (Joshua 6:1-25). Reflect for a moment and consider all these people were in one accord not only doing what God required for seven straight days but marching around a great city that was well protected. It was a fortified city. They were ready to apparently handle any battle. But this was the Lord's battle. There was no banging on the wall or attempting to climb over the wall. All that was required from the people of God was to TRUST the Lord!

Too often we rush into our own personal situations not considering that our battles are His battles. Why would God call us overcomers (I John 5:4-5), victors (Deuteronomy 20:4), ambassadors (II Corinthians 5:20), and conquerors (Romans 8:37), if He didn't see us in the capacity of knocking down what gets in the way? But not only just in the way, but what gets in the way of His purpose in your life. Often, when we face a roadblock or barrier in life, we attempt to go around it, look for another entrance, or just give up. But this wall came down because of the obedience of heeding the voice of God. No matter the size or height of whatever you face in life, your battles are really His battles. That is if we are willing to follow His word.

I mean walking around this great city seven times led to what most looked like a BOMB just went off. This battle was won when the people submitted to carry out the will of God. Today we may be missing how to demolish the 20 feet barriers in our lives that can collapse right in front of us because we have not accepted to follow the instructions of the Lord. Jesus said, "if you love me you will keep my commandments" (John 14:15). Jesus does not want to twist our arms and make us heed His word. When we OBEY, there is OUTCOME! Even if it is 20 FEET TALL.

## Day 113

# "SQUEEZED"

For many of us, I am sure we can seize a moment in life where it appeared like life was putting its tight grips on us, whether it be because of guilt, grief, or just the grind of life. For most of us, when we encounter one of these moments, we call it PRESSURE.

You might be going through some type of pressure right now, but I want to minister to you that if you are that person, consider this reality that experiencing pain and problems as children of the Most High God, the Word of God says that you are experiencing pressure now so that you can progress in life and become spiritually successful. The Bible says, "I will bring the one-third through the fire, will refine them as silver is refined, and test them as gold is tested. They will call on my name, and I will answer. I will say, this is my people and each one will say the lord is my God" (Zechariah 13:9).

Every day, people are experiencing pressure in every area of life, from friends and family, colleagues at work and so on. Often when we are trying to get ourselves out from one problem, another one rears its ugly head. As we are sorting one issue, people seem to bring out another to be resolved. Did you know that God sometimes allows problems in our lives so that we can experience breakthrough and become closer to Him? Remember also that God says, "I will not give to you much than you can bear" (I Corinthians 10:13).

You are being pressurized so that you can experience the glory of God in your life. The Lord says again, "I will bring you through the fire" (Isaiah 43:2), meaning you shall not die in your predicaments. Often, we allow the circumstance that we encounter to define how we will be defeated. For some, who we have become is because of what we face instead of becoming who we are because of what we have endured! Jesus said, "He that endures until the end shall be saved" (Matthew 24:13). Endurance has an outcome called DELIVERANCE.

We are bound to go through pressure in many ways as long as we have chosen to serve the Lord and Jesus Christ. We will certainly experience problems in our lives, and the enemy will wage war against us as long as we are a threat to the kingdom of the devil, because we and our households have chosen to serve the Lord Almighty.

I want you to change how you see pressure in the Spirit and understand that it is designed to squeeze out the treasure in you. Romans 5:3 says, "We glory in tribulations." Really? Sounds outside of human nature, right? Because it is. This is a divine nature reality! The rest of the verse says, "We glory in tribulation knowing that it produces perseverance, character, and hope." As we "serve the Lord with gladness," pressure will always PRODUCE something! Problems can refine us as silver and gold, and the result of God's supernatural glory is that we come out shining for the Lord. People want to be blessed but are afraid to go through anything. We all want something good in our lives but are we prepared to be SQUEEZED to see what comes out?

# Day 114

# LIVING IN NEWNESS

If for whatever reason something has taken your mind and heart towards your issues, your problems, and perhaps even a current loss, I want to extend to you that God loves you! You may say, "But CJ if God loves me, why I am going through what I am going through?" Circumstances and situations do not dictate or determine if God loves you. If we live based on circumstances, then who we are is based on what we go through. During whatever we are going through proves that we love Him.

Job said, "Thou He slay yet will I trust Him." In other words, no matter what manifests in my life, the trust I have in the Lord supersedes it. As a husband, I will go through stormy weather conditions where my wife will still have to TRUST in me. No matter what we face in this life, the Bible says, "TRUST in the Lord at all times."

In John 15:18-19, Jesus said, "If the world hates you, ye know that it hated me before it hated you. If ye were of the world, the world would love his own: but because ye are not of the world, but I have chosen you out of the world, therefore the world hateth you." Wait a minute Jesus, the world hates me? Why would the world hate me? Better yet, what truly is the world? The Greek biblical meaning of the word "world" is "kletos." It conveys the idea of refusing the invitation of the kingdom by the gospel.

Let us get something straight about HATE; it is an emotional response where a person opposes and detests a thing. That thing the world hates is the Word of God! Proverbs 1:29 says, "They hated knowledge and did not choose the fear of the LORD." That knowledge that the proverb writer was referring to is the Word of God! Jesus again said, "If you were of the world, the world would LOVE his own: but because you are not of the WORLD, but I have CHOSEN you out of the world the world hates you" (John 15:19). Your created intent in Christ is beyond the knowledge of this world. That is why the Bible shares, "If anyone is in Christ, He is new creation; old things have been passed away behold all things have become new" (II Corinthians 5:17). The benefits of being in Christ is always awakening NEWNESS!

Remember Jesus talked about putting NEW wine into old wineskins? How about when Isaiah said, "NEW things I declare to you" (Isaiah 42:9)? The Lord is in the business of delivering new things, and the spirit of the world is opposed to it. Today though, more and more people are inclined to trust everything but God. We trust in the news, we trust the stock market, and we trust our political system. Ladies and Gentlemen, the world is changing, but Jesus is the ultimate change agent. He came to change everything, while everything is trying to change YOU! Luke 5:32 says, "He came to call people to repentance." This is change. Let me also add that repentance is about welcoming the NEW. Repentance in any generation will change the generation!

Repentance is the expression of NEWNESS. It is the opportunity to leave what may want to reside inside, but true repentance is a spiritual change or new directions for your soul where you remove the things that have grown horribly in your life and begin to plant the life where you spring forth into the wonderful life in God.

## Day 115

# "What Is Your Form in God?"

*"This know also, that in the last days perilous times shall come. For men shall have a FORM of godliness but denying the power thereof."* (2 Timothy 3:1,5)

Whether we knew it or not, true holiness possesses power. Have you ever met a truly holy man or woman? There is a power in their godliness. Unless we are reaching and seeking for spiritual maturity, our immaturity shapes our perceptions of God. Shaping is really a sense of forming. Think about a diamond. Seldom do we consider that for a diamond to be formed there must be some intense shaping.

In becoming like God, we must understand that God is making us like Him. This process is a process of ELIMINATION. What we are eliminating is everything that godliness is not. When we are being formed into godliness, we must first take under consideration that godliness is really to be God-like. It is possessing the characteristics of God. For some, when they hear things like this, they see this as being impossible. But the Bible states in I Corinthians 11:1, "Imitate me as I imitate Christ."

To imitate anything is to follow it to the point that it becomes recognizable in your life. The Bible states in Titus 1:1, "I have been sent to proclaim faith to those God has chosen and to teach them to know the truth that shows them how to live in godliness." The truth of God's word transforms us into people who look like God! When God created us, He really wanted us to not just look like Him but to ACT like Him. Jesus said in John 17:17, "Sanctify them by Your truth. Your word is truth." In other words, the word has the power to sanctify or make you like God. Peter tells us, "Since you have purified your souls in obeying the truth through the Spirit in sincere love of the brethren, love one another fervently with a pure heart" (I Peter 1:22). The truth will purify us.

Our forming is a process of purification and sanctification that is manifested because we allow the Word of God to influence the totality of our spiritual lives. Forming into godliness is not incidentally or accidentally. It is not something that happens because you go to church or worship every opportunity, but it is accomplished because you allow the Word of God to have jurisdiction in more territory of your soul! No wonder Jesus said in Luke 6:46, "Why call me Lord Lord and DO NOT the things that I SAY." Whenever Jesus speaks, He is releasing His word, which is the agent of witnessing a transformation in our lives. Godliness is not something we put on to impress or please others, yet the godly believer is known by his or her works or fruits. The fruit of the Spirit is the evidence of the works of a godly Christian.

In fact, Jesus said, "By your fruit you are known." Fruit is the EVIDENCE of what God is creating and forming in one's life. Godliness is what Titus 2:7 said is "pattern of good works." A pattern is something that someone follows to become or to be like. It is to model. A pattern of good works is just the evidence of godliness. Today, before you take another step in your spiritual life, I challenge you to look at the evidence or FRUIT. I encourage you to observe, what is your FORM of God?

*Day 116*

# DELIGHT

*"Delight yourself also in the Lord, and He shall give you the desires of your heart."* (Psalms 37:4 NKJV)

We all have deep longings and desires towards something, but due to the circumstances of life, many of these so-called desires are not coming out the way we had hoped for or wanted. For some, these unfulfilled desires foster frustrations. For others, anguish and depression begins to creep in when unfulfilled desires are recognized. Solomon said, "Hope deferred makes the heart sick, but when the desire comes, it is a tree of life" (Proverbs 13:12). Here in our passage, King David said, "Delight yourself also in the Lord, and He shall give you the desires of your heart" (Psalms 37:4). But with everything that goes on in this life, this is where our faith then meets the promises of God. The key to keep moving beyond the unfulfilled is to truly TRUST the spoken word to the point that we begin to LIVE it. You may say, "This sounds simple enough, but I have waited, and waited and God still hasn't come through yet!"

As believers, we are to trust in verses like this, but for many, behind our smiling faces and exterior images reveals a frustrated interior of unfulfilled desires. We miss a major point of emphasis with this word from Proverbs, and that is, we must properly gage our DELIGHT in the Lord! So, the question is how do you acquire delight in the Lord? Here it is, "Commit your way to the Lord, trust also in Him, and He shall bring it to pass" (Psalms 37:5). But what is God going to bring to pass? "He shall bring forth your righteousness as the light, and your justice as the noonday" (Psalms 37:6). God will give us the desires of our hearts when we commit ourselves to fully follow Him and delight ourselves in Him rather than in what the world has to offer. God will give us the desires of our hearts when the desires of our hearts match His, that is, when it brings forth righteousness and justice. My righteousness is to become His RIGHTEOUSNESS! No wonder Jesus said, "Seek ye first the kingdom of God and all His righteousness and all these things will be given to you as well" (Matthew 6:33). God will give us the desires of our hearts when the desires of our hearts are in accordance with God's purpose in making a kingdom impact.

A young injured soldier crippled from the war wrote, "I asked for strength that I might achieve. I was made weak that I might obey. I asked for health that I might do greater things. I was given infirmity that I might do better things. I asked for riches that I might be happy. I was given poverty that I might be wise. I asked for power that I might have the praise of men. I was given weakness that I might feel the need for God. I asked for all things that I might enjoy life. I was given life that I might enjoy all things. I have received nothing I asked for; and in all that I hoped for, my prayers have been answered."

During our frustrating and our terrible situations we face, God will give us wisdom to deal with them. Our problem is that we live in a culture that believes it can fix everything, that it has a cure for whatever ails us, and the remedy is to be quick, painless, and inexpensive. God grants the desires of our heart, but not always in the way we want; rather it is in the way God ordains so His righteousness can shine through us to this darkened world. God's delight is that we become what He envisioned. That is, "Partakers of His Divine Nature" (II Peter 1:4). In other words, living a godly life will be far more satisfying than any other lifestyle! By doing so, we discover that pleasing the Lord is far more ETERNALLY beneficial than anything else! This is how you DELIGHT yourself in the Lord.

## Day 117

# "Learn of Me"

*"Take my yoke upon you and LEARN OF ME; for I am meek and lowly in heart: and ye shall find rest unto your souls."* (Matthew 11:29)

Someone said, "The bigger I grow in God, the smaller I become." What a concept. Today most people conclude that size matters in every capacity. Whether its possessions, popularity, or power, we equate success with how big anything is.

Jesus said, "Learn of Me; for I am meek and lowly in heart" (Matthew 11:29 KJV). Jesus is the holiest, most powerful voice, yet He described Himself as "meek and lowly in heart." Today, I want you to understand that holiness is the product of grace, and God gives grace only to the humble. So, our quest is to possess true humility. If we truly have a desire to be close to the Lord, it requires that we know that He resists the proud, but His grace is drawn to the humble (James 4:6). Humility brings grace to our need, and grace alone can change our hearts. Humility is the infrastructure of our transformation to be like Him and to be close to Him. God is so concerned about our phase development of humility that He allows the Holy Spirit to reveal our sinful condition. Not to condemn us or leave us walking in guilt, but on the contrary… to establish humility and to deepen the knowledge of our personal need for grace.

All of this leads us to what I call "PERSONAL PURITY." In truth, God created us to function and flow like Him, but our flesh nature (the toxic nature) always attempts to stifle the sifting of the Lord. Spiritual sifting is about removing what is not needed. When a baker sifts wheat, the objective is to spread and separate what is needed from what is not.

Our pursuit for purity begins with our determined commitment to open our hearts and not the refusal to hide from the current condition of our hearts. When we open our hearts, we are allowing the sifting to commence. We also discover that this causes us to HUMBLY yield to the truth of what we need. When we push away or hide away what revelation has been revealed, we are then personally convinced we do not need sifting, not realizing that this process opens the door to great grace!

In my past, I have found for myself that when I review all those that have hurt me, I exhausted all the energy in the world to find fault in those that hurt me, not realizing that this interrupts my "PERSONAL PURITY." The reason why is because the personal sifting has ceased, and now my intentions looks at the conditions of others, and not my own! In addition, we also miss the true heart of the humble. Remember Jesus said, "I will never desert you, nor will I ever forsake you." Wait a minute… Jesus are you saying you will not desert me even if I really want to desert you? True humility is not stuck on self. True humility accepts the conditions of oneself and at the same time the conditions of others. No wonder Jesus said, "He who is without sin among you, let him be the first to throw a stone" (John 8:7). I am not saying we cannot speak out about something that is wrong, but when we pursue looking for an outcome with the spirit of humility, then our objective is for God! Therefore, Jesus again said, "Learn of Me; for I am meek and lowly in heart."

## Day 118

# "REJOICE: AGAIN AND AGAIN!"

*"Rejoice in the Lord always; again, I will say, rejoice!"*
(Philippians 4:4)

Today we are prone to focus so much more on our problems than our divine PURPOSE! It is quite shocking to see so many people wallow and flounder in their problems when there is a plethora of areas that demand that we give God our praise. Little do we realize, when we soak our minds and hearts on our problems, we have just bathed our lives in unbelief. We wonder why the non-Christians do not run to give their lives to Christ. Perhaps the obstacle is not what exists in their hearts but what is in ours. Yes, we accepted Christ as Savior and gave Him our sins, but have we truly given Him our lives? In other words, do you believe and foresee your life in Christ based on circumstances, or do you live in Christ according to the author and finisher of your faith?

Often our so-called gloomy perspective on life negates what we claim we have in life according to Christ. The Lord desires to rescue us from the gloomy, unbelieving attitudes. He wants us to cancel our plans to be miserable and submit ourselves into His loving, wonderful hands. I understand that fear continues to fill the world with terrorism, death, poverty, and sickness. But the Lord plans on something different for us! In fact, He orders us, "Arise, shine; for your light has come." He tells us that His literal glory, which is now abiding within us, will "appear upon" us. The result? "Nations will come to your light, and kings to the brightness of your rising" (Isaiah 60:1-3).

When Scripture says, "The glory of the LORD will rise upon you," it is saying the GOODNESS of the Lord will be seen upon you. In other words, in contrast to the world all around, you will be one chosen to reveal how good God is. This is something that is worth rejoicing again and again! In our passage where the Apostle states, "Rejoice in the Lord always; again, I will say rejoice," he also adds, "For the Lord is near" (Philippians 4:5). Believe it or not, the Lord is not talking about the second coming but about how He is near to our spirits. He is near to our time of need. No wonder the Bible states, "God is our refuge and strength, an ever-present help in trouble" (Psalms 46:1). The Lord is always near!

Since this is the case, God is always in position for my good, and even when things are not good, He works them out for my good. This is my spiritual mindset. I must always trust the Lord! Even if the latest so-called "time" in my life is full of twists and turns, I know where my help comes from! We must make the choice to rejoice. Too many of us are cynics. Cynicism, contrary to popular opinion, is not a gift of the Holy Spirit. A cynic is a habitual doubter. He is always negative, expecting the worst, and probing for the worst when there is nothing negative visibly on the surface. Ultimately, a cynic will always discover something that confirms his or her expectations. My Spiritual Mentor, Adrian Taylor, told me once, "If you allow the enemy to take your joy, he'll also take your strength." Once our so-called strength is depleted, we are susceptible to giving up and giving in to anything that we do not have the strength to face. So today, I say rejoice again and again!

## Day 119

# "HUNGRY?"

*"Blessed are those who hunger and thirst for righteousness, for they will be filled."* (Matthew 5:6)

Today, many Christians have lost their hunger for God. Instead of coming into the Lord's presence hungry for more of His fullness, our thoughts are being held hostage to pursuits and distractions of the flesh. At best, we are merely curious about spiritual realities, but not truly hungry.

Let me elaborate on my point. Recently I witnessed that a survey stated that a great percentage of our nation believes in God, yet when asked how often they participate in a consistent operation that feeds into their spiritual lives, the shocking conclusion was the percentages dropped dramatically.

The reality on why we have lost an appetite for continual substance for the Lord is due mainly because our appetites have shifted for another kind of meal. This craving has captivated our desires so much that for many we settle for small portions and miniature snack size morsels of the presence of God!

Jesus said, "Blessed are those who hunger and thirst for righteousness, for they will be filled" (Matthew 5:6). Having a hunger for righteousness is what the Lord desired for His children. Keep in mind, our righteousness is as filthy rags if not for Him making us partakers of His righteousness. The Bible shares in II Corinthians 5:21, "For our sake he made him to be sin who knew no sin, so that in him we might become the righteousness of God."

Because we were made by the righteousness of God, the Lord wants every believer to want MORE! In fact, in this chapter of Matthew, Jesus quotes at least five times about righteousness. For example, in verse ten Jesus states, "Blessed are those who are persecuted for righteousness' sake, for theirs is the kingdom of heaven." In verse three He states, "Blessed are the poor in spirit, for theirs is the kingdom of heaven." What we may have overlooked is the fact that verse three really highlights that we are supposed to be truly HUNGRY.

This verse is about someone who is starving in the spirit, meaning someone who has a constant NEED of the Lord. Notice that Jesus shares that when we long for Him like a missed meal that the outcome is "The Kingdom." What is the Kingdom? It is God's way of doing things. It is the domain of His power, His purpose, His presence, His plan, and His productivity in our lives! The Kingdom is ours if we can have a consuming NEED for the Lord.

Unlike the Snicker's commercial that states, "You're not YOU when you're hungry," we must evaluate we are not like God when we have lost the appetite for RIGHTEOUSNESS.

Many are CURIOUS about God instead of being CONSUMED by God. The Lord is looking for hungry people. Blessed are they who hunger. He is seeking for a people who are truly seeking Him. Those that have a hunger that will not quench for His presence will possess a bread from Heaven that is always eternally SATISFYING!

## Day 120

# "Thinking Like God"

*"You are a stumbling block to me. You think as men think, not as God thinks."* (Matthew 16:23)

I am a firm believer that most of the roadblocks in this life are taking place because of how we THINK. Consider this—most people who struggle with their emotions do not understand that their thinking has everything to do with their ability to change their emotions.

Jesus said that when we think like men, we stumble. How we think and what we think is important. Wrong thinking trips us up. We need a new way of thinking; we need to think as God thinks!

God is the God of the possible. So, He thinks about the POSSIBLE! Impossible is not found in his vocabulary, and impossibility does not exist in his universe (Matthew 19:26). Everything is possible when you think the way God thinks. God is the SOURCE of all good THINGS. All that you are or have comes directly or indirectly from Him. There are no shortages in God's kingdom of love.

Everything that you need to live an abundant life is already present and available for those who think as God thinks. So, how does God think?

God thinks ABUNDANCE. Jesus said that He had come so that you might have life and have it more abundantly (John 10:10). God created the world and everything in it. What you need is no big deal to God. Supplying your needs will not break His back or bankrupt His kingdom. God enjoys giving you good things. His plan is to fill your cup with blessings until it runs over!

God thinks POSITIVE. The most positive force in the universe is God's love. It changes the way you think and creates a mindset that reflects Christ himself. No wonder the Bible says, "Let this MIND be in YOU that was also in Christ Jesus" (Philippians 2:5).

God's thinking has… EXPECTATIONS. When you get into agreement with God, your expectations change. Impossible becomes possible, and scarcity becomes abundance. God has a powerful positive plan for your life. God expects good things to happen in your life when you think the way He thinks.

God thinks FORGIVENESS. God forgives you for the wrong things that you have done (I John 1:9). He not only wipes the slate clean; He also throws the slate away!

God thinks FREEDOM, whether you are held captive over your past or captive from some outside influence (Luke 4:18). Jesus came to set free those that are held in their own prisons of the heart. He desires to remove the chains of lack and limitation when we think the way God thinks!

## Day 121

# "MOVING OUT THE SPIRIT OF MAMMON"

Over the past few years, I had the opportunity to read the book entitled *The Blessed Life* by Robert Morris. What a revelation God exposed to me on so many levels. For one, I realized that there is a spirit at work that draws people to it, who is called the spirit of MAMMON. This is not a word commonly used today in our society, but is nevertheless spoken in the Word of God on numerous occasions. What we discover about the spirit of Mammon is that this spirit specifically attacks the child of God. This spirit's objective is to impact the church in such a way that the body of Christ (the people) become something that resembles the characteristics of this spirit of Mammon.

What is Mammon? Well for starters it is in direct contrast with God. In fact, it is a spirit connected with the plots of the devil. Mammon says "buy and keep," while God says "sow and reap." Mammon says "cheat and steal," and God says "give and receive." The spirit of Mammon is filled with constant STRESS, constant STRUGGLES, and constant SUFFERING. Here is the reason why—Mammon is looking for servants, and it wants to rule your life and take the place of God (Luke 16:13). Mammon controls your thoughts and dreams where it is a consuming force that strives to be your form of worship. In other words, it occupies your thoughts and your time.

Mammon promises only what God can offer such as security, stability, and significance. But one thing always stands when the spirit of Mammon has jurisdiction in your life, everything is TEMPORAL! While on the other hand, God is about fruit "that shall REMAIN" (John 15:16). Mammon and God are on the opposite ends of the spectrum. Mammon is about selfishness, and God is about generosity. Mammon is an Aramaic word, which means consumption in riches. Money either has God's spirit on it or it has the Mammon spirit on it. Jesus said, "You can't serve God and mammon."

If we think that money can solve our problems instead of God, then the spirit of Mammon has already influenced us. Mammon has its roots in Babylon, and essentially it means "Sown in Confusion." In other words, when Mammon has become our master then we will manifest confusion. Mammon has a few relatives who are poverty, pride, and greed. These three provoke and stimulate us to the degree that many are oblivious to the schemes.

POVERTY causes the state of constant wanting, and it is the torment of never having enough. It will cause us to feel guilt and shame all the time for whatever blessings of the Lord we have in our lives. PRIDE, on the other hand, kills our ability to obey God and follow His plans and purposes. Pride is anti-God and is the very spirit which caused Lucifer's fall. It causes a turning away from God toward self-seeking and the pursuit of self-satisfaction of one's self. In other words, being one's own God. John 4:23-24 tells that "the hour is coming, and now is, when the true worshipers shall worship the Father in spirit and truth, for the Father seeks such to worship Him. God is a spirit, and they who worship Him must worship in spirit and in truth." Pride is a lie!

The Bible states in Haggai Chapter 1:6, "You have sown much, and bring in little; you eat but do not have enough; you drink, but you are not filled with drink; you clothe yourselves, but no one is warm; and he who earns wages, earns wages to put into a bag with holes." This text reveals the outcomes of never being fulfilled, fruitful, and favored. The culprit behind why these people of God kept missing the mark and ending up never satisfied was due to a spirit that was residing in them. The thing is, they could never figure it out! They continued to keep working the plan of Mammon not realizing that their pockets always seemed to be empty.

Tithing and giving offerings breaks the stronghold and spirit of Mammon. When we struggle to open our lives to give, but instead become consumed on hoarding or keeping things for ourselves, we have then been listening to the word of Mammon. When Jesus said, "you cannot serve two masters," that you will "either serve God or mammon," He was referring to whom you obey. How do you recognize if the spirit of God or the spirit of mammon is at work in your life? (1.) Do I look to PEOPLE to meet all my needs? (2.) Do I BLAME others for my current circumstances? (3.) When people fail to help me in the EXACT way I want, do I get unhappy, angry, or resentful? (4.) Do I feel like I will NEVER have enough?

If you said "Yes" to these questions, I want you to know that to break free from any spirit that is not of God requires deliverance. Obtaining more wealth, having a better employer, or getting your family or friends to admit it is their fault does not remove the conditions of this spirit. What is needed is a RESET. The Bible calls it repentance, which is giving up and surrendering your will to the will of God! Poverty, pride, and greed cannot quit or admit that they have dominion in someone's life because any spirit not of God does not want to give up control. Therefore, when we submit to the will of God, all spirits not of God must bow and break free.

## Day 122

# GIVING UP (A TALE OF GIVING UP CONTROL)

Have you noticed how much the word "control" is in our vocabulary? We have what is known as control freaks, remote controlled cars, and mission control, and we speak of someone who seems to be out of control. 2000 years ago, Jesus had to confront control issues. The Pharisees tried to control Jesus, and yet they found that to be hopeless. The disciples even tried to control certain events that Jesus was involved in and found it pointless. Pilate tried to control the crowd by offering our Savior or Barabbas, and he found himself worthless. Today, we all want control on some level do we not? One of the main reasons that prompts the need for control is the fear of losing what we think we have. Think about it. Have you ever gone on an amusement park ride like an intense roller coaster and even though you were strapped in you still felt like there was a place in your belly where you only had so much control? They strap you in and send you out into the wild blue yonder, and most of us just hang on for dear life (Like me)!

Controlling or being controlled is an age-old drama seen throughout mankind. It is as if we have watched it through the history of man since the notion of "I can be like God" (Genesis 3:5). Many have attempted to push down that this reality does not exist today, but the truth of the matter is that most want CONTROL over everything. Controlism is not prone to only the world or the unbeliever but the toxic ingredients of it has shuffled itself into the people of God. From those who refuse to be open to any other way but theirs, and those that demand for power, and those that bully, push, and even manipulate to achieve what they want is a tale tell sign of control.

Being fixed to want total control can be a horrible evil. Desiring absolute control is the absolute opposite of God. Control is a hopelessly additive operation of the fallen nature that was first introduced in Genesis. The only solution to remove it is to receive the authentic Spirit of God. Words like yield, surrender, and lordship all lean towards the removal of control. Even when the Bible shares, "Be a living SACRIFICE" (Romans 12:1), the point of it all is about GIVING up. Being a living sacrifice is a life where one is willing to openly sacrifice what is obviously not a walk in the park. Otherwise, it would not be a sacrifice! People who struggle with being a living sacrifice struggle with control, because in the depths of control is the place that refuses, rebels, and resists to do anything unless it benefits the person in control.

Control is at the root of genocide, rape, war, hatred, segregation, discrimination, racism, pornography, sex-trafficking, and several other forms of injustice (Galatians 5:19-21). Why? Because control is both motivational and operational in unleashing one thing… SIN. The Apostle Paul wrote to a group of Christians immersed in an evil culture. They lived for the moment and rejected God. Their whole world was focused on the satisfaction and pleasure of self. To keep these patterns of thinking from creeping into the hearts and minds of the believers, Paul urgently warned this group not to be CONTROLLED by the FLESH but by the SPIRIT. He said, "Walk in the Spirit and you shall not fulfill the lust of the flesh" (Galatians 5:16).

God gives us His word that if we WALK in the Spirit there will be an outcome where the CONTROL of the flesh will not empower or decide your outcome. This walking is really a living in the Spirit. When something is alive in you and is claiming territory of your life, it begins to readjust the space in your life, and now it is under the dominion of the one who is authority, namely God. The main problem with control is many refuse to consider that control is really about WHO is in authority of their lives, or should I say what is in authority of their lives. When the FLESH is in control, we "fulfill the lust of the flesh," which is basically the appetite to please what must be fulfilled from within yourself.

Conquering control is really conquering the flesh. How do we know if the flesh or control issues have taken place or have dominion in us? The Bible says it is known by its "WORKS" (Galatians 5:19). Works is labor. Think about it for a minute. What is laboring or working in your life for control? The Spirit or the flesh? When something is laboring it is using great effort, and there is exertion. These works consist of fornication, hatred, contentions, outbursts of wrath, ambitions, envy, dissensions, and murders to name a few (Galatians 5:19-21). These individuals wanted to do something as they existed with Christ, and that is to WALK in the flesh. This walk is an exercise. I have learned that whatever I open myself to exercise in my life will have jurisdiction in my life. Think about it, the flesh is an operation that none is unexposed from. We will all confront the flesh, fight the flesh, submit to the flesh, or have victory over it. The key is to WALK in the Spirit, and when we do, it involves GIVING UP.

## Day 123

# The Uplifting Quiz

*"All things are lawful for me, but not all things are helpful; all things are lawful for me, but not all things edify. Let no one seek his own, but each one the other's well-being… Therefore, whether you eat or drink, or whatever you do, do all to the glory of God."* (I Corinthians 10:23-24)

The word "edify" means to UPLIFT another and to encourage someone with hope. But unfortunately, many get caught in the trap of feeding into what they call their RIGHT. You may have a right to act like a fool over a situation where you are compelled to respond in a way that justifies your actions. Your conclusion is that you had the RIGHT to act this way. Our rights or liberties to function in any capacity has been given to us for serving and laying down our lives for the UPLIFTING of others. Too often we push and rush for our rights to be seen so much that in the process we do not lift anything or anyone but end up hurting and deflating the cause of connection with another.

If I am responsible for causing someone to stumble because of asserting my RIGHTS or LIBERTIES, then whether I knew it or not, I may have caused someone to stumble.

The Bible adds, "Therefore let us pursue the things which make for peace and the things by which one may EDIFY another" (Romans 14:29). We should make it our aim not to cause another person to stumble. But because of our personal liberties, many push our rights so much that in the process someone stumbles in their walk or faith. As our scripture highlights some things, and maybe a lot of things may be permissible or allowable for me to pursue, but in the end did it edify someone? In other words, even though I have a right to act out or show out because it was my right, did it EDIFY someone? We must use our liberty in Christ to help set others free and not keep them bound and broken spiritually. Asserting and moving where our lifestyle is always about our rights is a telltale sign that we are more consumed with ourselves than being consumed with the will of God for another.

Today, take a self-quiz and ask yourself, when you push to have things go your way, is anyone impacted? Is anyone hurt, wounded, or confused? If so, we are operating where those who are aware of our actions deal with sorrow, separation, and stumbling to their potential faith and lose the opportunity to be UPLIFTED!

## Day 124

# "MY LIFE"

*"I have been crucified with Christ and I no longer live, but Christ lives in me. The life I NOW live in the body, I live by faith in the Son of God, who loved me and gave himself for me."* (Galatians 2:20)

More than often I encounter those who tend to evaluate life and conclude "WHY ME?" Whether it is an unexplained situation, or a recent challenge with people, pain, or the current place they find themselves in. Many who claim the Lord see Him like a lottery ticket where they anticipate their number is about to be called, only to discover that the Lord wants to work more from within them than on what's on the outside of them. Many who have gotten in a fix find that they now have woven a desire for a quick release or breakthrough from the Lord. God is not an ATM machine! He does not operate where we just put in the numbers and we get to partake in being delivered from a situation!

The self-life is a stubborn, arrogant, and defiant life towards every correction. It will not obey God's word. The only way out is not to bend him down, but to uproot the self-life and crush it in DEATH. Nothing can be done to improve on him. Any little trace of the old man you PERMIT in your life will attempt to outgrow and choke up whatever spiritual life you think you are obtaining. As Cain slew Abel, as Esau sought to kill Jacob, as Ishmael persecuted Isaac, as Joseph's senior brothers bound him up in a dry pit, so does the self-life to everything spiritual. Or should I say, "The Me Life."

Carefully notice that in all these examples of scripture you find what I call "the Senior," which is the old man coming first. Many are more accustomed to the old man way and lifestyle than the new way. The self-man cannot crucify self. All we need to do is give up the self-life to the cross of the Christ-life. We have concluded that by the Death of Christ on the Cross that our old man also has been crucified with Him. But to truly find me, I must allow myself to die to have HIM! I have often stated, "You will never discover YOU until you find HIM!"

The challenge is we struggle and resist to destroy the old ME. Since the old man is the Senior who wants to run things, and plan things, and make things, we must be in the process of the destruction of the OLD ME. Here is why. For many of us, this senior position of the old man has been built over a period where it wants and desires to stand strong. He wants to cling and grip and have staying power even as you strive into your new life. Why? Because the old man sees himself as the dominant factor in your life, because he has had residence in you the longest.

No wonder Jesus says, "DIE DAILY." We are crucified with Christ, but the old self wants to keep living. The first step into a victorious new life is a clear manifestation of the resurrection life within your new life. Colossians 3:3 says, "For you DIED, and your life is hidden with Christ in God." The old man must be reminded that he's DEAD! We must declare to the old system of ourselves boldly that "I am crucified with Christ." The crucified life is a life that keeps putting to death the old man that is looking for opportunities to live again.

For the new life to manifest in your life, and for you to witness the fullness of God's purpose in your life, you must be ready to place a "NEVERTHELESS" on your daily encounter. In other words, "NEVERTHELESS, Christ lives in me!" The life that you now possess is the exact life of Christ. Is that not what the word says, "The life that I live NOW"? As God's people, when we function in the NOW, we function in our present that plows the movement for our future. What does it mean to you when you say "My Life"? Does it mean you dictate, operate, or orchestrate your direction? Does it mean the fulfillment of what pleases you, pushes you or propels you? Consider that to the Holy Spirit when we are introduced into the NEW MAN "it is no longer I that live, but the Christ in me." My complete self is now revamped, remade, and renewed to operate where who I am is because of who He is in me. This is "MY LIFE!"

## Day 125

# PURE

*"Every word of God is PURE: He is a shield to those who put their trust in Him."* (Proverbs 30:5)

/Pyoor/ Meaning: Not mixed or adulterated with any other substance or material. Purification on any level is to make something free from contaminations. In the spiritual life, the function is basically the same. Typically, when anything is purified, it is to take whatever it is to its intended state. God never designed you and me to operate and function where spiritual and emotional pollutants become our norm. No wonder the Bible shares, "There is a generation that is PURE in its own eyes yet is not washed from filthiness" (Proverbs 30:12). Have you ever asked the question why we struggle at times with consuming from God that which will create a divine dwelling place? The reason being is because we have become adjusted to consuming emotional and spiritual toxins.

A toxin is organism that can cause harm, pain, and destruction. It is unstable towards anything that thrives for stability. It is a virus and a poison. Its objective is to remove or replace what is needed with what is a toxin. Often, in the spiritual we meet toxins that wish to paralyze and even destroy us, from unresolved issues, contentious relationships, or our painful past, or believing we are just unforgiveable. Others deny that they exist with a toxin, and they push down unbeknown to them what is dwelling as a disease within. The Bible shares in Proverbs 16:2 that "all the ways of man are PURE in his own eyes, but the Lord weighs the spirits." In other words, man has concluded within himself that his ways, no matter what they look like, are PURE. God goes further by stating, "I know the way of man is not in himself; it is not in man who walks to direct his own steps" (Jeremiah 10:23).

Some say being PURE can be determined by our own personal perspective, and as a people we often make moves in life based on what we deem as right in our own eyes. But notice the Word of God reveals that it is impossible to direct our own steps. Let me break it down like this: Before I met my Lord and Savior, my life was convoluted, confused, and congested with TOXINS. I had no idea the contamination that dwelt in me was preventing me from having peace that surpasses all understanding. It was when I was open to the truth of God's Word that I discovered my life was saturated in spiritual fallacies.

My internal system had become so adjusted and accustomed to this kind of consumption, I was oblivious that I was dominated with TOXINS! But as I became more open and accessible to the Word of God (the Truth), my spiritual system began to consume God's truth. It was at this junction that I realized the need to renew my heart, humble myself, reconcile relationships, promote true forgiveness, and pursue HIS Righteousness. Therefore, the psalmist wrote, "Your word is very PURE; therefore, your servant loves it" (Psalms 119:140). As we ingest the Word of God, we not only see our current condition, but we see our purposed condition. "Every word of God is pure." In other words, even a single word from "The Word" has an objective and that is to PURIFY its recipients!

## Day 126

# THOUGHTS IN THE TEMPLE

> *"When a strong man, fully armed, guards his own house, his possessions are undisturbed. But when someone stronger than he attacks him and overpowers him, he takes away from him all his armor on which he had relied and distributes his plunder."* (Luke 11:21-22)

Whether you knew or not, the day the Lord stepped into your life (your Temple), He literally fought possession over the territory of your life being under the dominion of the adversary! The moment you were "saved" you were unleashed from being a hostage or a prisoner separated from God. The instant you received the salvation of the Lord was the moment "old things were passed away and all things became new" (II Corinthians 5:17). This is a divine result of the grace and power of God. The challenge after we are saved is to remove the residue of guilt and shame that clings to so many, that keeps us revolving in a state of perpetual pain in our minds! No wonder the Bible highlights to us after we have received Christ to "to take every thought captive" (II Corinthians 10:5). Many after their acceptance of Christ still struggle with thoughts that are a stronghold. In other words, it is a mental fortress that does not want to crumble down! These strongholds involve having chains of fear that keep us inferior in places, where God has ordained that we walk in His Supremacy. For others, they deal with being trapped in a loop of lust where they witness the same sequence of events that lead them into a spiritual slump.

For many, we excuse the revolving door of rerun thoughts by justifying and rationalizing its operation in our lives. In the end, it becomes a rotation of life. Because if we excuse ourselves so readily, it is difficult to discern the areas of oppression in our lives. After all, these are our thoughts, our attitudes, and our perceptions. Let us be honest, we justify and defend our thoughts with the same degree of intensity with which we justify and defend ourselves. As it is written, "As [a man] thinketh in his heart, so is he" (Proverbs 23:7 KJV). In other words, the nature of who we are exists in our thought-life. Therefore, before any lasting deliverance can truly be accomplished, we must honestly recognize and confess our need.

No wonder our Lord shared, "Blessed are the poor in spirit, for theirs is the kingdom of heaven" (Matthew 5:3), because when we possess a spirit like this it is a spirit that is aware of its NEED to be quenched by God. In other words, when we are needy for the Lord's provision, then we are open, honest, real, and HUMBLE to receive. It is pride, the opposite of humility, which brings misery. Pride establishes a condition where we refuse to confess, admit, and speak truth, thereby operating in a continual state in the mind where we learn to settle for the same series of events! The Bible states, "Do you not know that your body is a temple of the Holy Spirit within you, whom you have from God?" (I Corinthians 6:9). Our thoughts represent a part of the temple that is wanting an operation from God that resembles His nature where there is peace, joy, and comfort. Do not settle for the sequences of sadness and frustration that Christ already died for!

## Day 127

# "He's a Jealous God"

The Lord describes Himself often in the Bible as "a jealous God" (Exodus 20:5, 34:14; Deuteronomy 4:24, 5:9, etc.). We should expect He would be jealous since we have been created for His will and pleasure. While His covering, nurturing love accepts us as we are, a time comes when He begins to confront the false gods and the idols, which rule in our hearts. Indeed, anything in us that denies Him full access to our souls, or anything that stands between our hearts and His, becomes His enemy.

Have you ever considered that some of the things that may be causing a resistance on your path may not be the enemy at all, but really a jealous God? Often, we approach God seeking for breakthrough and desiring for alterations in places that we highlight for change, but have you ever just asked the Lord what pleases Him? Let us face it, when the Israelites grumbled and mumbled over the course God had taken them towards the promise land, they were more concerned about their needs then what would satisfy the Lord.

In fact, while Moses was communicating with God on the mountain, they decided they had waited long enough and rose up and created a new god for themselves. Why would they do that? Did they not witness the power and protection of Jehovah God? The answer is YES. They did see it and embrace it. The problem was and continues to be to this day that many had no real relationship with Him.

The Bible shares in Exodus 34:12-14, "Watch yourself that you make no covenant with the inhabitants of the land into which you are going, or it will become a snare in your midst. But rather, you are to tear down their altars and smash their sacred pillars and cut down their Asherim—for you shall not worship any other god, for the Lord, whose name is Jealous, is a jealous God."

Did you ever consider that the name "Jealous" is central to the nature of God? Therefore, the Lord states, "No one can serve two masters" (Matthew 6:24). The Bible also states I belong to God and that I was bought with a price. To God, we are personally connected and fused with Him. He invested everything for us by giving up His only begotten Son!

To live in the Lord and not consider that I may be hurting and damaging the relationship I have with God when I invite things into my heart that may turn me away from the Lord is to be spiritually distant with Him!

It creates an impulse within me that creates a great separation that over time becomes easier to live with. The Lord said, "Set no other Gods before me" (Exodus 20:3). In other words, nothing was supposed to have the preeminence in our lives but God. The reason being is because we are to not only be like Him, but to be with Him.

## Day 128

# STILL STANDING

*"If the foundations are destroyed, what can the righteous do?"* (Psalms 11:3)

I have known many people who could boldly speak the Word of God or pray for the sick or sing beautifully in church, but inwardly their spiritual lives were unstable. As soon as difficulties arose, they fell. Why? Something was missing from their inner spiritual life, and as soon as a storm was on the horizon of their lives, they crumbled during and after the storm.

Jesus put it this way, "Everyone who comes to Me and hears My words and acts on them, I will show you whom he is like: he is like a man building a house, who dug deep and laid a foundation on the rock; and when a flood occurred, the torrent burst against that house and could not shake it, because it had been well built" (Luke 6: 47-48).

The question is not "if" a storm is coming, but when. Life has a way of going from a calm and peaceful place to suddenly turning turbulent or adversarial. The only way one's house can stand during these times is if it is built well on a true foundation.

For years, I have witnessed people attempt to try to build a foundation through a storm. In other words, while they are going through calamity and tribulation is when they want to build. Any home builder will tell you nothing can be built properly when there is a turbulent storm. Your house must be built before the storm comes.

Many do not want foundation, they only desire relief. Case in point, someone is going through a financial hardship for the tenth time, and instead of building a proper foundation that will last, they want a quick RELIEF!

We want relief in our marriages, with our issues with our children, with our personal circumstances, and all throughout life, not realizing that only fortified foundations can support the onslaught of a severe storm. All temporary relief is capable of is providing for the MOMENT when the Lord envisioned us victorious for the entire MISSION.

Here is a question: What is the condition of your spiritual life when you are going through a storm? What was the Psalmist saying when he said, "If the foundations are destroyed, what can the righteous do?" His point was if there is no definite, true foundation in our lives then whatever righteous life you have, its grounding is temperamental.

In fact, whether we knew it or not, God uses storms that we face in life to determine what kind of foundation we have. No wonder the Bible shares in Matthew 7:24-26 that no matter if you build on the Rock (the foundation) or on sinking sand, it is still going to storm! It is going to rain eventually in all our lives, and we need to know after every storm that we are STILL STANDING.

# Day 129

# "LEARNING TO WORSHIP IN ANY DISRUPTION"

> "Why, my soul, are you downcast?
> Why so disturbed within me?
> Put your hope in God,
> for I will yet praise him,
> my Savior and my God." (Psalms 42:11)

One of the most quoted comments I hear from believers is, "I can't worship or keep God on my mind when all around me spins stress, situations, and strains!" The truth of the matter is the Bible states, "Trust the Lord at ALL TIMES" (Psalms 62:8). It also shares, "Give thanks in all circumstances; for this is God's will for you in Christ Jesus" (Thessalonians 5:18). It is apparent that God uses interruptions as an opportunity to discover TRUE WORSHIP.

We have confined worship to a ritual and a practice and not as a lifestyle! True worship is a constant journey where no matter what we bump into, we seize that time to give God praise. Clocks, schedules, and routines may be interfered with in life by the interruption to worship. A true worshiper understands that the key of worshiping God is when it is inconvenient. Let me break this down. On Sunday when we typically have our so-called corporate or scheduled worship, it is a time set up to prompt praising, singing, praying, and sharing with one another. But when we are asked to worship God during controversy and conflicts, it seems like uncharted territory. Why is this? Because we have established worship as a part of life and not for the whole of life!

Personally, in my life, I have discovered that worship is authentic when I am going through tough terrain and tense moments. Learning to worship when disruptions have confronted our lives is one of the functions for which we were created. You and I were created to worship. To truly capitalize on being true to worship, we must recognize that stuff happens. Sometimes we cannot avoid calamities and challenges, but we can worship through them. I must also confess that the reason it seems awkward to worship when going through tough terrain is because the flesh nature has become a normal protocol for us. In other words, we have adapted to operating with anxiety, strife, and contentions instead of transitioning towards worship.

The FLESH is about inner turmoil, inner struggles, and inner despair. Worship though transitions guides us straight towards the Spirit of God. The Spirit is about… "Love, joy, peace, patience, kindness, goodness, faithfulness, gentleness, and self-control" (Galatians 5:22-23). I have discovered that every disruption in life is an opportunity to possess what worship is all about. Worship was created by God. It is a divine thing that is designed to glorify

God. When genuine worship is activated, it draws the closeness and the connection of God. The Bible shares, "Come near to God and he will come near to you" (James 4:8). When God is drawn closer to us, that means His presence draws closer, His power draws closer, and His protection draws closer. Today, do not limit worship to just one place; learn to worship in any disruption!

## Day 130

# "When Pride is HIGH"

*"Command those who are rich in this present age not to be high-minded, nor to trust in uncertain riches but in the living God, who gives us richly all things to enjoy."*
(I Timothy 6:17)

According to the Word of God, being high-minded is to be prideful, and when pride is high, it has become a form of worship. When pride is high in our lives, we justify whatever we are seeking to satisfy our needs. When pride is high, we rationalize with whatever we are considering just to have it. When pride is high, we struggle to admit our ways.

Therefore, the Lord stated, "If my people who are called by my name will humble themselves and pray and seek my face and turn from their wicked ways, then will I hear from heaven and will forgive their sin and will heal their land." This passage is really about worship. When our worship is perverted, it stifles our ability to witness the majesty of God!

Being high-minded is worshipping ourselves. It is called idolatry in the Bible. Idolatry is really to have an appetite for the flesh. Therefore, the Lord says, "Taste the Lord and see that He is good" (Psalms 34:8). Because there are many entrees from the flesh that are hoping that the craving cannot be quenched, you cannot stop going after it. If you did not know it, power, pleasure, popularity, possessions, pornography, and positions can all become idols.

Worship is about something that consumes you. No wonder Jesus states, "The Father is seeking for true worshipers" (John 4:23). In other words, the Lord is sifting through the masses to determine the proof of true worship. Being high-minded or prideful stifles true worship.

The biggest idol that most struggle with is the idol of SELF. We say it is not so, but upon further investigation, we can survey from our own lives and determine just how much attention God truly has. Check this: If Sunday is the summation of what you offer God, may I suggest to you to observe the other 90% of your time to see who is truly receiving the serving?

Remember this: "All worship is not acceptable." Did you know that you can even worship depression and stress? How is that possible? Because if you are constantly stressed, then stress has your attention, it has your attraction, and you even adore it. How could that be? Because when you adore something it is high in your life. And many have stress and depression high in their lives! Worship is about something that consumes you. I encourage you today to determine what is HIGH in your life.

## Day 131

# "YOUR WILL NOT MINE"

*"Saying, Father, if thou be willing, remove this cup from me: nevertheless, not my will, but thine, be done."* (Luke 22:42)

When we are so fixated on ourselves rather than the will of God, this is a form of worship. It is the idol worshipping of self. Here is the thing, the Lord wants to reshape our wills. He realizes that people struggle with turning their wills into His will. Their wills are on SELF. God's intent is about altering the will of man. The thing is many are confused about what their WILL is.

Jesus as He prepared for the cross shared, "Lord let your WILL be done" (Luke 22:42). He had to submit to the will of the Father as He faced the greatest time before giving His life. Also remember when the enemy asked Him while He was hungry on one occasion to turn rocks into bread to satisfy his personal will and not consider the outcome with God's will (Luke Chapter 4). To live in the will of God is to obey the Word of God. Sounds simple? What gets in the way is your will!

Your will is more than just your conscience. It involves your ability to choose and decide what direction you will take in life. Here is the thing, we are told how good it is in our world to be an independent soul, but let me help you today with independency.

If you did not know, independency is "I Rule Me." But the Bible states that Jesus wants to be your Lord, which means He rules the TOTAL ME. Do not get me wrong, having some independency has its place, but too much independence creates what my professor told me—a displaced EGO. My acronym for EGO is Etching God Out. The Bible states that "God is a jealous God" (Deuteronomy 6:13). What is He jealous over? On what we are worshipping!

Now worshipping anything or other things can be so subtle. It is like not cleaning your room or the garage, and before long, there is so much stuff in there that you are trying to figure out how in the world all this stuff got there. It is like my storage room in my home. It is so full that all I can do is stand at times and look at it. Have you ever noticed when you are congested with stuff that you immediately get tired or lose interest? I know I do.

That is why some of us keep certain things barricaded and covered up. Listen, when our worship experience has become a place of clutter, we look for easy ways to exist with it. Others come to worship on Sunday, but by Monday morning the disarray is overwhelming again.

Therefore, so many have struggles with change and focus. Is your worship full of laziness, stagnation, distractions, and doubt? Today, let us remove the clutter that is keeping us from worshipping the Lord. How you ask? Here is how—by submitting to the will of God. Submission is an admission of giving something up. It is to yield your life to enrich your life. When we yield to God, He yields to us!

## Day 132

# "Managing Emotions Through the Inner-Man"

*"That he would grant you, according to the riches of his glory, to be strengthened with might by his Spirit in the inner man."* (Ephesians 3:16)

Emotions were never designed to be evil. Emotions allow us to rejoice over the birth of a child or celebrate friendships, milestones, and victories. Emotions allow us to be angry at the evil of evildoers, and yet praise at the faithfulness of God. Emotions allow us to demonstrate a response to the world around us. Those emotions that are out of control emotions hurt people. Joyce Meyers stated that, "Hurting people will always hurt people." Emotions in control or out of control come from the heart. Jeremiah 17:9 tells us that our "hearts are desperately wicked and deceptive." The heart is a way of describing the inner man.

When Jeremiah says the heart is desperately wicked and deceptive, he is simply saying we can fool ourselves about the condition of our heart and the outflow of our emotions.

The great tragedy of our society is that nearly all people mature physically, and a lot of us mature mentally somewhat, but very few ever grow up emotionally or spiritually. To be honest, it appears that emotional immaturity is becoming the norm rather than the exception. The problem with our emotions is the problem with our INNER MAN. Paul prayed that we would be strengthened in the inner man because that is the source where we defeat or deflect our problems, especially our spiritual and emotional ones. We almost always try to tackle the problem from the wrong direction. We tackle it from the outside instead of the inside out.

Years ago, in my back yard we had a fig tree. Every year it would bear more fruit than my family could use. Even when we invited others over to pick the fruit, we would end up with fruit still on the ground. That is alright for a while, until you walk out in the yard and carry fig mush in the house on your shoes. For many of us, that is how we handle our emotional problems most of the time. We pick up and apologize for our anger outbreaks, anxiety attacks, fears, etc. We pick up all the emotional bad fruit that others have dropped off along the path of life. Then many give out all our apologies, but Paul has already given us the solution. If we want to deal with the FRUIT that we bear, we must deal with the ROOT that we have.

The example of the fig tree teaches us that the solution is not just trying harder to deal with our emotional problems, but we must be able to remove the roots by replacing them. In our text, the writer states that we would be strengthened in the inner man and that Jesus would dwell or take root and control our inner selves. Whether you knew it or not, the inner man or the heart holds our true core emotions. It is the objective of Jesus that we cooperate with the indwelling of the Holy Spirit. The Holy Spirit works not on the outward but the inward. The Holy Spirit works to renew our minds, redirect our wills, and renovate our emotions. All of these are inward workings. Why is God so concerned with the inner man? Because that is where true and lasting transformation takes places. If you want to stop picking up all the rotten and smashed emotional fruit, then you must submit to the Holy Spirit's inner working. This is how we embrace managing our emotions.

## Day 133

# "THE PALM TREE"

*"The righteous shall flourish like the palm tree: he shall grow like a cedar in Lebanon. Those that be planted in the house of the LORD shall flourish in the courts of our God. They shall still bring forth fruit in old age; they shall be fat and flourishing."* (Psalms 92:12-14)

Did you know that the palm tree that existed in Judea could reach a height of eighty feet, but more commonly forty to fifty? It could also bear fruit for a century. The palm is, in truth, a beautiful and most useful tree.

Its fruit is the daily food of millions; its sap furnishes an agreeable wine; the fibers of the base of its leaves are woven into ropes and rigging; its tall stem supplies a valuable timber; and its leaves are manufactured into brushes, mats, bags, couches, and baskets. This one tree supplies almost all the wants of the people.

The Bible states "the righteous shall flourish like the palm tree." The palm tree is fruitful in every way, and like the palm tree, the Lord is wanting us to witness an experience of flourishing where we can provide a difference in the total operation of our lives in Christ.

What we fail to recognize for this to manifest is the key component of RIGHTEOUSNESS. The Bible stated, "The righteous shall flourish!" Many believe that being righteous is completely on us, but the truth of the matter is that we inherited righteousness from God; it was given to us. We did not work for it. We are declared righteous by the blood of Jesus.

Now our objective is to blossom in His righteousness! Therefore, Jesus said, "Seek first the kingdom of God and all His RIGHTEOUSNESS."

Righteousness is really the will of God. It was formerly spelled "right-wiseness," which clearly expresses the meaning. It holds the truth, the promises, and the divine nature of God.

When we live as the righteous, the Bible says, "I have never seen the righteous forsaken" (Psalms 37:25). This does not mean we will be obsolete of challenges, but through whatever we face in this life, if we maintain a righteous life, we will never be alone. We will never be deserted or abandoned by God!

Today, be like the palm tree. Even though they may encounter storms, winds, and rough conditions, they grow into what God envisioned. As the people of God, let's fulfill our flourished state of being the RIGHTEOUS!

## Day 134

# PEARLS

*"Again, the kingdom of heaven is like a merchant looking for fine pearls. When he found one of great value, he went away and sold everything he had and bought it."* (Matthew 13:45-46)

Pearls in the first century were viewed much like diamonds are today. They were the most valuable gem in the world at that time. If you owned a pearl, you owned a fortune. And there was a good reason for it. The fine quality of pearls are obtained from the pearl oyster, which thrives at an average depth of 40 feet. Many people died while pearl hunting. A first century pearl diver would tie a large rock to his body and jump over the side of a little boat, allowing the weight of the rock to carry him down to the oyster beds. He risked danger from sharks, moray eels, and other predators to scour the mud below for oysters.

Typically, a pearl merchant would average about one oyster in a thousand to obtain a pearl! All the while, he had to hold his breath and hope he would not drown. You can see why pearls were so precious. The Jewish Talmud shares that "pearls are beyond price." The pearl merchant in this parable represents many parallels to a person who is seeking after Christ. Christ and salvation are not earned because of labor; instead, Christ is gained by knowledge and discovery. To know Christ and surrender to Him is to know eternal life. Just as this merchant found something that was of immense value, so the finding of Christ is the discovery of that which is of ultimate VALUE.

Upon further discovery, you will find that the pearl merchant did four things. First, he sought; next, he found; third, he sold his accumulated wealth; and lastly, he obtained his goal by buying. His goal was to SEEK and FIND pearls! When one is a seeker of something specific such as pearls, then his mind is engaged on thinking massively about pearls. In fact, he spends a surmountable amount of energy in the discovery of pearls. He does not waste time binging on movies or spending tons of time on pleasure seeking. No, his intent is to capture, contain, and pay the COST to establish something considered PRICELESS! The pearl merchant's life is mission driven. If you were to ask him, "What are you doing with your life?" He would answer, "I am searching for quality pearls." Today, the masses in general when asked this question struggle to share with certainty their purpose.

Purpose has an a.m. The pearl merchant did not settle for any other type of jewel or stone. He did not shrink his passion to searching for granite, slate, or flint. In other words, he did not minimize his overall objective to a lesser target. He stuck with obtaining PEARLS. He did not shrink his vision. Today, many reduce and decrease the purpose God intended for everyone. This pearl merchant's aim was for something extremely valuable, and he wanted to extend his life for a worthy PURPOSE.

It is normal for pearl traders to travel all over the world to the areas where the prime oyster beds of pearls are discovered to find prized ones. Their search might take them to places far off the tourist treks or to places that are dangerous, but they are determined to brave whatever conditions to get the BEST. If you have not figured it out yet, Jesus and His Kingdom are the PEARLS. The Lord desires for everyone that wants to know Him to discover something He possesses that is far greater than any jewel! Christ is the pearl of great wealth! Many claim to have Him, but their everyday investments do not consist of faith, hope, and love. Their pursuit to obtain the finest possessions offered in the kingdom seems wavering and shallow. When we HAVE Christ, we have power, peace, and prosperity! Today, determine the authenticity of the great pearl you are after.

## Day 135

# "Greatness in Thankfulness"

*"Giving thanks always and for everything to God the Father in the name of our Lord Jesus Christ."* (Ephesians 5:20)

While shopping at Sam's Club recently, a mother and her three children were picking out food items to place in the basket, and as they walked past the isle for video games, they pushed and pricked at Mom to consider purchasing one or two of the games. But Mom had said, "We just bought you guys some new games last month." The trio almost in unison said, "WE DON'T LIKE THOSE GAMES!"

Then there is the husband who decides he is going to cook a special meal for his wife and surprises her by cooking her favorite meal… Blackened Catfish! But when she takes a bite of the prepared dish, she discovers it is not to her satisfaction, and shares to her husband, "Did you taste this mess?"

Others complain in major doses every day about their jobs and their bosses. Sometimes so much that they vocalize it to their colleagues. Yet, they come back day after day to collect a paycheck. The operation of the ungrateful is fully operational in our current everyday world. We witness on the regular what appears to be more and more a spirit of ungratefulness. Instead of learning to accept, many learn to only reject. Instead of being satisfied over any gift, many stay dissatisfied over what they did not receive.

As a child, I was used to receiving something that was either worn by someone else or played with by someone else. I was taught no matter the condition, the contents, or the cost, I should always be THANKFUL. If you knew it or not, the very quality of your life, whether you love it or hate it, is based upon how thankful you are toward God. It is one's attitude that determines whether life unfolds into a place of blessedness or wretchedness. Indeed, even looking at the rose bush, some people complain that the roses has thorns while others rejoice that some thorns come with roses. It all depends on your perspective. If you want to find joy, you must first find thankfulness. Indeed, the one who is thankful for even a little enjoys much. But the unappreciative soul is always miserable, always complaining. He or she lives outside the shelter of the Highest God.

Today, I witness more people who have become "specialists in MISERY." They are experts in discovering everything that does not measure up to their standards. They dwell in the land of THE CRITICAL. They constantly pick and probe for anything that is wrong in their eyes, and they miss what was right in their sight! Ungratefulness is a condition that separates us from the FAVOR of GOD. It is in the will of God that we be thankful in all things. I Thessalonians 5:18 says, "In everything give thanks: for this is the will of God in Christ Jesus concerning you." As far as God is concerned, thankfulness leads to greatness. Psalms 100:4 says, "Enter His gates with Thanksgiving." Gates are used as an entrance into a place. For the people of God to dwell where God is GREAT, we must enter in with Thanksgiving in our hearts!

## Day 136

# "WHAT'S GROWING... FROM YOU?"

The Bible states, "A man that hath friends must shew himself friendly" (Proverbs 18:24). In other words, there is something being displayed, or that is presently being identified as something prevalent in a person, that is impacting another.

Though this is a reality towards having healthy relationships that surrounds us, the truth of the matter is that there are many who struggle with LONLINESSS. They feel that not only does no one love them, but no one likes them. They search for connection and embracing from others, and many in the long run wind up feeling abandoned and rejected. Some conclude that something must be wrong with who they are as the reason no one in their own assessment wishes to be close to them.

Possessing the traits of a friend is like the growth of the plant. If proper cultivation and the manifestation of fruit is to be recognized in the plant, then it will stand OUT! My mother used to tell me, "You can't give what you don't have." In other words,

LOVE begets love; and love requires love as its recompense. When love is vacant or missing in a person, then the ability to give it will not be the outcome.

Jesus said, "There is no greater love than to lay down one's life for one's friends" (John 15:13). Great love is a demonstration of unselfishness. The sad truth about many relationships is that the objective of obtaining something in the relationship seems to be for SELF.

In other words, there is the lack of freely giving, but a place where the motive is for self. When a person struggles with giving respect or showing trust, then they will struggle with having genuine friendships!

The key is to change what your plant (your life) looks like, or the way it is currently growing. I have never been one that had the ability to have a green thumb. I have had several plants that did not fare well under my care from forgetting to give the plants water, having no proper sunlight available, and making sure the soil was exactly right. My poor plants never had a chance!

Plants were meant to be seen flourishing, beautiful, and colorful. Jesus said, "So let your light so shine that men may see your good works and glorify your Father in heaven." When we are growing properly, we are an attraction.

When there is the LACK of love, patience, goodness, trust, and respect blossoming from our lives, then it will impact our relationships. So, ask yourself today, "What's growing from YOU?"

## Day 137

# "Thinking of You"

Ponder this. Jesus said, "Can you not buy five sparrows for two pennies? And yet not one is forgotten in God's sight. Why, every hair on your head has been counted. There is no need to be afraid; you are worth more than hundreds of sparrows" (Luke 12:6-7).

Have you ever dwelt on this fact—God is thinking about you to the degree that every hair on your head is recognized by Him? That is some detail, which makes me consider that if God has that kind of observation over me then I must embrace that not only does He care for me but that He has a plan for me.

God has never stopped THINKING OF ME! It is woven in His being to ALWAYS WATCH AFTER ME. He makes it so simple to TRUST in HIM with all my HEART. To be loved in totality from the one responsible for my creation causes me to pause and give Him recognition and reverence.

I will always remember when I was a child, long before my siblings came, my mother watched me with eyes behind her head.

She knew when I was frustrated and sad. She knew when I was hungry and when I needed a hug. Like my mother, the Lord is connected to me that He knows when I feel lost and discouraged.

The Bible states, "When I am most afraid, I put my trust in you, in God whose word I praise, in God I put my trust, fearing nothing; what can man do to me?" (Psalms 56:3-4).

When I face unrest, uncertainty, and just being uncomfortable, the Lord is wired and fused with me to the point that He showers me with His love. When I am troubled, I can depend on "He rescued me, since He loves me" (Psalms 18:19).

Lord, thank you for always thinking of me!

## Day 138

# ELEVATE

*"I am MORE than a Conqueror."* (Romans 8:37)

What is the first thing you think of when you hear the word "elevate"? For most of us, we tend to think of escalating, rising, and growing. Interesting enough, I have discovered that many would love to elevate in several places, but what puts the brakes on in most cases is a push. I am referring to a force that is a necessity for you to press through. No wonder the Bible states, "Fight the good fight of faith" (I Timothy 6:12), and "Run the race set before you" (Hebrews 12:1). Before we can transition, shift, or move to a place of promotion, we must be willing to press through what we need to break through. No more evading or shuffling to dodge what is tough, a trial, and a test of our spiritual fortitude. Jesus said, "He that endures until the end shall be saved." Many give up way before the season of breakthrough!

To elevate, you must PENETRATE what perhaps you have avoided or evaded. To elevate, you must be willing to BREAK

THROUGH what you MUST GO THROUGH. Many of us want a promotion without facing the commotion that has been hidden in the crevices of our souls. No wonder the Bible says, "Lay aside every weight, and the sin which so EASILY ensnares us" (Hebrews 12:12:1a). So many are trying to escalate with WEIGHTS and LUGGAGE that has been a burden and barrier towards their breakthrough.

Moreover, we want to be promoted in life, but we try to shift and dive away from the pain that often comes with the promotion. In my life, I have personally encountered that every promotion comes with commotion. The Bible confirms that we are "More than a Conqueror." In Greek, the word signifies that our spiritual level is where we operate as "Hyper-conquerors," meaning we surpass just having victory, but we are to maintain a surpassing gaining victory. Think about it. If we are more than being just a conqueror, then we are beyond just existing as just conquerors!

God has a level for us to operate on that you may have not obtained mainly because to truly elevate, you must face forces that resist elevation. To be just a conqueror, we must subdue some things, and defeat some things, and resist some things. We want to be more than a conqueror, but what we may be lacking is what being more must faced. Romans 8:38-39 tells us it involves "not be being persuaded by death nor life, nor angels, nor principalities nor powers nor present things to come, nor height nor depth nor any other created thing, shall be able to separate you from the love of God which is in Christ Jesus."

To elevate to be MORE, we must not allow anything to separate us from the love of God, which comes from Jesus. This love is intentional and deliberate. It is the kind of love that uses the phrase "Nothing can separate you from." Far too often we find ourselves being challenged by the Love we claim for the Christ. Before you give up where your elevation level may be your ability to prove that LOVE, I implore you to trust what God said that you already possess. You are already more than a conqueror, just walk in what God has already spoke about you and start to ELEVATE!

## Day 139

# REAL LOVE vs. FALSE LOVE

*"And so we know and rely on the love God has for us. God is love. Whoever lives in love lives in God, and God in them."*
(I John 4:16)

REAL LOVE expresses itself by giving the best and not thinking about what an individual is receiving, while false love is focused and fixed only with giving the impression of giving the best and being motivated to do so only because of the expected outcome they wish to see (Read John 3:16).

REAL LOVE survives the storms of life, while on the other hand false love proves they lack depth by how they handle storms.

REAL LOVE is grounded, sound, and coachable, while false love is unstable, unsure, indecisive, and closed.

REAL LOVE reveals itself through problems and so does false love.

REAL LOVE has learned to be flexible, while false love tends to be frustrated.

REAL LOVE can embrace input as guidance, while false love has learned to turn it into personal guilt.

REAL LOVE is GOD- DRIVEN! "God so loved the world that He gave His only begotten Son" (John 3:16). Real love DRIVES people to operate like God.

REAL LOVE serves others!

REAL LOVE is not conditional, but is saturated in the UNCONDTIONAL, meaning it is not based on stipulations, or meeting one's expectations. Jesus said, "Greater love hath no man than this, that a man lay down his life for his friends" (John 15:13).

REAL LOVE is divine because it was originated and woven into the nature of God.

REAL LOVE is open, transparent, and vulnerable.

REAL LOVE walks with God, "And walk in love, just as Christ also loved you and gave Himself up for us, an offering and a sacrifice to God as a fragrant aroma." (Ephesians 5:2); therefore, you walk in FAITH.

REAL LOVE is SELFLESS and not SELFISH.

REAL LOVE is MATURE and does not reflect characteristics consistently identified as IMMATURE. Jesus said, "If you love me keep my commandments" (John 14:15). When we are willing to submit to Jesus, we can then see that operation in the totality of our lives. This is spiritual maturity.

REAL LOVE is spiritual and supernatural. The Bible says, "God is Spirit" (John 4:24).

REAL LOVE is SACRIFICIAL. The Bible says, "Christ also loved the church and gave himself for her" (Ephesians 5:25).

The question we should pose is where do we stand? In REAL LOVE or FALSE LOVE?

## Day 140

# "DENIAL"

*"Jesus answered, 'I tell you, Peter, before the rooster crows today, you will DENY three times that you know me.'"*
(Luke 22:34)

What is denial? It is a defense mechanism used by individuals to push away the TRUTH. It is an operation where the evidence and the reality of the situation is so substantial that many feel denials are the only way they can survive their situation. This is where the truth is just too uncomfortable for a person to accept. Whenever confronted with the truth, some feel that they must find an escape route from receiving the truth, and this is denial. Take for instance the person who refuses to talk about their actions after excessively drinking. Then of course there are those who struggle with what is impacting a tussle on the soul that requires accountability. They are also in DENIAL.

It is the guy who says, "I can control my drinking," only to find himself over and over in a state of a stupor. It is camouflaging and hiding real areas in one's life. It is where people avoid confronting a reality. Denial is seen in children as a coping skill to deal with moments where they confront circumstances that are just too hard and painful to accept or deal with. Areas like death, divorce, separation. But denial goes much further. It is also seen when someone is attempting to cover up something. It is when someone is willing to lie to push away what they are up against. It is seen when a person just cannot accept the truth. People use denial when something that hits their emotional button causes them to react with conflict in their thoughts. Dealing with denial can be so overwhelming that many feel they have no choice but to use it.

Denial is not something new. Remember Peter after Jesus was arrested? He dealt with a challenging moment that tested an area he did not want to face. He hid, he lied, and he avoided the questions about his relationship with Jesus. Peter was obviously close to Jesus. So how could it be that a person with his connection with the Lord comes to this point? If he really loved the Lord, how could he deny him three times? The question we need to glean from this is how did he get to this point?

You may recall the occasion where Jesus shared, *"He must go to Jerusalem and suffer many things at the hands of the elders, chief priests and teachers of the law, and that he must be killed and on the third day be raised to life. Peter took him aside and began to rebuke him. 'Never, Lord!' he said. 'This shall never happen to you!' Jesus turned and said to Peter, 'Get behind me, Satan! You are a stumbling block to me; you do not have in mind the things of God, but the things of men.' Then Jesus said to his disciples, 'If anyone would come after me, he must DENY himself and take up his cross and follow me. For whoever wants to save his life will lose it, but whoever loses his life for me will find it'"* (Matthew 16:21-26).

When the way of Jesus is different than the way we thought it would be or should be in our own eyes, then we just might have a controversy with him. We may feel we may have to DENY Him. Everyday most of us are tested like Peter in some area where it is pulling us to deny. Many also deal with struggles where someone close to them is in the world of denial. Our position should be like the example of God to stand on the truth! Peter avoided the truth, even when he watched His Lord being dragged away and convicted of a crime He did not commit, and when spotted, he denied He knew Him. He even cursed to boot to make it appear there was no connection to the one called Jesus Christ. Jesus prophesied to Peter he would reach this place of personal denial. He knew that Peter must come face to face with what he was denying. I pray today that whatever you may be avoiding or saying that you claim is too hard to face, that you allow yourself to be submerged in the truth.

## Day 141

# NO WORRIES

*"Therefore, I say to you, do not worry about your life, what you will eat or what you will drink; nor about your body, what you will put on. Is not life more than food and the body more than clothing? Look at the birds of the air, for they neither sow nor reap nor gather into barns; yet your heavenly Father feeds them. Are you not of more value than they? Which of you by worrying can add one cubit to his stature?"* (Matthew 6:25-27)

Today, it appears on every corner and in every community across the globe the one thing that seems to be synonymous with people in general is that we are soaking up WORRY. We tend to worry over who is in the White House and what the future holds for America, or if we can handle the impact of change in any direction.

Wait a second, I thought Jesus shared to His people to "Don't Worry" (Matthew 6:25:34)? Yet we worry about everything from family to finances. Some are so saturated with worry that when they are squeezed by the conditions of life they witness the result of what comes out. When squeezed, many unleash everything from stress, frustration, anger, and the killer… Hopelessness. In other words, when pushed, poked, and prodded from the situations in this life, there is a tendency to "give up." But Jesus still wants us to trust what He said and have NO WORRIES. You say it cannot be done? Well, think about why that position may have taken root in your heart. The Bible states, "As a man thinks in his heart so is, he." So, if you allow worry to consume you, it becomes a spiritual digestive source for consumption. In other words, we have munched so much on worry as meal in life when it is the time to face the challenges in this life that now it becomes our spiritual meal.

A common expression is, "You are what you eat." Jesus said, "Man cannot live by bread alone but by every word that comes from God." The Word of God is a spiritual meal that helps us to live. No wonder the Bible states, "Taste the Lord and see that He is good." God wants such an operation of consumption from His Word that something happens in how we walk out life. When worry hits home, many navigate towards dealing with it by feeding it not by the Word of God, but by feeding it things like alcohol, gambling, pornography, and soaking themselves in pleasure to avoid the reality of their problems.

The thing is, these things may temporarily be a quick fix, but it does not promote power, purpose, and genuine prosperity. So why do so many find themselves soaking up worry? Mainly because of poor spiritual eating habits! Remember in the Lord's prayer, Jesus said to pray, "Give us this day our daily bread, and forgive us our debts, as we forgive our debtors. And do not lead us into temptation but deliver us from the evil one. For yours is the kingdom and the power and the glory forever. Amen" (Matthew 6:9-13). Notice that there is an emphasis to have the "Bread of God" before we journey into forgiveness and face temptation.

When we are depleted of the right kind of spiritual nourishment, it will show up when we are confronted with the things of life like worry and the things that tempt us. Worriedness is a condition that is established because it is fueled by doubt, dread, and depression. Feeding on worry has become synonymous with how people function because they keep allowing their lives to become accessible to it. In our text, Jesus basically says, "Why do you worry?" As if it is not spiritually in our DNA. We must confront worry with TRUSTING in the Word of God to perform just like He did for the birds.

# Day 142

# "ARE YOU TRULY READY TO LOVE?"

Love is the highest value of the kingdom (I Corinthians 13:13). It is the central motivation of all the commandments (Mark 12:30-31). It is the character of God Himself (I John 4:8). It is the motivation behind the life mission of Jesus (John 3:16). And it involves pain.

Love involves a relationship, which in turn involves another human being. All of us human beings cause trouble. We sin. Sin hurts other people. If we love people, we have to deal with the pain that sin causes.

I have wonderful, loving, faithful relationships with people in all spheres of my life—marriage, family, work, congregation, partners, and friends. Yet they all involve pain. Faithfulness and patience mean that there will be the bearing of pain in relationships for perhaps a long period of time. The beauty of love is well worth the pain involved, but it does cost the price.

Pain is the price of love. Jesus was willing to suffer all the way to the CROSS for LOVE!

The pain of loving relationships comes in several dimensions. First, we bear the weight when those we are in relationship that are weak. They cannot do all they should, so we need to "make up the difference." Here there is no intended harm meant. It is more of a weight than a pain. Romans 15:1 says, "We who are strong should bear the weaknesses of the weak."

The second level is that we feel vicariously the pains of others. Jesus would weep in His daily prayer times (Hebrews 5:7) as He felt the suffering of others. Paul (Saul) said that he felt the suffering of those in the congregations under his authority. This pain is a spiritual pain, not your own pain. It is the loving identification of compassion and intercession. I Corinthians 12:26 says, "If one member is hurting, then all the members suffer."

The third level of pain is when someone you love hurts you. Here the pain is more direct. The depth of love is intimacy. Intimacy demands openness. Openness makes way for vulnerability. That means you can be hurt or wounded. When we are hurt, we have the grace of Jesus to help us forgive, overlook, communicate, and receive healing. Yet the process still hurts. I Corinthians 13:7 says, "Love covers all things… suffers all things." In other words, this level of LOVE has matured to become accessible to be wounded. Did you ever consider that this is LOVE?

If we have struggled and separated ourselves from places and people that have thrown things that have worn us down, made us weak, and caused us pain, then please let's ask ourselves daily, are we ready to LOVE?

# Day 143

# "MIND MOVE"

*"Let this MIND be in you that was also in Jesus Christ."* (Philippians 2:5)

Have you ever noticed that we tend to focus more on our problems? Often, we enter our day with our countenance darkened by the gloom of the day from whatever we still have not given over to God from our past, or perhaps the latest issue that has caused a rise in anxiety or tension.

We wonder why people do not run to give their lives to Christ. Perhaps the obstacle is not what exists in their hearts but what they see coming from our hearts. Yes, we accepted Christ as Savior and gave Him our sins, but have we truly given Him our lives?

I mean to live in Christ is GAIN, but for some (maybe many), we flop around as if we are walking in messy situations every day. This is not the will of God! Our gloom reveals our trust in God. The Lord desires to rescue us from gloomy, unbelieving attitudes. He wants us to cancel our plans to be miserable and submit ourselves into His loving, wonderful hands. Therefore, I am fighting for the best life I can possibly have. I am fighting powers of darkness so that I can experience the fullness of joy.

It is a MIND MOVE that we need. We so often want God to change or alter the stuff we face, the situations we encounter, and the silliness that drops in our lives, and the Lord wants to CHANGE YOU TO DEAL WITH IT!

In a world where spiritual darkness is increasing, the Lord plans something different for us. In fact, He orders us, "Arise, shine; for your light has come" (Isaiah 60:1). He tells us that His literal glory, which is now abiding within us, will "appear upon" us. The result? "Nations will come to your light, and kings to the brightness of your rising" (Isaiah 60:1-3).

What does that mean? Well, in essence it means that people, organizations, establishments, those in power, and those that are in the place of providing or promoting things to transpire in your community, in your town, and in your company will be impacted by the LIGHT that exudes from your LIFE!

For this to unfold, we must ask ourselves, where are our MINDS?

The Bible says, "Let NOTHING be done through selfish ambition or conceit, but in lowliness of MIND let each esteem others BETTER than himself" (Philippians 2:3). This was the MIND of Christ. He expected His mind to become the MIND you POSSESS.

When we focus on ourselves all the time, we are never escalating towards where the mind of Christ dwells. The challenge is the enemy draws us to lumber around in life where we cannot get our minds off anyone but ourselves.

Think about it, when we are feeling down, dejected, and depressed, we typically do not gravitate towards thinking about others, for that sake even going out of our way to be a benefit towards another. The reason being is because we are wrapped up in ourselves. When the mind of Christ is active in your life, it is MOVING. You are witnessing a shift that is not based on your MOMENT but based on His MOTIVE!

For Jesus, His Father exalted Him because He had the mind to become obedient without any fanfare, props, and others that were seeking Him, because He saw Himself as somebody (Philippians 2:7). He was ridiculed, disrespected, and talked about. Yet He humbled himself to the point of death (Philippians 2:8).

When we have this MIND MOVE, people may ask, "Why are you so happy especially given your difficult circumstances?" You respond, "I can't tell you why, I just know, despite my battle, I'm fully loved by God. He's in charge of me and my future." 1 Peter 1:8 says, "You greatly rejoice with joy inexpressible..." Add it up and see how much we have—peace beyond comprehension, love beyond knowledge, and joy beyond our ability to express and articulate!

All I can say is who does not desire a MIND MOVE?

## Day 144

# "Self-Esteem in Recovery"

*"So, remove grief and anger from your heart and put away pain from your body, because childhood and the prime of life are fleeting."* (Ecclesiastics 11:10)

The first goal in the recovery process of low self-esteem is to address the *distorted* thinking, feelings, and behaviors that resulted from the sources of your low self-esteem. To accomplish this goal, you need to establish a trusting relationship in which these three issues can be addressed. To correct your thinking, you will need to learn what is the reality in your life. You will need to dispel your irrational beliefs. You will need to identify, discard, and replace negative self-scripts with daily self-affirmations.

To heal your feelings, you will need to be taught how to *identify* and *label* your feelings. You will need to give yourself permission to have both negative and positive feelings. You will need to be encouraged to get in touch with how you are feeling about the reality in your life. You will need to feel the power of self-affirmation, which results in you are growing in self-love and self-caring. You will need practice in expressing feelings and listening to others express their feelings.

To change your unhealthy behaviors, you will need to begin to act only on rational thinking and true self-felt feelings. You will need to accept personal responsibility for your own actions and no longer blame others. This is normally one of the biggest moves to make. The reason being is because it is typically a way of life to blame someone else for who you are or where you are! In addition, you will need to identify your self-defeating behaviors and change them. This part is also huge due to rationalizing those behaviors and attempting to hide them. They must be exposed!

As a result of corrected thinking, healed feelings, and healthy behaviors, your compulsively driven behavioral pattern can change. This will occur by rewriting the old behavioral scripts. In your new script, you need to keep the positive elements of your personality and replace the unhealthy aspects. You can change your old pattern by getting in touch with the feelings you have ignored for too long. You can "let go" of the compulsive nature of your old unhealthy personality traits and work at thinking before you act. You can redefine yourself by letting go of self-defeating behaviors with their negative consequences. This is what the scriptures expose as well when we read, "Be renewed in the spirit of your mind, and that you put on the NEW MAN which was created according to God, in true righteousness and holiness" (Ephesians 4:23-24).

Here is a summary of the concerns that impact the low self-esteem:

1. **Loss issues**—to let go of the unresolved grief over losses you have experienced in your life.
2. **Self–destructive behaviors**—to eliminate these behaviors and gain outside support to ensure your continued abstinence.
3. **Control issues**—to let go of the uncontrollable and the unchangeable in life and to accept self-control over your behaviors and feelings over what is not under your control.
4. **Anger issues**—to let go of unresolved anger through systematic anger workout efforts. Anger is typically a secondary emotion, which means something is the key that often we are not in tune.
5. **Faulty communications**—to learn how to focus your feelings on content by active listening and reflecting your feelings on reality and not something that is not real. This prevents the ability for problem solving based on the expression of your honest feelings.
6. **Personal adjustment**—to let go of self-defeating behaviors and to adopt new, healthy behaviors by accepting personal responsibility for self.
7. **Interpersonal relationships**—to work on improving personal behaviors to strengthen personal, work, and social relationships.

## Day 145

# "The Culture of the Angry"

With all that is happening on our streets and neighborhoods, and with being shut in for most likely the most days we have ever faced due to COVID-19, I am not surprised by the increased of anger. My concern is that, unless this anger regenerates into something more redemptive, more Christlike, we will not see our cities renewed. Indeed, anger that does not awaken in us redemptive action ultimately degrades into bitterness and unbelief.

While hell advances into our world on many levels, I want to discuss two primary areas. The first manifestation is brazened, widespread, and alarming. For example, a corrupt law gets passed or a corrupt officer of the law activates anger, and violence breaks out.

It is on the news and people are talking about it. The shock waves caused by this demonic intrusion smash against the sensibilities of our hearts—we are disappointed, offended, stunned, and, often, outraged. In this state of mind, hell launches the second area of attack. There is no newscast dragging our attention to this next stage of warfare. On this front, the devil does not come flaunting himself. In seething whispers, he stirs the pot of our discontent until it boils! Ultimately, where once the heart of the Christian was full of faith and love, now bitterness, hatred, and malice churn in the souls of God's people. This is the second prong of the attack—the hardening of our hearts in reaction to evil.

The Bible states in Hebrews Chapter 3, "Do not harden your hearts" more than a few times, as if God is warning His children of a subtle avenue that can easily become stealth and slick and take on the appearance of something good when in its really the promotion of rebellion! In many places where God says "Don't harden your hearts," He is encouraging us not to become STUBBORN against His ways. How could that be? For instance, someone refuses to admit the need to ask for forgiveness. Or they refuse to take ownership of something they have allowed that has caused havoc and confusion to another or even an entire culture.

So, while we must fight the spiritual wars of our times, we must not compromise our capacity to love if we will win our war. We must remember we are not fighting against "flesh and blood, but against principalities, against powers, against the rulers of the darkness of this world" (Ephesians 6:12 KJV).

Sadly, I have heard many people say recently that they've lost their vision for America. What they lost was not their vision, but their love. For "love believes all things, hopes all things, and endures all things. Love never fails" (1 Corinthians 13:7-8).

I believe that if the Lord's plan were to end evil on Earth, He could do so in a flash. Why does He wait? He desires to bring believers to Christlike maturity. In a moment, evil would be gone! Just like He created the heaven and the earth, He could remove evil. So why does it still exist among us?

God is waiting for our spiritual maturity. Our Father desires to bring many sons and daughters to glory, and this world, even with all its evil. This is the setting for God to accomplish His eternal purpose.

Yes, we should be angry about what is wrong, but we must be Christlike in making things right. We cannot be political; we must be spiritual.

Rightly there are times when we must defend the helpless among us, but concerning ourselves, let us consider again what Jesus commanded, "You have heard that it was said, 'You shall love your neighbor and hate your enemy.' But I say to you, love your enemies and pray for those who persecute you, so that you may be sons of your Father who is in Heaven" (Matthew 5:43-45).

To see our nation transformed, we must be transformed. We cannot become those whose hearts are given over to anger. Otherwise, we will risk becoming hypocrites—angry that the world is not Christian but untroubled that we are not Christlike.

Made in the USA
Monee, IL
10 November 2021